The Wisdom of Andrew Murray Volume I

Humility
With Christ in the School of Prayer
Abide in Christ

The Wisdom Of Andrew Murray Vol I

by Andrew Murray

Humility

Table of Contents

Preface

There are three great motives that urge us to humility. It becomes me as a creature, as a sinner, as a saint. The first we see in the heavenly hosts, in unfallen man, in Jesus as Son of Man. The second appeals to us in our fallen state, and points out the only way through which we can return to our right place as creatures. In the third we have the mystery of grace, which teaches us that, as we lose ourselves in the overwhelming greatness of redeeming love, humility becomes to us the consummation of everlasting blessedness and adoration.

In our ordinary religious teaching, the second aspect has been too exclusively put in the foreground, so that some have even gone to the extreme of saying that we must keep sinning if we are indeed to keep humble. Others again have thought that the strength of self-condemnation is the secret of humility. And the Christian life has suffered loss, where believers have not been distinctly guided to see that, even in our relation as creatures, nothing is more natural and beautiful and blessed than to be nothing, that God may be all; or where it has not been made clear that it is not sin that humbles most, but grace, and that it is the soul, led through its sinfulness to be occupied with God in His wonderful glory as God, as Creator and Redeemer, that will truly take the lowest place before Him.

In these meditations I have, for more than one reason, almost exclusively directed attention to the humility that becomes us as creatures. It is not only that the connection between humility and sin is so abundantly set forth in all our religious teaching, but because I believe that for the fullness of the Christian life it is indispensable that prominence be given to the other aspect. If Jesus is indeed to be our example in His lowliness, we need to understand the principles in which it was rooted, and in which we find the common ground on which we stand with Him, and in which our likeness to Him is to be attained. If we are indeed to be humble, not only before God but towards men, if humility is to be our joy, we must see that it is not only the mark of shame, because of sin, but, apart from all sin, a being clothed upon with the very beauty and blessedness of heaven and of Jesus. We shall see that just as Jesus found His glory in taking the form of a servant, so when He said to us, "Whosoever would be first among you, shall be your servant," He simply taught us the blessed truth that there is nothing so divine and heavenly as being the servant and helper of all. The faithful servant, who recognizes his position, finds a real pleasure in supplying the wants of the master or his guests. When we see that humility is something infinitely deeper than contrition, and accept it as our participation in the life of Jesus, we shall begin to learn that it is our true nobility, and that to prove it in being servants of all is the highest fulfillment of our destiny, as men created in the image of God.

When I look back upon my own religious experience, or round upon the Church of Christ in the world, I stand amazed at the thought of how little humility is sought after as the distinguishing feature of the discipleship of Jesus. In preaching and living, in the daily intercourse of the home and social life, in the more special fellowship with Christians, in the direction and performance of work for Christ,—alas! how much proof there is that humility is not esteemed the cardinal virtue, the only root from which the graces can grow, the one indispensable condition of true fellowship with Jesus. That it should have been possible for men to say of those who claim to be seeking the higher holiness, that the profession has not been accompanied with increasing humility, is a loud call to all earnest Christians, however much or little truth there be in the charge, to prove that meekness and lowliness of heart are the chief mark by which they who follow the meek and lowly Lamb of God are to be known.

Humility: the Glory of the Creature

"They shall cast their crowns before the throne, so saying: Worthy art Thou, our Lord and our God, to receive the glory, and the honor and the power: for Thou didst create all things, and because of Thy will then are, and were created. "—Rev. 4:11

When God created the universe, it was with the one ob;ect of making the creature partaker of His perfection and blessedness, and so showing forth in it the glory of His love and wisdom and power. God wished to reveal Himself in and through created beings by communicating to them as much of His own goodness and glory as they were capable of receiving. But this communication was not a giving to the creature something which it could possess in itself, a certain life or goodness, of which it had the charge and disposal. By no means. But as God is the ever-living, ever-present, ever-acting One, who upholdeth all things by the word of His power, and in whom all things exist, the relation of the creature to God could only be one of unceasing, absolute, universal dependence. As truly as God by His power once created, so truly by that same power must God every moment maintain. The creature has not only to look back to the origin and first beginning of existence, and acknowledge that it there owes everything to God; its chief care, its highest virtue, its only happiness, now and through all eternity, is to present itself an empty vessel, in which God can dwell and manifest His power and goodness.

The life God bestows is imparted not once for all, but each moment continuously, by the unceasing operation of His mighty power. Humility, the place of entire dependence on God, is, from the very nature of things, the first duty and the highest virtue of the creature, and the root of every virtue.

And so pride, or the loss of this humility, is the root of every sin and evil. It was when the now fallen angels began to look upon themselves with self-complacency that they were led to disobedience, and were cast down from the light of heaven into outer darkness. Even so it was, when the serpent breathed the poison of his pride, the desire to be as God, into the hearts of our first parents, that they too fell from their high estate into all the wretchedness in which man is now sunk. In heaven and earth, pride, self-exaltation, is the gate and the birth, and the curse, of hell. (See Note "A" at end of chapter.)

Hence it follows that nothing can be our redemption, but the restoration of the 'lost humility, the original and only true relation of the creature to its God. And so Jesus came to bring humility back to earth, to make us partakers of it, and by it to save us. In heaven He humbled Himself to become man. The humility we see in Him possessed Him in heaven; it brought Him, He brought it, from there. Here on earth "He humbled Himself, and became obedient unto death"; His humility gave His death its value, and so became our redemption. And now the salvation He imparts is nothing less and nothing else than a communication of His own life and death, His own disposition and spirit, His own humility, as the ground and root of His relation to God and His redeeming work. Jesus Christ took the place and fulfilled the destiny of man, as a creature, by His life of perfect humility. His humility is our salvation. His salvation is our humility.

And so the life of the saved ones, of the saints, must needs bear this stamp of deliverance from sin, and full restoration to their original state; their whole relation to God and man marked by an all-pervading humility. Without this there can be no true abiding in God's presence, or experience of His favor and the power of His Spirit; without this no abiding faith, or love or joy or strength. Humility is the only soil in which the graces root; the lack of humility is the sufficient explanation of every defect and failure. Humility is not so much a grace or virtue along with others; it is the root of all, because it alone takes the right attitude before God, and allows Him as God to do all.

God has so constituted us as reasonable beings, that the truer the insight into the real nature or the absolute need of a command, the readier and fuller will be our obedience to it. The call to humility has been too little regarded in the Church because its true nature and importance has been too little apprehended. It is not a something which we bring to God, or He bestows; it is simply the sense of entire nothingness, which comes when we see how truly God is all, and in which we make way for God to be all. When the creature realizes that this is the true nobility, and consents to be with his will, his mind, and his affections, the form, the vessel in which the life and glory of God are to work and manifest themselves, he sees that humility is simply acknowledging the truth of his position as creature, and yielding to God His place.

In the life of earnest Christians, of those who pursue and profess holiness, humility ought to be the chief mark of their uprightness. It is often said that it is not so. May not one reason be that in the teaching and example of the Church, it has never had that place of supreme importance which belongs to it? And that this, again, is owing to the neglect of this truth, that strong as sin is as a motive to humility, there is one of still wider and mightier influence, that which makes the angels, that which made Jesus, that which makes the holiest of saints in heaven, so humble; that the first and chief mark of the relation of the creature, the secret of his blessedness, is the humility and nothingness which leaves God free to be all?

I am sure there are many Christians who will confess that their experience has been very much like my own in this, that we had long known the Lord without realizing that meekness and lowliness of heart are to be the distinguishing feature of the disciple as they were of the Master. And further, that this humility is not a thing that will come of itself, but that it must be made the object of special desire and prayer and faith and practice. As we study the word, we shall see what very distinct and oft-repeated instructions Jesus gave His disciples on this point, and how slow they were in understanding Him. Let us, at the very commencement of our meditations, admit that there is nothing so natural to man, nothing so insidious and hidden from our sight, nothing so difficult and dangerous, as pride. Let us feel that nothing but a very determined and persevering waiting on God and Christ will discover how lacking we are in the grace of humility, and how impotent to obtain what we seek. Let us study the character of Christ until our souls are filled with the love and admiration of His lowliness. And let us believe that, when we are broken down under a sense of our pride, and our impotence to cast it out, Jesus Christ Himself will come in to impart this grace too, as a part of His wondrous life within us.

NOTE A—"All this is to make it known the region of eternity that pride can degrade the highest angels into devils, and humility raise fallen flesh and blood to the thrones of angels. Thus, this is the great end of God raising a new creation out of a fallen kingdom of angels: for this end it stands in its state of war betwixt the fire and pride of fallen angels, and the humility of the Lamb of God, that the last trumpet may sound the great truth through the depths of eternity, that evil can have no beginning but from pride, and no end but from humility. The truth is this: Pride may die in you, or nothing of heaven can live in you. Under the banner of the truth, give yourself up to the meek and humble spirit of the holy Jesus. Humility must sow seed, or there can be no reaping in Heaven. Look not at pride only as an unbecoming temper, nor at humility only as a decent virtue: for the one is death, and the other is life; the one is all hell, the other is all heaven. So much as you have of pride within you, you have of the fallen angels alive in you; so much as you have of true humility, so much you have of the Lamb of God within you. Could you see what every stirring of pride does to your soul, you would beg of everything you meet to tear the viper from you, though with the loss of a hand or an eye. Could you see what a sweet, divine, transforming power there is in humility, how it expels the poison of your nature, and makes room for the Spirit of God to live in you, you would rather wish to be the footstool of all the world than want the smallest degree of it." —Spirit of Prayer, Pt.II, p.73, Edition of Moreton, Canterbury, 1893.

Humility: the Secret of Redemption

"Have this mind in you which was also in Christ Jesus: who emptied Himself; taking the form of a servant; and humbled Himself; becoming obedient even unto death. Wherefore God also highly exalted Him. "Phil. 2: 5-9.

No tree can grow except on the root from which it sprang. Through all its existence it can only live with the life that was in the seed that gave it being. The full apprehension of this truth in its application to the first and the Second Adam cannot but help us greatly to understand both the need and the nature of the redemption there is in Jesus.

The Need.—When the Old Serpent, he who had been cast out from heaven for his pride, whose whole nature as devil was pride, spoke his words of temptation into the ear of Eve, these words carried with them the very poison of hell. And when she listened, and yielded her desire and her will to the prospect of being as God, knowing good and evil, the poison entered into her soul and blood and life, destroying forever that blessed humility and dependence upon God which would have been our everlasting happiness. And instead of this, her life and the life of the race that sprang from her became corrupted to its very root with that most terrible of all sins and all curses, the poison of Satan's own pride. All the wretchedness of which this world has been the scene, all its wars and bloodshed among the nations, all its selfishness and suffering, all its ambitions and jealousies, all its broken hearts and embittered lives, with all its daily unhappiness, have their origin in what this cursed, hellish pride, either our own, or that of others, has brought us. It is pride that made redemption needful; it is from our pride we need above everything to be redeemed. And our insight into the need of redemption will largely depend upon our knowledge of the terrible nature of the power that has entered our being.

No tree can grow except on the root from which it sprang. The power that Satan brought from hell, and cast into man's life, is working daily, hourly, with mighty power throughout the world. Men suffer from it; they fear and fight and flee it; and yet they know not whence it comes, whence it has its terrible supremacy. No wonder they do not know where or how it is to be overcome. Pride has its root and strength in a terrible spiritual power, outside of us as well as within us; as needful as it is that we confess and deplore it as our very own, is to know it in its Satanic origin. If this leads us to utter despair of ever conquering or casting it out, it will lead us all the sooner to that supernatural power in which alone our deliverance is to be found—the redemption of the Lamb of God. The hopeless struggle against the workings of self and pride within us may indeed become still more hopeless as we think of the power of darkness behind it all; the utter despair will fit us the better for realizing and accepting a power and a life outside of ourselves too, even the humility of heaven as brought down and brought nigh by the Lamb of God, to cast out Satan and his pride.

No tree can grow except on the root from which it sprang. Even as we need to look to the first Adam and his fall to know the power of the sin within us, we need to know well the Second Adam and His power to give within us a life of humility as real and abiding and overmastering as has been that of pride. We have our life from and in Christ, as truly, yea more truly, than from and in Adam. We are to walk "rooted in Him," "holding fast the Head from whom the whole body increaseth with the increase of God." The life of God which in the incarnation entered human nature, is the root in which we are to stand and grow; it is the same almighty power that worked there, and thence onward to the resurrection, which works daily in us. Our one need is to study and know and trust the life that has been revealed in Christ as the life that is now ours, and waits for our consent to gain possession and mastery of our whole being.

In this view it is of inconceivable importance that we should have right thoughts of what Christ is, of what really constitutes Him the Christ, and specially of what may be counted His chief characteristic, the root and essence of all His character as our Redeemer. There can be but one answer: it is His humility. What is the incarnation but His heavenly humility, His emptying Himself and becoming man? What is His life on earth but humility; His taking the form of a servant? And what is His atonement but humility? "He humbled Himself and became obedient unto death." And what is His ascension and His glory, but humility exalted to the throne and crowned with glory? "He humbled Himself, therefore God highly exalted Him." In heaven, where He was with the Father, in His birth, in His life, in His death, in His sitting on the throne, it is all, it is nothing but humility. Christ is the humility of God embodied in human nature; the Eternal Love humbling itself, clothing itself in the garb of meekness and gentleness, to win and serve and save us. As the love and condescension of God makes Him the benefactor and helper and servant of all, so Jesus of necessity was the Incarnate Humility. And so He is still in the midst of the throne, the meek and lowly Lamb of God.

If this be the root of the tree, its nature must be seen in every branch and leaf and fruit. If humility be the first, the all-including grace of the life of Jesus,—if humility be the secret of His atonement,—then the health and strength of our spiritual life will entirely depend upon our putting this grace first too, and making humility the chief thing we admire in Him, the chief thing we ask of Him, the one thing for which we sacrifice all else. See Note B (at end of this chapter)

Is it any wonder that the Christian life is so often feeble and fruitless, when the very root of the Christ life is neglected, is unknown? Is it any wonder that the joy of salvation is so little felt, when that in which Christ found it and brings it, is so little sought? Until a humility which will rest in nothing less than the end and death of self; which gives up all the honor of men as Jesus did, to seek the honor that comes from God alone; which absolutely makes and counts itself nothing, that God may be all, that the Lord alone may be exalted,—until such a humility be what we seek in Christ above our chief joy, and welcome at any price, there is very little hope of a religion that will conquer the world.

I cannot too earnestly plead with my reader, if possibly his attention has never yet been specially directed to the want there is of humility within him or around him, to pause and ask whether he sees much of the spirit of the meek and lowly Lamb of God in those who are called by His name. Let him consider how all want of love, all indifference to the needs, the feelings, the weakness of others; all sharp and hasty judgments and utterances, so often excused under the plea of being outright and honest; all manifestations of temper and touchiness and irritation; all feelings of bitterness and estrangement, have their root in nothing but pride, that ever seeks itself, and his eyes will be opened to see how a dark, shall I not say a devilish pride, creeps in almost everywhere, the assemblies of the saints not excepted. Let him begin to ask what would be the effect, if in himself and around him, if towards fellow-saints and the world, believers were really permanently guided by the humility of Jesus; and let him say if the cry of our whole heart, night and day, ought not to be, Oh for the humility of Jesus in myself and all around me! Let him honestly fix his heart on his own lack of the humility which has been revealed in the likeness of Christ's life, and in the whole character of His redemption, and he will begin to feel as if he had never yet really known what Christ and His salvation is.

Believer! study the humility of Jesus. This is the secret, the hidden root of thy redemption. Sink down into it deeper day by day. Believe with thy whole heart that this Christ, whom God has given thee, even as His divine humility wrought the work for thee, will enter in to dwell and work within thee too, and make thee what the Father would have thee be.

Note B.— "We need to know two things: 1. That our salvation consists wholly in being saved from ourselves, or that which we are by nature; 2. That in the whole nature of things nothing could be this salvation or savior to us but such a humility of God as is beyond all expression. Hence the first unalterable term of the Savior to fallen man: Except a man denies himself, he cannot be My disciple. Self is the whole evil of fallen nature; self-denial is our capacity of being saved; humility is our savior ... Self is the root, the branches, the tree, of all the evil of our fallen state. All the evils of fallen angels and men have their birth in the pride of self. On the other hand, all the virtues of the heavenly life are the virtues of humility. It is humility alone that makes the unpassable gulf between heaven and hell. What is then, or in what lies, the great struggle for eternal life? It all lies in the strife between pride and humility: pride and humility are the two master powers, the two kingdoms in strife for the eternal possession of man. There never was, nor ever will be, but one humility, and that is the one humility of Christ. Pride and self have the all of man, till man has his all from Christ. He therefore only fights the good fight whose strife is that the self-idolatrous nature which he hath from Adam may be brought to death by the supernatural humility of Christ brought to life in him."—W. Law, Address to the Clergy, p. 52. [I hope that this book of Law on the Holy Spirit may be issued by my publisher in the course of the year.]

Humility in the Life of Jesus

"I am in the midst of you as he that serveth." Luke 22: 27.

In the Gospel of John we have the inner life of our Lord laid open to us. Jesus speaks frequently of His relation to the Father, of the motives by which He is guided, of His consciousness of the power and spirit in which He acts. Though the word humble does not occur, we shall nowhere in Scripture see so clearly wherein His humility consisted. We have already said that this grace is in truth nothing but that simple consent of the creature to let God be all, in virtue of which it surrenders itself to His working alone. In Jesus we shall see how both as the Son of God in heaven, and as man upon earth, He took the place of entire subordination, and gave God the honor and the glory which is due to Him— And what He taught so often was made true to Himself: "He that humbleth him: shall be exalted." As it is written, "He humbled Himself, therefore God highly exalted Him."

Listen to the words in which our Lord speaks of His relation to the Father, and how unceasingly He uses the words not, and nothing, of Himself. The not I, in which Paul expresses his relation to Christ, is the very spirit of what Christ says of His relation the Father.

"The Son can do nothing of Himself" (John 5: 19).

"I can of My own self do nothing; My judgment is just, because I seek not Mine own will" (John 5: 30).

"I receive not glory from men" (John 5: 41).

"I am come not to do Mine own will" (John 6:38).

"My teaching is not Mine" (John 7:16)

"I am not come of Myself" (John 7:28)

"I do nothing of Myself" (John 8:28)

"I have not come of Myself, but He sent Me" (John 8: 42).

"I seek not Mine own glory" (John 8:50)

"The words that I say, I speak not from Myself" (John 14: 10).

"The word which ye hear is not Mine" (John 14: 24).

These words open to us the deepest roots of Christ's life and work. They tell us how it was that the Almighty God was able to work His mighty redemptive work through Him. They show what Christ counted the state of heart which became Him as the Son of the Father. They teach us what the essential nature and life is of that redemption which Christ accomplished and now communicates. It is this: He was nothing, that God might be all. He resigned Himself with His will and His powers entirely for the Father to work in Him. Of His own power, His own will, and His own glory, of His whole mission with all His works and His teaching, of all this He said, It is not I; I am nothing; I have given Myself to the Father to work; I am nothing, the Father is all.

This life of entire self-abnegation, of absolute submission and dependence upon the Father's will, Christ found to be one of perfect peace and joy. He lost nothing by giving all to God. God honored His trust, and did all for Him, and then exalted Him to His own right hand in glory. And because Christ had thus humbled Himself before God, and God was ever before Him, He found it possible to humble Himself before men too, and to be the Servant of all. His humility was simply the surrender of Himself to God, to allow Him to do in Him what He pleased, whatever men around might say of Him, or do to Him.

It is in this state of mind, in this spirit and disposition, that the redemption of Christ has its virtue and efficacy. It is to bring us to this disposition that we are made partakers of Christ. This is the true self-denial to which our Savior calls us, the acknowledgment that self has nothing good in it, except as an empty vessel which God must fill, and that its claim to be or do anything may not for a moment be allowed. It is in this, above and before everything, in which the conformity to Jesus consists, the being and doing nothing of ourselves, that God may be all.

Here we have the root and nature of true humility. It is because this is not understood or sought after, that our humility is so superficial and so feeble. We must learn of Jesus, how He is meek and lowly of heart. He teaches us where true humility takes its rise and finds its strength—in the knowledge that it is God who worketh all in all, that our place is to yield to Him in perfect resignation and dependence, in full consent to be and to do nothing of ourselves. This is the life Christ came to reveal and to impart—a life to God that came through death to sin and self. If we feel that this life is too high for us and beyond our reach, it must but the more urge us to seek it in Him; it is the indwelling Christ who will live in us this life, meek and lowly. If we long for this, let us, meantime, above everything, seek the holy secret of the knowledge of the nature of God, as He every moment works all in all; the secret, of which all nature and every creature, and above all, every child of God, is to be the witness,—that it is nothing but a vessel, a channel, through which the living God can manifest the riches of His wisdom, power, and goodness. The root of all virtue and grace, of all faith and acceptable worship, is that we know that we have nothing but what we receive, and bow in deepest humility to wait upon God for it.

It was because this humility was not only a temporary sentiment, wakened up and brought into exercise when He thought of God, but the very spirit of His whole life, that Jesus was just as humble in His intercourse with men as with God. He felt Himself the Servant of God for the men whom God made and loved; as a natural consequence, He counted Himself the Servant of men, that through Him God might do His work of love. He never for a moment thought of seeking His honor, or asserting His power to vindicate Himself. His whole spirit was that of a life yielded to God to work in. It is not until Christians study the humility of Jesus as the very essence of His redemption, as the very blessedness of the life of the Son of God, as the only true relation to the Father, and therefore as that which Jesus must give us if we are to have any part with Him, that the terrible lack of actual, heavenly, manifest humility will become a burden and a sorrow, and our ordinary religion be set aside to secure this, the first and the chief of the marks of the Christ within us.

Brother, are you clothed with humility? Ask your daily life. Ask Jesus. Ask your friends. Ask the world. And begin to praise God that there is opened up to you in Jesus a heavenly humility of which you have hardly known, and through which a heavenly blessedness you possibly have never yet tasted can come in to you.

Humility in the Teaching of Jesus

"Learn of Me, for I am meek and lowly of heart. "—Matt. xi. 29. "Whosoever will be chief among you, let him be your servant, even as the Son of Man came to server." Matt.10:27.

We have seen humility in the life of Christ, as He laid open His heart to us: let us listen to His teaching. There we shall hear how He speaks of it, and how far He expects men, and specially His disciples, to be humble as He was. Let us carefully study the passages, which I can scarce do more than quote, to receive the full impression of how often and how earnestly He taught it: it may help us to realize what He asks of us.

I. Look at the commencement of His ministry. In the Beatitudes with which the Sermon on the Mount opens, He speaks:"Blessed are the poor in spirit; for theirs is the kingdom of heaven. Blessed are the meek; for they shall inherit the earth." The very first words of His proclamation of the kingdom of heaven reveal the open gate through which alone we enter. The poor, who have nothing in themselves, to them the kingdom comes. The meek, who seek nothing in themselves, theirs the earth shall be. The blessings of heaven and earth are for the lowly. For the heavenly and the earthly life, humility is the secret of blessing.

2. "Learn of Me; for I am meek and lowly of heart, and ye shall find rest for your souls."Jesus offers Himself as Teacher. He tells what the spirit both is, which we shall find Him as Teacher, and which we can learn receive from Him. Meekness and lowliness the one thing He offers us; in it we shall find perfect rest of soul. Humility is to be a salvation.

3. The disciples had been disputing who would be the greatest in the kingdom, and had agreed to ask the Master (Luke 9:46; Matt. 18:3).

He set a child in their midst and said, "Whosoever shall humble himself as this little child, shall be exalted. " "Who the greatest in the kingdom of heaven?" The question is indeed a far-reaching one. What will be the chief distinction in the heavenly kingdom? The answer, none but Jesus would have given. The chief glory of heaven, the true heavenly-mindedness, the chief of the graces, is humility. "He that is least among you, the same shall be great. "

4. The sons of Zebedee had asked Jesus to sit on His right and left, the highest place in the kingdom. Jesus said it was not His to give, but the Father's, who would give it to those for whom it was prepared. They must not look or ask for it. Their thought must be of the cup and the baptism of humiliation. And then He added, "Whosoever will be chief among you, let him be your servant. Even as the Son of Man came to serve. " Humility, as it is the mark of Christ the heavenly, will be the one standard of glory in heaven: the lowliest is the nearest to God. The primacy in the Church is promised to the humblest.

5. Speaking to the multitude and the disciples, of the Pharisees and their love of the chief seats, Christ said once again (Matt. 23:11), "He that is greatest among you shall be your servant." Humiliation is the only ladder to honor in God's kingdom.

6. On another occasion, in the house of a Pharisee, He spoke the parable of the guest who would be invited to come up higher (Luke 14:1-11), and added, "For whosoever exalteth himself shall be abased; and he that humbleth himself shall be exalted." The demand is inexorable; there is no other way. Self-abasement alone will be exalted.

7. After the parable of the Pharisee and the Publican, Christ spake again (Luke18: 14), "Everyone that exalteth himself shall be abased; and he that humbleth himself shall be exalted." In the temple and presence and worship of God, everything is worthless that is not pervaded by deep, true humility towards God and men.

8. After washing the disciples' feet, Jesus said (John 13:14), "If I then, the Lord and Master, have washed your feet, ye also ought to wash one another's feet." The authority of command, and example, every thought, either of obedience or conformity, make humility the first and most essential element of discipleship.

9. At the Holy Supper table, the disciples still disputed who should be greatest (Luke 22:26). Jesus said, "He that is greatest among you, let him be as the younger; and he that is chief, as he that doth serve. I am among you as he that serveth." The path in which Jesus walked, and which He opened up for us, the power and spirit in which He wrought out salvation, and to which He saves us, is ever the humility that makes me the servant of all.

How little this is preached. How little it is practice. How little the lack of it is felt or confessed. I do not say, how few attain to it, some recognizable measure of likeness to Jesus in His humility. But how few ever think, of making it a distinct object of continual desire or prayer. How little the world has seen it. How little has it been seen even in the inner circle of the Church.

"Whosoever will be chief among you, let him be your servant." Would God that it might be given us to believe that Jesus means this! We all know what the character of a faithful servant or slave implies. Devotion to the master's interests, thoughtful study and care to please him, delight in his prosperity and honor and happiness. There are servants on earth in whom these dispositions have been seen, and to whom the name of servant has never been anything but a glory. To how many of us has it not been a new joy in the Christian life to know that we may yield ourselves as servants, as slaves to God, and to find that His service is our highest liberty,—the liberty from sin and self? We need now to learn another lesson,—that Jesus calls us to be servants of one another, and that, as we accept it heartily, this service too will be a most blessed one, a new and fuller liberty too from sin and self. At first it may appear hard; this is only because of the pride which still counts itself something. If once we learn that to be nothing before God is the glory of the creature, the spirit of Jesus, the joy of heaven, we shall welcome with our whole heart the discipline we may have in serving even those who try to vex us. When our own heart is set upon this, the true sanctification, we shall study each word of Jesus on self-abasement with new zest, and no place will be too low, and no stooping too deep, and no service too mean or too long continued, if we may but share and prove the fellowship with Him who spake, "I am among you as he that serveth".

Brethren, here is the path to the higher life. Down, lower down! This was what Jesus ever said to the disciples who were thinking of being great in the kingdom, and of sitting on His right hand and His left. Seek not, ask not for exaltation; that is God's work. Look to it that you abase and humble yourselves, and take no place before God or man but that of servant; that is your work; let that be your one purpose and prayer. God is faithful. Just as water ever seeks and fills the lowest place, so the moment God finds the creature abased and empty, His glory and power flow in to exalt and to bless. He that humbleth himself—that must be our one care shall be exalted; that is God's care; by His mighty power and in His great love He will do it.

Men sometimes speak as if humility and meekness would rob us of what is noble and bold and manlike. Oh that all would believe that this is the nobility of the kingdom of heaven, that this is the royal spirit that the King of heaven displayed, that this is Godlike, to humble oneself, to become the servant of all! This is the path to the gladness and the glory of Christ's presence ever in us, His power ever resting on us.

Jesus, the meek and lowly One, calls us to learn of Him the path to God. Let us study the words we have been reading, until our heart is filled with the thought: My one need is humility. And let us believe that what He shows, He gives; what He is, He imparts. As the meek and lowly One, He will come in and dwell in the longing heart.

Humility in the Disciples of Jesus

"Let him that is chief among you be as he that doth serve." —Luke 22:26.

We have studied humility in the person and teaching of Jesus; let us now look for it in the circle of His chosen companions—the twelve apostles. If, in the lack of it we find in them, the contrast between Christ and men is brought out more clearly, it will help us to appreciate the mighty change which Pentecost wrought in them, and prove how real our participation can be in the perfect triumph of Christ's humility over the pride Satan had breathed into man.

In the texts quoted from the teaching of Jesus, we have already seen what the occasions were on which the disciples had proved how entirely wanting they were in the grace of humility. Once, they had been disputing the way which of them should be the greatest Another time, the sons of Zebedee with their mother had asked for the first places—the seat on the right hand and the left. And, later on, at the Supper table on the last night, there was again a contention which should be accounted the greatest. Not that there were not moments when they indeed humbled themselves before their Lord. So it was with Peter when he cried out, "Depart from me, Lord, for I am a sinful man." So, too, with the disciples when they fell down and worshiped Him who had stilled the storm. But such occasional expressions of humility only bring out into stronger relief what was the habitual tone of their mind, as shown in the natural and spontaneous revelation given at other times of the place and the power of self. The study of the meaning of all this will teach us most important lessons.

First,. How much there may be of earnest and active, religion while humility is still sadly wanting.—See it in the disciples. There was in them fervent attachment to Jesus. They had forsaken all for Him. The

Father had revealed to them that He was the Christ of God. They believed in Him, they loved Him, they obeyed His commandments. They had forsaken all to follow Him. When others went back, they clave to Him. They were ready to die with Him. But deeper down than all this there was a dark power, of the existence and the hideousness of which they were hardly conscious, which had to be slain and cast out, ere they could be the witnesses of the power of Jesus to save. It is even so still. We may find professors and ministers, evangelists and workers, missionaries and teachers, in whom the gifts of the Spirit are many and manifest, and who are the channels of blessing to multitudes, but of whom, when the testing time comes, or closer intercourse gives fuller knowledge, it is only too painfully manifest that the grace of humility, as an abiding characteristic, is scarce to be seen. All tends to confirm the lesson that humility is one of the chief and the highest graces; one of the most difficult of attainment; one to which our first and chiefest efforts ought to be directed; one that only comes in power, when the fullness of the Spirit makes us partakers of the indwelling Christ, and He lives within us.

Second, How impotent all external teaching and all personal effort is, to conquer pride or give the meek and lowly heart.—For three years the disciples had been in the training school of Jesus. He had told them what the chief lesson was He wished to teach them: "Learn of Me, for I am meek and lowly in heart." Time after time He had spoken to them, to the Pharisees, to the multitude, of humility as the only path to the glory of God. He had not only lived before them as the Lamb of God in His divine humility, He had more than once unfolded to them the inmost secret of His life: "The Son of Man came not to be served, but to serve"; "I am among you as one that serveth." He had washed their feet, and told them they were to follow His example. And yet all had availed but little. At the Holy Supper there was still the contention as to who should be greatest. They had doubtless often tried to learn His lessons, and firmly resolved not again to grieve Him. But all in vain. To teach them and us the much needed lesson, that no outward instruction, not even of Christ Himself; no argument however convincing; no sense of the beauty of humility, however deep; no personal resolve or effort, however sincere and earnest,—can cast out the devil of pride. When Satan casts out Satan, it is only to enter afresh in a mightier, though more hidden power. Nothing can avail but this, that the new nature in its divine humility be revealed in power to take the place of the old, to become as truly our very nature as that ever was.

Third, It is only by the indwelling of Christ in His divine humility that we become truly humble. We have our pride from another, from Adam; we must have our humility from Another too. Pride is ours, and rules in us with such terrible power, because it is ourself, our very nature. Humility must be ours in the same way; it must be our very self, our very nature. As natural and easy as it has been to be proud, it must be, it will be, to be humble. The promise is, "Where," even in the heart, "sin abounded, grace did abound more exceedingly." All Christ's teaching of His disciples, and all their vain efforts, were the needful preparation for His entering into them in divine power, to give and be in them what He had taught them to desire. In His death He destroyed the power of the devil, He put away sin, and effected an everlasting redemption. In His resurrection He received from the Father an entirely new life, the life of man in the power of God, capable of being communicated to men, and entering and renewing and filling their lives with His divine power. In His ascension He received the Spirit of the Father, through whom He might do what He could not do while upon earth, make Himself one with those He loved, actually live their life for them, so that they could live before the Father in a humility like His, because it was Himself who lived and breathed in them. And on Pentecost He came and took possession. The work of preparation and conviction, the awakening of desire and hope which His teaching had effected, was perfected by the mighty change that Pentecost wrought. And the lives and the epistles of James and Peter and John bear witness that all was changed, and that the spirit of the meek and suffering Jesus had indeed possession of them.

What shall we say to these things? Among my readers I am sure there is more than one class. There may be some who have never yet thought very specially of the matter, and cannot at once realize its immense importance as a life question for the Church and its every member. There are others who have felt condemned for their shortcomings, and have put forth very earnest efforts, only to fail and be discouraged. Others, again, may be able to give joyful testimony of spiritual blessing and power, and yet there has never been the needed conviction of what those around them still see as wanting. And still others may be able to witness that in regard to this grace too the Lord has given deliverance and victory, while He has taught them how much they still need and may expect out of the fullness of Jesus. To whichever class we belong, may I urge the pressing need there is for our all seeking a still deeper conviction of the unique place that humility holds in the religion of Christ, and the utter impossibility of the Church or the believer being what Christ would have them be, as long as His humility is not recognized as His chief glory, His first command, and our highest blessedness. Let us consider deeply how far the disciples were advanced while this grace was still so terribly lacking, and let us pray to God that other gifts may not so satisfy us, that we never grasp the fact that the absence of this grace is the secret cause why the power of God cannot do its mighty work. It is only where we, like the Son, truly know and show that we can do nothing of ourselves, that God will do all.

It is when the truth of an indwelling Christ takes the place it claims in the experience of believers, that the Church will put on her beautiful garments and humility be seen in her teachers and members as the beauty of holiness.

Humility in Daily Life

"He that loveth not his brother whom he hath seen, how can he love God whom he hath not seen?"—1 John 4:20.

What a solemn thought, that our love to God will be measured by our everyday intercourse with men and the love it displays; and that our love to God will be found to be a delusion, except was its truth is proved in standing the test of daily life with our fellow-men. It is even so with our humility. It is easy to think we humble ourselves before God: humility towards men will be the only sufficient proof that our humility before God is real; that humility has taken up its abode in us; and become our very nature; that we actually, like Christ, have made ourselves of no reputation. When in the presence of God lowliness of heart has become, not a posture we pray to Him, but the very spirit of our life, it will manifest itself in all our bearing towards our brethren. The lesson is one of deep import: the only humility that is really ours is not that which we try to show before God in prayer, but that which we carry with us, and carry out, in our ordinary conduct; the insignificances of daily life are the importances and the tests of eternity, because they prove what really is the spirit that possesses us. It is in our most unguarded moments that we really show and see what we are. To know the humble man, to know how the humble man behaves, you must follow him in the common course of daily life.

Is not this what Jesus taught? It was when the disciples disputed who should be greatest; when He saw how the Pharisees loved the chief place at feasts and the chief seats in the synagogues; when He had given them the example of washing their feet,—that He taught His lessons of humility. Humility before God is nothing if not proved in humility before men.

It is even so in the teaching of Paul. To the Romans He writes: "In honor preferring one another"; "Set not your mind on high things, but condescend to those that are lowly." "Be not wise in your own conceit." To the Corinthians: "Love," and there is no love without humility as its root, "vaunteth not itself, is not puffed up, seeketh not its own, is not provoked." To the Galatians: "Through love be servants one of another. Let us not be desirous of vainglory, provoking one another, envying one another." To the Ephesians, immediately after the three wonderful chapters on the heavenly life: "Therefore, walk with all lowliness and meekness, with long-suffering, forbearing one another in love"; "Giving thanks always, subjecting yourselves one to another in the fear of Christ." To the Philippians: "Doing nothing through faction or vainglory, but in lowliness of mind, each counting other better than himself. Have the mind in you which was also in Christ Jesus, who emptied Himself, taking the form of a servant, and humbled Himself." And to the Colossians: "Put on a heart of compassion, kindness, humility, meekness, long-suffering, forebearing one another, and forgiving each other, even as the Lord forgave you." It is in our relation to one another, in our treatment of one another, that the true lowliness of mind and the heart of humility are to be seen. Our humility before God has no value, but as it prepares us to reveal the humility of Jesus to our fellow-men. Let us study humility in daily life in the light of these words.

The humble man seeks at all times to act up to the rule, "In honor preferring one another; Servants one of another; Each counting others better than himself Subjecting yourselves one to another." The question is often asked, how we can count others better than ourselves, when we see that they are far below us in wisdom and in holiness, in natural gifts, or in grace received. The question proves at once how little we understand what real lowliness of mind is. True humility comes when, in the, light of God, we have seen ourselves to be nothing, have consented to part with and cast away self, to let God be all. The soul that has done this, sand can say, So have I lost myself in finding Thee, no longer compares itself with others. It has given up forever every thought of self in God's presence; it meets its fellow-men as one who is nothing, and seeks nothing for itself; who is a servant of God, and for His sake a servant of all. A faithful servant may be wiser than the master, and yet retain the true spirit and posture of the servant. The humble man looks upon every, the feeblest and unworthiest, child of God, and honors him and prefers him in honor as the son of a King. The spirit of Him who washed the disciples' feet, makes it a joy to us to be indeed the least, to be servants one of another.

The humble man feels no jealousy—or envy. He can praise God when others are preferred and blessed before him. He can bear to hear others praised and himself forgotten, because in God's presence he has learnt to say with Paul, "I am nothing." He has received the spirit of Jesus, who pleased not Himself, and sought not His own honor, as the spirit of his life.

Amid what are considered the temptations to impatience and touchiness, to hard thoughts and sharp words, which come from the failings and sins of fellow-Christians, the humble man carries the oft-repeated injunction in his heart, and shows it in his life, "Forbearing one another, and forgiving one another, even as the Lord forgave you." He has learnt that in putting on the Lord Jesus he has put on the heart of compassion, kindness, humility, meekness, and long-suffering. Jesus has taken the place of self, and it is not an impossibility to forgive as Jesus forgave. His humility does not consist merely in thoughts or words of self-depreciation, but, as Paul puts it, in "a heart of humility," encompassed by compassion and kindness, meekness and longsuffering,—the sweet and lowly gentleness recognized as the mark of the Lamb of God.

In striving after the higher experiences of the Christian life, the believer is often in danger of aiming at and rejoicing in what one might call the more human, the manly, virtues, such as boldness, joy, contempt of the world, zeal, self-sacrifice,—even the old Stoics taught and practice these,—while the deeper and gentler, the diviner and more heavenly graces, those which Jesus first taught upon earth, because He brought them from heaven; those which are more distinctly connected with His cross and the death of self,—poverty of spirit, meekness, humility, lowliness,—are scarcely thought of or valued. Therefore, let us put on a heart of compassion, kindness, humility, meekness, long-suffering; and let us prove our Christlikeness, not only in our zeal for saving the lost, but before all in our intercourse with the brethren, forbearing and forgiving one another, even as the Lord forgave us.

Fellow-Christians, do let us study the Bible portrait of the humble man. And let us ask our brethren, and ask the world, whether they recognize in us the likeness to the original. Let us be content with nothing less than taking each of these texts as the promise of what God will work in us, as the revelation in words of what the Spirit of Jesus will give as a birth within us. And let each failure and shortcoming simply urge us to turn humbly and meekly to the meek and lowly Lamb of God, in the assurance that where He is enthroned in the heart, His humility and gentleness will be one of the streams of living water that flow from within us. 1

(1— I knew Jesus, and He was very precious to my soul: but I found something in me that would not keep sweet and patient and kind. I did what I could to keep it down, but it was there. I besought Jesus to do something for me, and when I gave Him my will, He came to my heart, and took out all that would not be sweet, all that would not be kind, all that would not be patient, and then He shut the door."—George Foxe)

Once again I repeat what I have said before. I feel deeply that we have very little conception of what the Church suffers from the lack of this divine humility,—the nothingness that makes room for God to prove His power. It is not long since a Christian, of an humble, loving spirit, acquainted with not a few mission stations of various societies, expressed his deep sorrow that in some cases the spirit of love and forbearance was sadly lacking. Men and women, who in Europe could each choose their own circle of friends, brought close together with others of uncongenial minds, find it hard to bear, and to love, and to keep the unity of the Spirit in the bond of peace. And those who should have been fellow-helpers of each other's joy, became a hindrance and a weariness. And all for the one reason, the lack of the humility which counts itself nothing, which rejoices in becoming and being counted the least, and only seeks, like Jesus, to be the servant, the helper and comforter of others, even the lowest and unworthiest.

And whence comes it that men who have joyfully given up themselves for Christ, find it so hard to give up themselves for their brethren? Is not the blame with the Church? It has so little taught its sons that the humility of Christ is the first of the virtues, the best of all the graces and powers of the Spirit. It has so little proved that a Christlike humility is what it, like Christ, places and preaches first, as what is in very deed needed, and possible too. But let us not be discouraged. Let the discovery of the lack of this grace stir us to larger expectation from God. Let us look upon every brother who tries or vexes us, as God's means of grace, God's instrument for our purification, for our exercise of the humility Jesus our Life breathes within us. And let us have such faith in the All of God, and the nothing of self, that, as nothing in our own eyes, we may, in God's power, only seek to serve one another in love.

Humility and Holiness

"Which say, Stand by thyself;—,for I am holier than thou. " —Isa. 65: 5.

We speak of the Holiness movement in our times, and praise God for it. We hear a great deal of seekers after holiness and professors of holiness, of holiness teaching and holiness meetings. The blessed truths of holiness in Christ, and holiness by faith, are being emphasized as never before. The great test of whether the holiness we profess to seek or to attain, is truth and life, will be whether it be manifest in the increasing humility it produces. In the creature, humility is the one thing needed to allow God's holiness to dwell in him and shine through him. In Jesus, the Holy One of God who makes us holy, a divine humility was the secret of His life and His death and His exaltation; the one infallible test of our holiness will be the humility before God and men which marks us. Humility is the bloom and the beauty of holiness.

The chief mark of counterfeit holiness is its lack of humility. Every seeker after holiness needs to be on his guard, lest unconsciously what was begun in the spirit be perfected in the flesh, and pride creep in where its presence is least expected. Two men went up into the temple to pray: the one a Pharisee, the other a publican. There is no place or position so sacred but the Pharisee can enter there. Pride can lift its head in the very temple of God, and make His worship the scene of its self exaltation. Since the time Christ so exposed his pride, the Pharisee has put on the garb of the publican, and the confessor of deep sinfulness equally with the professor of the highest holiness, must be on the watch. Just when We are most anxious to have our heart the temple of God, we shall find the two men coming up to pray. And the publican will find that his danger is not from the Pharisee beside him, who despises him, but the Pharisee within who commends and exalts.

In God's temple, when we think we are in the holiest of all, in the presence of His holiness, let us beware of pride. "Now there was a day when the sons of God came to present themselves before the Lord, and Satan came also among them."

"God, I thank thee, I am not as the rest of men, or even as this publican." It is in that which is just cause for thanksgiving, it is in the very thanksgiving which we render to God, it may be in the very confession that God has done it all, that self finds its cause of complacency. Yes, even when in the temple the language of penitence and trust in God's mercy alone is heard, the Pharisee may take up the note of praise, and in thanking God be congratulating himself. Pride can clothe itself in the garments of praise or of penitence. Even though the words, "I am not as the rest of men" are rejected and condemned, their spirit may too often be found in our feelings and language towards our fellow-worshipers and fellow-men. Would you know if this really is so, just listen to the way in which Churches and Christians often speak of one another. How little of the meekness and gentleness of Jesus is to be seen. It is so little remembered that deep humility must be the keynote of what the servants of Jesus say of themselves or each other. Is there not many a Church or assembly of the saints, many a mission or convention, many a society or committee, even many a mission away in heathendom, where the harmony has been disturbed and the work of God hindered, because men who are counted saints have proved in touchiness and haste and impatience, in self-defense and self-assertion, in sharp judgments and unkind words, that they did not each reckon others better than themselves, and that their holiness has but little in it of the meekness of the saints? In their spiritual history men may have had times of great humbling and brokenness, but what a different thing this is from being clothed with humility, from having an humble spirit, from having that lowliness of mind in which each counts himself the servant of others, and so shows forth the very mind which was also in Jesus Christ.

"Stand by; for I am holier than thou!" What a parody on holiness! Jesus the Holy One is the humble One: the holiest will ever be the humblest. There is none holy but God: we have as much of holiness as we have of God. And according to what we have of God will be our real humility, because humility is nothing but the disappearance of self in the vision that God is all. The holiest will be the humblest. Alas! though the bare-faced boasting Jew of the days of Isaiah is not often to be found, even our manners have taught us not to speak thus, how often his spirit is still seen, whether in the treatment of fellow saints or of the children of the world. In the spirit in which opinions are given, and work is undertaken, and faults are exposed, how often, though the garb be that of the publican, the voice is still that of the Pharisee: "Oh God, I thank Thee that I am not as other men."

And is there, then, such humility to be found, that men shall indeed still count themselves "less than the least of all saints," the servants of all? There is. "Love vaunteth not itself, is not puffed up, seeketh not its own." Where the spirit of love is shed abroad in the heart, where the divine nature comes to a full birth where Christ the meek and lowly Lamb of God is truly formed within, there is given the power of a perfect love that forgets itself and finds its blessedness in blessing others, in bearing with them and honoring them, however feeble they be. Where this love enters, there God enters. And where God has entered in His power, and reveals Himself as All, there the creature becomes nothing. And where the creature becomes nothing before God; it cannot be anything but humble towards the fellow-creature. The presence of God becomes not a thing of times and seasons, but the covering under which the soul ever dwells, and its deep abasement before God becomes the holy place of His presence whence all its words and works proceed.

May God teach us that our thoughts and words and feelings concerning our fellow men are His test of our humility towards Him, and that our humility before Him is the only power that can enable us to be always humble with our fellow-men. Our humility must be the life of Christ, the Lamb of God, within us.

Let all teachers of holiness, whether in the pulpit or on the platform, and all seekers after holiness, whether in the closet or the convention, take warning. There is no pride so dangerous, because none so subtle and insidious, as the pride of holiness. It is not that a man ever says, or even thinks, "Stand by; I am holier than thou." No, indeed, the thought would be regarded with abhorrence. But there grows up, all unconsciously, a hidden habit of soul, which feels complacency its attainments, and cannot help seeing how far it is in advance of others. It can be recognized, not always in any special self-assertion or self-laudation, but simply in the absence of that deep self-abasement which cannot but be the mark of the soul that has seen the glory of God (Job 42: 5, 6; Isa.6: 5). It reveals itself, not only in words or thoughts, but in a tone, a way of speaking of others, in which those who have the gift of spiritual discernment cannot but recognize the power of self. Even the world with its keen eyes notices it, and points to it as a proof that the profession of a heavenly life does not bear any specially heavenly fruits. O brethren! let us beware. Unless we make, with each advance in what we think holiness, the increase of humility our study, we may find that we have been delighting in beautiful thoughts and feelings, in solemn acts of consecration and faith, while the only sure mark of the presence of God, the disappearance of self, was all the time wanting. Come and let us flee to Jesus, and hide ourselves in Him until we be clothed upon with His humility. That alone is our holiness.

Humility and Sin

"Sinners, of whom I am chief."—1 Tim.1:15

Humility is often identified with penitence and contrition. As a consequence, there appears to be no way of fostering humility but by keeping the soul occupied with its sin. We have learned, I think, that humility is something else and something more. We have seen in the teaching of our Lord Jesus and the Epistles how often the virtue is inculcated without any reference to sin. In the very nature of things, in the whole relation of the creature to the Creator, in the life of Jesus as He lived it and imparts it to us, humility is the very essence of holiness as of blessedness. It is the displacement of self by the enthronement of God. Where God is all, self is nothing.

But though it is this aspect of the truth I have felt it specially needful to press, I need scarce say what new depth and intensity man's sin and God's grace give to the humility of the saints. We have only to look at a man like the Apostle Paul, to see how, through his life as a ransomed and a holy man, the deep consciousness of having been a sinner lives inextinguishably. We all know the passages in which he refers to his life as a persecutor and blasphemer. "I am the least of the apostles, that am not worthy to be called an apostle, because I persecuted the Church of God ...I labored more abundantly than they all; yet not I, but the grace of God which was with me" (I Cor. 15: 9,10). "Unto me, who am less than the least of all saints, was this grace given, to preach to the heathen" (Eph.3: 8). "I was before a blasphemer, and a persecutor, and injurious; howbeit I obtained mercy, because I did it ignorantly in unbelief ...Christ Jesus came into the world to save sinners, of whom I am chief" (1 Tim. I. 13, 15). God's grace had saved him; God remembered his sins no more for ever; but never, never could he forget how terribly he had sinned. The more he rejoiced in God's salvation, and the more his experience of God's grace filled him with joy unspeakable, the clearer was his consciousness that he was a saved sinner, and that salvation had no meaning or sweetness except as the sense of his being a sinner made it precious and real to him. Never for a moment could he forget that it was a sinner God had taken up in His arms and crowned with His love.

The texts we have just quoted are often appealed to as Paul's confession of daily sinning. One has only to read them carefully in their connection, to see how little this is the case. They have a far deeper meaning, they refer to that which lasts throughout eternity, and which will give its deep undertone of amazement and adoration to the humility with which the ransomed bow before the throne, as those who have been washed from their sins in the blood of the Lamb. Never, never, even in, glory, can they be other than ransomed sinners: never for a moment in this life can God's child live in the full light of His love, but as he feels that the sin, out of which he has been saved, is his one only right and title to all that grace has promised to do. The humility with which first he came as a sinner, acquires a new meaning when he learns how it becomes him as a creature. And then ever again, the humility, in which he was born as a creature, has its deepest, richest tones of adoration, in the memory of what it is to be a monument of God's wondrous redeeming love.

The true import of what these expressions of St. Paul teach us comes out all the more strongly when we notice the remarkable fact that, through his whole Christian course, we never find from his pen, even in those epistles in which we have the most intensely personal unbosomings, anything like confession of sin. Nowhere is there any mention of shortcoming or defect, nowhere any suggestion to his readers that he has failed in duty, or sinned against the law of perfect love. On the contrary, there are passages not a few in which he vindicates himself in language that means nothing if it does not appeal to a faultless life before God and men. "Ye are witnesses, and God also, how holy, and righteously, and un-blameably we behaved ourselves toward you" (1 Thess.2:10). "Our glorying is this, this testimony of our conscience, that in holiness and sincerity of God we .behaved ourselves in the world, and more abundantly to you ward" (2 Cor.1:12). This is not an ideal or an aspiration; it is an appeal to what his actual life had been. However we may account for this absence of confession of sin, all will admit that it must point to a life in the power of the Holy Ghost, such as is but seldom realized or expected in these our days.

The point which I wish to emphasize is this—that the very fact of the absence of such confession of sinning only gives the more force to the truth that it is not in daily sinning that the secret of the deeper humility will be found, but in the habitual, never for a moment to be forgotten position, which just the more abundant grace will keep more distinctly alive, that our only place,, the only place of blessing, our one abiding position before God, must be that of those whose highest joy it is to confess that they are sinners saved by grace.

With Paul's deep remembrance of having sinned so terribly in the past, ere grace had met him, and the consciousness of being kept from present sinning, there was ever coupled the abiding remembrance of the dark hidden power of sin ever ready to come in, and only kept out by the presence and power of the indwelling Christ. "In me, that is, in my flesh, dwelleth no good thing;"—these words of Rom. 7 describe the flesh as it is to the end. The glorious deliverance of Rom.8—"The law of the Spirit of life in Christ Jesus hath now made me free from the law of sin, which once led me captive"—is neither the annihilation nor the sanctification of the flesh, but a continuous victory given by the Spirit as He mortifies the deeds of the body. As health expels disease, and light swallows up darkness, and life conquers death, the indwelling of Christ through the Spirit is the health and light and life of the soul. But with this, the conviction of helplessness and danger ever tempers the faith in the momentary and unbroken action of the Holy Spirit into that chastened sense of dependence which makes the highest faith and joy the handmaids of a humility that only lives by the grace of God.

The three passages above quoted all show that it was the wonderful grace bestowed upon Paul, and of which he felt the need every moment, that humbled him so deeply. The grace of God that was with him, and enabled him to labor more abundantly than they all; the grace to preach to the heathen the unsearchable riches of Christ; the grace that was exceeding abundant with faith and love which is in Christ Jesus, it was this grace of which it is the very nature and glory that it is for sinners, that kept the consciousness of his having once sinned, and being liable to sin, so intensely alive. "Where sin abounded, grace did abound more exceedingly." This reveals how the very essence of grace is to deal with and take away sin, and how it must ever be the more abundant the experience of grace, the more intense the consciousness of being a sinner. It is not sin, but God's grace showing a man and ever reminding him what a sinner he was, that, will keep him truly humble. It is not sin, but grace, that will make me indeed know myself a sinner, and— make the sinner's place of deepest self-abasement the place I never leave.

I fear that there are not a few who, by strong expressions of self-condemnation and self-denunciation, have sought to humble themselves, and have to confess with sorrow that a humble spirit, a "heart of humility," with its accompaniments of kindness and compassion, of meekness and forbearance, is still as far off as ever. Being occupied with self, even amid the deepest self-abhorrence, can never free us from self. It is the revelation of God, not only by the law condemning sin but by His grace delivering from it, that will make us humble. The law may break the heart with fear; it is only grace that works that sweet humility which becomes a joy to the soul as its second nature. It was the revelation of God in His holiness, drawing nigh to make Himself known in His grace, that made Abraham and Jacob, Job and Isaiah, bow so low. It is the soul in which God the Creator, as the All of the creature in its nothingness, God the Redeemer in His grace, as the All of the sinner in his sinfulness, is waited for and trusted and worshiped, that will find itself so filled with His presence, that there will be no place for self. So alone can the promise be fulfilled: "The haughtiness of man shall be brought low, and the Lord alone be exalted in that day."

It is the sinner dwelling in the full light of God's holy, redeeming love, in the experience of that full indwelling of divine love, which comes through Christ and the Holy Spirit, who cannot but be humble. Not to be occupied with thy sin, but to be occupied with God, brings deliverance from self.

Humility and Faith

"How can ye believe, which receive glory from one another, and the glory that cometh from the only God ye seek not?"—John 5: 44.

In an address I lately heard, the speaker said that the blessings of the higher Christian life were often like the objects exposed in a shop window,—one could see them clearly and yet could not reach them. If told to stretch out his hand and take, a man would answer, I cannot; there is a thick pane of plate-glass between me and them. And even so Christians may see clearly the blessed promises of perfect peace and rest, of overflowing love and joy, of abiding communion and fruitfulness, and yet feel that there was something between hindering the true possession. And what might that be? Nothing but pride. The promises made to faith are so free and sure; the invitations and encouragements so strong; the mighty power of God on which it may count is so near and free,—that it can only be something that hinders faith that hinders the blessing being ours. In our text Jesus discovers to us that it is indeed pride that makes faith impossible. "How can ye believe, which receive glory from one another?" As we see how in their very nature pride and faith are irreconcilably at variance, we shall learn that faith and humility are at root one, and that we never can have more of true faith than we have of true humility; we shall see that we may indeed have strong intellectual conviction and assurance of the truth while pride is kept in the heart, but that it makes the living faith, which has power with God, an impossibility.

We need only think for a moment what faith is. Is it not the confession of nothingness and helplessness, the surrender and the waiting to let God work? Is it not in itself the most humbling thing there can be, the acceptance of our place as dependents, who can claim or get or do nothing but what grace bestows?! Humility is 'simply the disposition which prepares the soul for living on trust. And every, even the most secret breathing of pride, in self-seeking, self-will, self-confidence, or self exaltation, is just the strengthening of that self which cannot enter the kingdom, or possess the things of the kingdom, because it refuses to allow God to be what He is and must be there—the All in All.

Faith is the organ or sense for the perception and apprehension of the heavenly world and its blessings. Faith seeks .the glory that comes from God, that only comes where God is All. As long as we take glory from one another, as long as ever we seek and love and jealously guard the glory of this life, the honor and reputation that comes from men, we do not seek, and cannot receive the glory that comes from God. Pride renders faith impossible. Salvation comes through a cross and a crucified Christ. Salvation is the fellowship with the crucified Christ in the Spirit of His cross. Salvation is union with and delight in, salvation is participation in, the humility of Jesus. Is it wonder that our faith is so feeble when pride still reigns so much, and we have scarce learnt even to long or pray for humility as the most needful and blessed part of salvation?

Humility and faith are more nearly allied in Scripture than many know. See it in the life of Christ. There are two cases in which He spoke of a great faith. Had not the centurion, at whose faith He marveled, saying, "I have not found so great faith, no, not in Israel!" spoken, "I am not worthy that Thou shouldst come under my roof"? And had not the mother to whom He spoke, "O woman, great is thy faith!" accepted the name of dog, and said, "Yea, Lord, yet the dogs eat of the crumbs'? It is the humility that brings a soul to be nothing before God, that also removes every hindrance to faith, and makes it only fear lest it should dishonor Him by not trusting Him wholly.

Brother, have we not here the cause of failure in the pursuit of holiness? Is it not this, though we knew it not, that made our consecration and our faith so superficial and so short-lived? We had no idea to what an extent pride and self were still secretly working within us, and how alone God by His incoming and His mighty power could cast them out. We understood not how nothing but the new and divine nature, taking entirely the place of the old self, could make us really humble. We knew not that absolute, unceasing, universal humility must be the root disposition of every prayer and every approach to God as well as of every dealing with man; and that we might as well attempt to see without eyes, or live without breath, as believe or draw nigh to God or dwell in His love, without an all-pervading humility and lowliness of heart.

Brother, have we not been making a mistake in taking so much trouble to believe, while all the time there was the old self in its pride seeking to possess itself of God's blessing and riches? No wonder we could not believe. Let us change our course. Let us seek first of all to humble ourselves under the mighty hand of God: He will exalt us. The cross, and the death, and the grave, into which Jesus humbled Himself, were His path to the glory of God. And they are our path. Let our one desire and our fervent prayer be, to be humbled with Him and like Him; let us accept gladly whatever can humble us before God or men;—this alone is the path to the glory of God.

You perhaps feel inclined to ask a question. I have spoken of some who have blessed experiences, or are the means of bringing blessing to others, and yet are lacking in humility. You ask whether these do not prove that they have true, even strong faith, though they show too clearly that they still seek too much the honor that cometh from men. There is more than one answer can be given. But the principal answer in our present connection is this: They indeed have a measure of faith, in proportion to which, with the special gifts bestowed upon them, is the blessing they bring to others. But in that very blessing the work of their faith is hindered, through the lack of humility. The blessing is often superficial or transitory, just because they are not the nothing that opens the way for God to be all. A deeper humility would without doubt bring a deeper and fuller blessing. The Holy Spirit not only working in them as a Spirit of power, but dwelling in them in the fullness of His grace, and specially that of humility, would through them communicate Himself to these converts for a life of power and holiness and steadfastness now all too little seen.

"How can ye believe, which receive glory from one another?" Brother! nothing can cure you of the desire of receiving glory from men, or of the sensitiveness and pain and anger which come when it is not given, but giving yourself to seek only the glory that comes from God. Let the glory of the All glorious God be everything to you. You will be freed from the glory of men and of self, and be content and glad to be nothing. Out of this nothingness you will grow strong in faith, giving glory to God, and you will find that the deeper you sink in humility before Him, the nearer He is to fulfill the every desire of your Faith.

Humility and Death to Self

"He humbled Himself and became obedient unto death." —Phil.2: 8.

Humility is the path to death, because in death it gives the highest proof of its perfection. Humility is the blossom of which death to self, is the ,perfect. fruit. Jesus humbled Himself unto death, and opened the path in which we too must walk. As there was no way for Him to prove His surrender to God to the very uttermost, or to give up and rise out of our human nature to the glory of the Father but through death, so with us too. Humility must lead us to die to self: so we prove how wholly we have given ourselves up to it and to God; so alone we are freed from fallen nature, and find the path that leads to life in God, to that full birth of the new nature, of which

We have spoken of what Jesus did for His disciples when He communicated His resurrection life to them, when in the descent of the Holy Spirit He, the glorified and enthroned Meekness, actually came from heaven Himself to dwell in them. He won the power to do this through death: in its inmost nature the life He imparted was a life out of death, a life that had been surrendered to death, and been won through death. He who came to dwell in them was Himself One who had been dead and now lives for evermore. His life, His person, His presence, bears the marks of death, of being a life begotten out of death. That life in His disciples ever bears the death marks too; it is only as the Spirit of the death, of the dying One, dwells and works in the soul, that the power of His life can be known. The first and chief of the marks of the dying of the Lord Jesus, of the death-marks that show the true follower of Jesus, is humility. For these two reasons: Only humility leads to perfect death; Only death perfects humility. Humility and death are in their very nature one: humility is the bud; in death the fruit is ripened to perfection.

Humility leads to perfect death. Humility means the giving up of self and the taking of the place of perfect nothingness before God. Jesus humbled Himself, and became obedient unto death. In death He gave the highest, the perfect proof of having given up His will to the will of God. In death He gave up His self, with its natural reluctance to drink the cup; He gave up the life He had in union with our human nature; He died to self, and the sin that tempted Him; so, as man, He entered into the perfect life of God. If it had not been for His boundless humility, counting Himself as nothing except as a servant to do and suffer the will of God, He never would have died.

This gives us the answer to the question so often asked, and of which the meaning is so seldom clearly apprehended: How can I die to self? The death to self is not your work, it is God's work. In Christ you are dead to sin the life there is in you has gone through the process of death and resurrection; you may be sure you are indeed dead to sin. But the full manifestation of the power of this death in your disposition and conduct. depends upon the measure in which the Holy Spirit imparts the power of the death of Christ And here it is that the teaching is needed: if you would enter into full fellowship with Christ in His death, and know the full deliverance from self, humble yourself. This is your one duty. Place yourself before God in your utter helplessness; consent heartily to the fact of your impotence to slay or make alive yourself; sink down into your own nothingness, in the spirit of meek and patient and trustful surrender to God. Accept every humiliation,. look upon every fellow-man who tries or vexes you, as a means of grace to humble you. Use every opportunity of humbling' yourself before your fellow-men as a help to abide humble before God. God will accept such humbling of yourself as the proof that your whole heart desires it, as the very best prayer for it, as your preparation for His mighty work of grace, when, by the mighty strengthening of His Holy Spirit, He reveals Christ fully in you, so that He, in His form of a servant, is truly formed in you, and dwells in your heart. It is the path of humility which leads to perfect death, the full and perfect experience that we are dead in Christ.

Then follows: Only this death leads to perfect humility. Oh, beware of the mistake so many make, who would fain be humble, but are afraid to be too humble. They have so many qualifications and limitations, so many reasonings and questionings, as to what true humility is to be and to do, that they never unreservedly yield themselves to it. Beware of this. Humble yourself unto the death. It is in the death to self that humility is perfected. Be sure that at the root of all real experience of more grace, of all true advance in consecration, of all actually increasing conformity to the likeness of Jesus, there must be a deadness to self that proves itself to God and men in our dispositions and habits. It is sadly possible to speak of the death-life and the Spirit-walk, while even the tenderest love cannot but see how much there is of self. The death to self has no surer death-mark than a humility which makes itself of no reputation, which empties out itself, and takes the form of a servant. It is possible to speak much and honestly of fellowship with a despised and rejected Jesus, and of bearing His cross, while the meek and lowly, the kind and gentle humility of the Lamb of God is not seen, is scarcely sought. The Lamb of God means to two things—meekness and death. Let us seek to receive Him in both forms. In Him they are inseparable: they must be in us too.

What a hopeless task if we had to do the work! Nature never can overcome, —nature, not even with—the help of grace. Self can never cast out self, even in the regenerate man. Praise God! the work has been done, and finished and perfected for ever. The death of Jesus, once and forever, is our death to self. And the ascension of Jesus, His entering once and for ever into the Holiest, has given us the Holy Spirit to communicate to us in power, and make our very own, the power of the death-life. As the soul, in the pursuit and practice of humility, follows in the steps of Jesus, its consciousness of the need of something more is awakened, its desire and hope is quickened, its faith is strengthened, and it learns to look up and claim and receive that true fullness of the Spirit of Jesus, which can daily maintain His death to self and sin in its full power, and make humility the all pervading spirit of our life. (See note "C" at end of this chapter.)

"Are ye ignorant that all we who were baptized into Jesus Christ were baptized into His death? Reckon yourselves to be dead unto sin, but alive unto God in Christ Jesus. Present yourself unto God, as alive from the dead. " The whole self consciousness of the Christian is to be imbued and characterized by the spirit that animated the death of Christ. He has ever to present himself to God as one who has died in Christ, and in Christ is alive from the dead, bearing about in his body the dying of the Lord Jesus. His life ever bears the two-fold mark: its roots striking in true humility deep into the grave of Jesus, the death to sin and self; its head lifted up in resurrection power to the heaven where Jesus is.

Believer, claim in faith the death and the life of Jesus as thine. Enter in His grave into the rest from self and its work—the rest of God.— With Christ, who committed His spirit into the Father's hands, humble thyself and descend each— day into that perfect, helpless dependence upon God. God will raise thee up and exalt thee. Sink every morning in deep, deep nothingness into the grave of Jesus; every day the life of Jesus will be manifest in thee, Let a willing, loving, restful, happy humility be the mark that thou hast indeed claimed thy birthright—the baptism into the death of Christ. "By one offering He has perfected for ever them that are sanctified."The souls that enter into His humiliation will find in Him the power to see and count self dead, and, as those who have learned and received of Him, to walk with all lowliness and meekness, forbearing one another in love. The death-life is seen in a meekness and lowliness like that of Christ.

Note C— "To die to self, or come from under its power, is not, cannot be done, by
any active resistance we can make to it by the powers of nature. The one true way of dying to self is the way of patience, meekness, humility, and resignation to God. This is the truth and perfection of dying to self ...For if I ask you what the Lamb of God means, must you not tell me that it is and means the perfection of patience, meekness, humility, and resignation to God? Must you not therefore say that a desire and faith of these virtues is an application to Christ, is a giving up yourself to Him and the perfection of faith in Him? And then, because this inclination of your heart to sink down in patience, meekness, humility, and resignation to God, is truly giving up all that you are and all that

you have from fallen Adam, it is perfectly leaving all you have to follow Christ; it is your highest act of faith in Him. Christ is nowhere but in these virtues; when they are there, He is in His own kingdom. Let this be the Christ you follow.

"The Spirit of divine love can have no birth in any fallen creature, till it wills and chooses to be dead to all self, in a patient, humble resignation to the power and mercy of God. "I seek for all my salvation through the merits and mediation of the meek, humble, patient, suffering Lamb of God, who alone hath power to bring forth the blessed birth of these heavenly virtues in my soul. There is no possibility of salvation but in and by the birth of the meek, humble, patient, resigned Lamb of God in our souls. When the Lamb of God hath brought forth a real birth of His own meekness, humility, and full resignation to God in our souls, then it is the birthday of the Spirit of love in our souls, which, whenever we attain, will feast our souls with such peace and joy in God as will blot out the remembrance of everything that we called peace or joy before.

"This way to God is infallible. This infallibility is grounded in the twofold character of our Savior: 1. As He is the Lamb of God, a principle of all meekness and humility in the soul; 2. As He is the Light of heaven, and blesses eternal nature, and turns it into a kingdom of heaven,—when we are willing to get rest to our souls in meek, humble resignation to God, then it is that He, as the Light of God and heaven, joyfully breaks in upon us, turns our darkness into light, and begins that kingdom of God and of love within us, which will never have an end." —See Wholly For God. (The whole passage deserves careful study, showing most remarkably how the continual sinking down in humility before God is, from man's side, the only way to die to self.)

Humility and Happiness

"Most gladly therefore will I rather glory in my weaknesses, that the strength of Christ may rest upon me. Wherefore I take pleasure in weakness: for when I am weak then am I strong. " —2 Cor.12:9,10.

Lest Paul should exalt himself, by reason of the exceeding greatness of the revelations, a thorn in the flesh was sent him to keep him humble. Paul's first desire was to have it removed, and he besought the Lord thrice that it might depart. The answer came that the trial was a blessing; that, in the weakness and humiliation it brought, the grace and strength of the Lord could be the better manifested. Paul at once entered upon a new stage in his relation to the trial: instead of simply enduring it, he most gladly gloried in it; instead of asking for deliverance, he took pleasure in it. He had learned that the place of humiliation is the place of blessing, of power, of joy.

Every Christian virtually passes through these two stages in his pursuit of humility. In the first he fears and flees and seeks deliverance from all that can humble him. He has not yet learnt to seek humility at any cost. He has accepted the command to be humble, and seeks to obey it, though only to find how utterly he fails. He prays for humility, at times very earnestly; but in his secret heart he prays more, if not in word, then in wish, to be kept from the very things that will make him humble. He is not yet so in love with humility as the beauty of the Lamb of God, and the joy of heaven, that he would sell all to procure it. In his pursuit of it, and his prayer for it, there is still somewhat of a sense of burden and of bondage; to humble himself has not yet become the spontaneous expression of a life and a nature that is essentially humble. It has not yet become his joy and only pleasure. He cannot yet say, "Most gladly do I glory in weakness, I take pleasure in whatever humbles me."

But can we hope to reach the stage in which this will be the case? Undoubtedly. And what will it be that brings us there? That which brought Paul there—a new revelation of the Lord Jesus. Nothing but the presence of God can reveal and expel self. A clearer insight was to be given to Paul into the deep truth that the presence of Jesus will banish every desire to seek anything in ourselves, and will make us delight in every humiliation that prepares us for His fuller manifestation. Our humiliations lead us, in the experience of the presence and power of Jesus, to choose humility as our highest blessing. Let us try to learn the lessons the story of Paul teaches us.

We may have advanced believers, eminent teachers, men of heavenly experiences, who have not yet fully learnt the lesson of perfect humility, gladly glorying in weakness. We see this in Paul. The danger of exalting himself was coming very near. He knew not yet perfectly what it was to be nothing; to die, that Christ alone might live in him; to take pleasure in all that brought him low. It appears as if this were the highest lesson that he had to learn, full conformity to his Lord in that self-emptying where he gloried in weakness that God might be all.

The highest lesson a believer has to learn is humility. Oh that every Christian who seek to advance in holiness may remember this well! There may be intense consecration, and fervent zeal and heavenly experience, and yet, if it is not prevented by very special dealings of the Lord, there may be an unconscious self-exaltation with it all. Let us learn the lesson,—the highest holiness is the deepest humility; and let us remember that comes not of itself, but only as it is made matter of special dealing on the part of our faithful Lord and His faithful servant.

Let us look at our lives in the light of this experience, and see whether we gladly glory in weakness, whether we take pleasure, as Paul did, in injuries, in necessities, in distresses. Yes, let us ask whether we have learnt to regard a reproof, just or unjust, a reproach from friend or enemy, an injury, or trouble, or difficulty into which others bring us, as above all an opportunity of proving Jesus is all to us, how our own pleasure or honor are nothing, and , how humiliation is in very truth what we take pleasure in. It is indeed blessed, the deep happiness of heaven, to be so free from self that whatever is said of us or done to us is lost and swallowed up, in the thought that Jesus is all.

Let us trust Him who took charge of Paul to take charge of us too. Paul needed special discipline, and with it special instruction, to learn, what was more precious than even the unutterable things he had heard in heaven what it is to glory in weakness and lowliness. We need it, too, oh so much. He who cared for him will care for us too. He watches over us with a jealous, loving care, "lest we exalt ourselves". When we are doing so, He seeks to discover to us the evil, and deliver us from it. In trial and weakness and trouble He seeks to bring us low, until we so learn that His grace is all, as to take pleasure in the very thing that brings us and keeps us low. His strength made perfect in our weakness, His presence filling and satisfying our emptiness, becomes the secret of a humility that need never fail. It can, as Paul, in full sight of what God works in us, and through us, ever say, "In nothing was I behind the chiefest apostles, though I am nothing." His humiliations had led him to true humility, with its wonderful gladness and glorying and pleasure in all that humbles.

"Most gladly will I glory in my weaknesses, that the power of Christ may rest upon me; wherefore I take pleasure in weaknesses. "The humble man has learnt the secret of abiding gladness. The weaker he feels, the lower he sinks; the greater his humiliations appear, the more the power and the presence of Christ are his portion, ,until, as he says, " I am nothing," the word of his Lord brings ever deeper joy: "My grace is sufficient for thee."

I feel as if I must once again gather up all in the two lessons: the danger of pride is greater and nearer than we think, and the grace for humility too.

The danger of pride is greater and nearer than we think, and that especially at the time of our highest experiences. The preacher of spiritual truth with an admiring congregation hanging on his lips, the gifted speaker on a Holiness platform expounding the secrets of the heavenly life, the Christian giving testimony to a blessed experience, the evangelist moving on as in triumph, and made a blessing to rejoicing multitudes,—no man knows the hidden, the unconscious danger to which these are exposed. Paul was in danger without knowing it; what Jesus did for him is written for our admonition, that we may know our danger and know our only safety. If ever it has been said of a teacher or professor of holiness, he is so full of self; or, he does not practice what he preaches; or, his blessing has not made him humbler or gentler,—let it be said no more. Jesus, in whom we trust, can make us humble.

Yes, the grace for humility is greater and nearer, too, than we think. The humility of Jesus is our salvation: Jesus Himself is our humility. Our humility is His care and His work. His grace is sufficient for us, to meet the temptation of pride too. His strength will be perfected in our weakness. Let us choose to be weak, to be low, to be nothing. Let humility be to us joy and gladness. Let us gladly glory and take pleasure in weakness, in all that can humble us and keep us low; the power of Christ will rest upon us. Christ humbled Himself, therefore God exalted Him. Christ will humble us, and keep us humble; let us heartily consent, let us trustfully and joyfully accept all that humbles; the power of Christ will rest upon us. We shall find that the deepest humility is the secret of the truest happiness, of a joy that nothing can destroy.

Humility and Exaltation

"He that humbleth himself shall be exalted. "Luke 14:11, 18:14.

"God giveth grace to the humble. Humble yourself in the sight of the Lord, and He shall exalt you." Jas. 4:10.

"Humble yourselves therefore under the mighty hand of God, that He may exalt you in due time. "1 Pet.5:6.

Just yesterday I was asked the question, How am I to conquer this pride? The answer; was simple. Two things are needed. Do what; God says is your work: humble yourself. Trust Him to do what He says is His work: He will exalt you.

The command is clear: humble yourself. That does not mean that it is your work to conquer and cast out the pride of your nature, and to form within yourself the lowliness of the holy Jesus. No, this is God's work; the very essence of that exaltation, wherein He lifts you up into the real likeness of the beloved Son. What the command does mean is this: take every opportunity of humbling yourself before God and man. In the faith of the grace that is already working in you; in the assurance of the more grace for victory that is coming; up to the light that conscience each time flashes upon the pride of the heart and its workings; notwithstanding all there may be of failure and falling, stand persistently as under the unchanging command: humble yourself. Accept with gratitude everything that God allows from within or without, from friend or enemy, in nature or in grace, to remind you of your need of humbling, and to help you to it. Reckon humility to be indeed the mother-virtue, your very first duty before God, the one perpetual safeguard of the soul, and set your heart upon it as the source of all blessing. The promise is divine and sure: He that humbleth himself shall be exalted. See that you do the one thing God asks:

humble yourself. God will see that does the one thing He has promised. He will give more grace; He will exalt you in due time.

All God's dealings with man are characterized by two stages. There is the time of preparation, when command and promise, with the mingled experience of effort and impotence, of failure and partial success, with the holy expectancy of something better which these waken, train and discipline men for a higher stage. Then comes the time of fulfillment, when faith inherits the promise, and enjoys what it had so often struggled for in vain. This law holds good in every part of the Christian life, and in the pursuit of every separate virtue. And that because it is grounded in the very nature of things. In all that concerns our redemption, God must needs take the initiative. When that has been done, man's turn comes. In the effort after obedience and attainment, he must learn to know his impotence, in self-despair to die to himself, and so be fitted voluntarily and intelligently to receive from God the end, the completion of that of which he had accepted the beginning in ignorance. So, God who had been the Beginning, ere man rightly knew Him, or fully understood what His purpose was, is longed for and. welcomed as the End, as the All in All.

It is even thus, too, in the pursuit of humility. To every Christian the command comes from the throne of God Himself: humble yourself. The earnest attempt to listen and obey will be rewarded yes, rewarded—with the painful discovery of two things. The one, what depth of pride, that is of unwillingness to count oneself and to be counted nothing, to submit absolutely to God, there was, that one never knew. The other, what utter impotence there is in all our efforts, and in all our prayers too for God's help, to destroy the hideous monster. Blessed the man who now learns to put his hope in God, and to persevere, notwithstanding all the power of pride within him, in acts of humiliation before God and Men. We know the law of human nature: acts produce habits, habits breed dispositions, dispositions form the will, and the rightly-formed will is character. It is no otherwise in the work of grace. As acts, persistently repeated, beget habits and dispositions, and these strengthened the will, He who works both to will and to do comes with His mighty power and Spirit; and the humbling of the proud heart with which the' penitent saint cast himself so often before God, is rewarded with the "more grace" of the humble heart, in which the Spirit of Jesus has conquered, and brought the new nature to its maturity, and He the meek and lowly One now dwells for ever.

Humble yourselves in the sight of the Lord, and He will exalt you. And wherein does the exaltation consist? The highest glory of the creature is in being only a vessel, to receive and enjoy and show forth the glory of God. It can do this only as it is willing to be nothing in itself, that God may be all. Water always fills first the lowest places. The lower, the emptier a man lies before God, the speedier and the fuller will be the inflow of the divine glory. The exaltation God promises is not, cannot be, any external thing apart from Himself: all that He has to give or can give is only more of Himself, Himself to take more complete possession. The exaltation is not, like an earthly prize, something arbitrary, in no necessary connection with the conduct to be rewarded. No, but it is in its very nature the effect and result of the humbling of ourselves. It is nothing but the gift of such a divine indwelling humility, such a conformity to and possession of the humility of the Lamb of God, as fits us for receiving fully the indwelling of God.

He that humbleth himself shall be exalted. Of the truth of these words Jesus Himself is the proof; of the certainty of their fulfillment to us He is the pledge. Let us take His yoke upon us and learn of Him, for He is meek and lowly of heart. If we are but willing to stoop to Him, as He has stooped to us, He will yet stoop to each one of us again, and we shall find ourselves not unequally yoked with Him. As we enter deeper into the fellowship of His humiliation, and either humble ourselves or bear the humbling of men, we can count upon it that the Spirit of His exaltation, "the Spirit of God and of glory," will rest upon us. The presence and the power of the glorified Christ will come to them that are of an humble spirit. When God can again have His rightful place in us, He will lift us up. Make His glory thy care in humbling thyself; He will make thy glory His care in perfecting thy humility, and breathing into thee, as thy abiding life, the very Spirit of His Son. As the all-pervading life of God possesses thee, there will be nothing so natural, and nothing so sweet, as to be nothing, with not a thought or wish for self, because all is occupied with Him who filleth all. "Most gladly will I glory in my weakness, that the strength of Christ may rest upon me."

Brother, have we not here the reason that our consecration and our faith have availed so little in the pursuit of holiness? It was by self and its strength that the work was done under the name of faith; it was for self and its happiness that God was called in; it was, unconsciously, but still truly, in self and its holiness that the soul rejoiced. We never knew that humility, absolute, abiding, Christlike humility and self-effacement, pervading and marking our whole life with God and man, was the most essential element of the life of the holiness we sought for.

It is only in the possession of God that I lose myself. As it is in the height and breadth and glory of the sunshine that the littleness of the mote playing in its beams is seen, even so humility is the taking our place in God's presence to be nothing but a mote dwelling in the sunlight of His love.

"How great is God! how small am I! .Lost, swallowed up in Love's immensity! God only there, not I."

May God teach us to believe that to be humble, to be nothing in His presence, is the highest attainment, and the fullest blessing of the Christian life. He speaks to us: "I dwell in the high and holy place, and with him the is of a contrite and humble spirit." Be this our portion!

"Oh, to be emptier, lowlier,
Mean, unnoticed, and unknown,
And to God a vessel holier,
Filled with Christ, and Christ alone!"

Note D.—A Secret of Secrets: Humility the Soul of True Prayer.—Till the spirit of the heart be renewed, till it is emptied of all earthly desires, and stands in an habitual hunger and thirst after God, which is the true spirit of prayer; till then, all our prayer will be, more or less, but too much like lessons given to scholars; and we shall mostly say them, only because we dare not neglect them. But be not discouraged; take the following advice, and then you may go to church without any danger of mere lip-labor or hypocrisy, although there should be a hymn or a prayer, whose language is higher than that of your heart. Do this: go to the church as the publican went to the temple; stand inwardly in the spirit of your mind in that form which he outwardly expressed, when he cast down his eyes, and could only say, "God be merciful to me, a sinner." Stand unchangeably, at least in your desire, in this form or state of heart; it will sanctify every petition that comes out of your mouth; and when anything is read or sung or prayed, that is more exalted than your heart is, if you make this an occasion of further sinking down in the spirit of the publican, you will then be helped, and highly blessed, by those prayers and praises which seem only to belong to a heart better than yours.

This, my friend, is a secret of secrets; it will help you to reap where you have not sown, and be a continual source of grace in your soul; for everything that inwardly stirs in you, or outwardly happens to you, becomes a real good to you, if it finds or excites in you this humble state of mind. For nothing is in vain, or without profit to the humble soul; it stands always in a state of divine growth; everything that falls upon it is like a dew of heaven to it. Shut up yourself, therefore, in this form of Humility; all good is enclosed in it; it is a water of heaven, that turns the fire of the fallen soul into the meekness of the divine life, and creates that oil, out of which the love to God and man gets its flame. Be enclosed, therefore, always in it; let it be as a garment wherewith you are always covered, and a girdle with which you are girt; breathe nothing but in and from its spirit; see nothing but with its eyes; hear nothing but with its ears. And then, whether you are in the church or out of the church, hearing the praises of God or receiving wrongs from men and the world, all will be edification, and everything will help forward your growth in the life of God. (The Spirit of Prayer, PtII, p. 121)

A Prayer for Humility

I will here give you an infallible touchstone, that will try all to the truth. It is this: retire from the world and all conversation, only for one month; neither write, nor read, nor debate anything with yourself; stop all the former workings of your heart and mind: and, with all the strength of your heart, stand all this month, as continually as you can, in the following form of prayer to God. Offer it frequently on your knees; but whether sitting, walking, or standing, be always inwardly longing, and earnestly praying this one prayer to God: "That of His great goodness He would make known to you, and take from your heart, every kind and form and degree of Pride, whether it be from evil spirits, or your own corrupt nature; and that He would awaken in you the deepest depth and truth of that Humility, which can make you capable of His light and Holy Spirit." Reject every thought, but that of waiting and praying in this matter from the bottom of your heart, with such truth and earnestness, as people in torment wish to pray and be delivered from it ...If you can and will give yourself up in truth and sincerity to this spirit of prayer, I will venture to affirm that, if you had twice as many evil spirits in you as Mary Magdalene had, they will all be cast out of you, and you will be forced with her to weep tears of love at the feet of the holy Jesus.—The Spirit of Prayer, Pt. II, p. 124

With Christ in the School of Prayer
Table of Contents

Preface

Of all the promises connected with the command, abide in me,' there is none higher, and none that sooner brings the confession, `Not that I have already attained, or am already made perfect,' than this: `If ye abide in me, ask whatsoever ye will, and it shall be done unto you.' Power with God is the highest attainment of the life of full abiding.

And of all the traits of a life like *Christ* there is none higher and more glorious than conformity to Him in the work that now engages Him without ceasing in the Father's presence—His all-prevailing intercession. The more we abide in Him, and grow unto His likeness, will His priestly life work in us mightily, and our life become what His is, a life that ever pleads and prevails for men.

Thou hast made us kings and priests unto God. Both in the king and the priest the chief thing is power, influence, blessing. In the king it is the power coming downward; in the priest the power rising upward, prevailing with God. In our blessed Priest-King, Jesus Christ, the kingly power is founded on the priestly `He is able to save to the uttermost, because He ever liveth to make intercession.' in us, His priests and kings, it is no otherwise: it is in intercession that the Church is to find and wield its highest power, that each member of the, Church is to prove his descent from Israel, who as a prince had power with God and with men, and prevailed

It is under a deep impression that the place and power of prayer in the Christian life is too little understood that this book has been written. I feel sure that as long as we look on prayer chiefly as the means of maintaining our own Christian life, we shall not know fully what it is meant to be. But when we learn to regard it as the highest part of the work entrusted to us, the root and strength of all other work, we shall see that there is nothing that we so need to study and practice as the art of praying aright. If I have at all succeeded in pointing out the progressive teaching of our Lord in regard to prayer and the distinct reference the wonderful promises , of the last night (John 16:16) have to the works we are to do in His name, to the greater works, and to the bearing much fruit, we shall all admit that it is only when the Church gives herself up to this holy work of intercession that we can expect the power of Christ to manifest itself in her behalf. It is my prayer that God may use this little book to make clearer to some of His children the wonderful place of power and influence which He is waiting for them to occupy, and for which a weary world is waiting too.

In connection with this there is another truth that has come to me with wonderful clearness as I studied the teaching of Jesus on prayer. It is this: that the Father waits to hear every prayer of faith,: to give us whatsoever we will and whatsoever we ask in Jesus' name. We have become so accustomed to limit the wonderful love and the large promises of our God, that we cannot read the simplest and clearest statements of our Lord without the qualifying clauses by which we guard and expound them. If there is one thing I think the Church needs to learn, it is that God means prayer to have an answer, and that it hath not entered into the heart of man to conceive what God will do for His child who gives himself to believe that his prayer will be heard. God hears prayer; this is a truth universally admitted, but of which very few understand the meaning, or experience the power. If what I have written stirs my reader to go to the Master's words, and take His wondrous promises simply and literally as they stand, my object has been attained.

And then just one thing more. Thousands have in these last years found an unspeakable blessing in learning how completely Christ is our life, and how He undertakes to be and to do all in us that we need. I know not if we have yet learned to apply this truth to our prayer-life. Many complain that they have not the power to pray in faith, to pray the effectual prayer that availeth much. The message I would fain bring them is that the blessed Jesus is waiting, is longing, to teach them this. Christ is our life: in heaven He ever liveth to pray; His life in us is an ever-praying life, if we will but trust Him for it. Christ teaches us to pray not only by example, by instruction, by command, by promises, but by showing us *Himself* the ever-living Intercessor, as our Life. It is when we believe this, and go and abide in Him for our prayer-life too, that our fears of not being able to pray aright will vanish, and we shall joyfully and triumphantly trust our Lord to teach us to pray, to be Himself the life and the power of our prayer.

May God open our eyes to see what the holy ministry of intercession is, to which, as His royal priesthood, we have been set apart. May He give us a large and strong heart to believe what mighty influence our prayers can exert. And may all fear as to our being able to fulfil our vocation vanish as we see Jesus, living ever to pray, living and standing surety for our prayer-life.

Andrew Murray

Lord, Teach Us to Pray

And it came to pass, as He was praying in a certain place, that when He ceased, one of His disciples said to Him, Lord, teach us to pray. Luke 11:1

The disciples had been with Christ, and seen him pray. They had learnt to understand something of the connection between His wondrous life in public, and His secret life of prayer. They had learnt to believe in Him as a Master in the art of prayer—none could pray like Him. And so they came to Him with the request, `Lord, teach us to pray.' And in after years they would have told us that there were few things more wonderful or blessed that He taught them than His lessons on prayer.

And now still it comes to pass, as He is praying in a certain place, that disciples who see Him thus engaged feel the need of repeating the same request, `Lord, teach us to pray.' As we grow in the Christian life, the thought and the faith of the Beloved Master in His never-failing intercession becomes ever more precious, and the hope of being Like Christ in His intercession gains an attractiveness before unknown. And as we see Him pray, and remember that there is none who can pray like Him, and none who can teach like Him, we feel the petition of the disciples, `Lord, teach us to pray,' is just what we need. And as we think how all He is and has, how He Himself is our very own, how He is Himself our life, we feel assured that we have but to ask, and He will be delighted to take us up into closer fellowship with Himself, and teach us to pray even as He prays.

Come, my brothers! Shall we not go to the Blessed Master and ask Him to enroll our names too anew in that school which He always keeps open for those who long to continue their studies in the Divine art of prayer and intercession? Yes, let us this very day say to the Master, as they did of old `Lord, teach us to pray.' As we meditate we shall find each word of the petition we bring to be full of meaning.

'Lord, teach us to pray.' Yes, to pray. This is what we need to be taught. Though in its beginnings prayer is so simple that the feeblest child can pray, yet it is at the same time the highest and holiest work to which man can rise. It is fellowship with the Unseen and Most Holy One. The powers of the eternal world have been placed at its disposal. It is the very essence of true religion the channel of all blessings, the secret of power and life. Not only for ourselves, but for others, for the Church for the world, it is to prayer that God has given the right to take hold of Him and His strength. It is on prayer that the promises wait for their fulfilment the kingdom for its coming, the glory of God for its full revelation. And for this blessed work, how slothful and unfit we are. It is only the Spirit of God can enable us to do it aright. How speedily we are deceived into a resting in the form, while the power is wanting. Our early training, the teaching of the Church, the influence , of habit, the stirring of the emotions—how easily these lead to prayer which has no Spiritual power, and avails but little. True prayer, —that takes hold of God's strength; 'that availeth much, to which the gates of heaven are really opened wide—who would not cry, Oh for some one to teach me thus to pray?

Jesus has opened a school, in which He trains His redeemed ones, who specially desire it, to have power in prayer. Shall we not enter it with the petition, Lord! it is just this we need to be taught! O teach us to pray.

'Lord, teach us to pray.' Yes, us, Lord. We have read in Thy Word with what power Thy believing people of old used to pray, and what mighty wonders were done in answer to their prayers. And if this took place under the Old Covenant, in the time of preparation, how much more wilt Thou not now, in these days of fulfilment, give Thy people this sure sign of Thy presence in their midst. We have heard the promises given to Thine apostles of the power of prayer in Thy name, and have seen how gloriously they experienced their truth: we know for certain. they can become true to us too. We hear continually even in these days what glorious tokens of Thy power Thou dost still give to those who trust Thee fully. Lord! these all are men of like passions with ourselves; teach us to pray so too. The promises are for us, the powers and gifts of the heavenly world are for us. O teach us to pray so that we may receive abundantly. To us too Thou hast entrusted Thy work, on our prayer too the coming of Thy kingdom depends, in our prayer too Thou canst glorify Thy name; 'Lord, teach us to pray.' Yes, us, Lord; we offer ourselves as learners; we would indeed be taught of Thee. 'Lord, teach us to pray.'

'Lord, teach us to pray.' Yes, we feel the need now of being taught to pray. At first there is no work appears so simple; later on, none that is more difficult; and the confession is forced from us: We know not how to pray as we ought. It is true we have God's Word, with its clear and sure promises; but sin has so darkened our mind, that we know not always how to apply the Word. In spiritual things we do not always seek the most needful things, or fail in praying according to the law of the sanctuary. In temporal things we are still less able to avail ourselves of the wonderful liberty our Father has given us to ask what we need. And even when we know what to ask, how much there is still needed to make prayer acceptable. It must be to the glory of God, in full surrender to His will, in full assurance of faith, in the name of Jesus, and with a perseverance that, if need be, refuses to be denied. All this must be learned. It can only be learned in the school of much prayer, for practice makes perfect. Amid the painful consciousness of ignorance and unworthiness, in the struggle between believing and doubting, the heavenly art of effectual prayer is learned. Because, even when we do not remember it, there is One, the Beginner and Finisher of faith and prayer, who watches over our praying, and sees to it that in all who trust Him for it their education in the school of prayer shall be carried on to perfection. Let but the deep undertone of all our prayer be the teachable— that comes from a sense of ignorance, and from faith in Him as a perfect teacher, and we may be sure we shall be taught, we shall learn to pray in power. Yes, we may depend upon it, *He* teaches to pray.

'Lord, teach us to pray.' None can teach like Jesus, none but Jesus; therefore we call on Him, `Lord, teach us to pray.' A pupil needs a teacher, who knows his work, who has the gift of teaching, who in patience and love will descend to the pupil's needs. Blessed be God! Jesus is a this and much more. He knows what prayer is. It is Jesus, praying Himself, who teaches to pray. He knows what prayer is. He learned it amid the trials and tears of His earthly life. In heaven it is still His beloved work: His life there is prayer. Nothing delights Him more than to find those whom He can take with Him into the Father's presence, whom He can clothe with power to pray down God's blessing on those around them, whom He can train to be His fellow-workers in the intercession by which the kingdom is to be revealed on earth. He knows how to teach. Now the urgency of felt need, then by the confidence with which joy inspires. Here by the teaching of the Word, there by the testimony of another believer who knows what it is to have prayer beard. By His Holy Spirit, He has access to our heart, and teaches us to pray by showing us the sin that hinders the prayer, or giving us the assurance than we please God. He teaches, by giving not only thoughts of what to ask or how to ask, but by breathing within us the very spirit of prayer, by living within us as the Great Intercessor. We may indeed and most joyfully say, `Who teacheth like Him?' Jesus never taught His disciples how to preach, only how to pray. He did not speak much of what was needed to preach well but much of praying well. To know how to speak to God is more than knowing how to speak to man. Not power with men; 'but power with God is, the first thing. Jesus loves to teach us how to pray:

What think you, my beloved fellow-disciples! would it not be just what we need, to ask the Master for a month to give us a course of special lessons on the art of prayer? As we meditate on the words He spake on earth, let us yield ourselves to His teaching in the fullest confidence that, with such a teacher, we shall make progress. Let us take time not only to meditate, but to pray, to tarry at the foot of the throne, and be trained to the work of intercession. Let us do so in the assurance that amidst our, stammerings and fears He is carrying on His work most beautifully. He will breathe His own life which is all prayer, into us. As he makes us partakers of His righteousness and His life, He will of His intercession too. As the members of His body, as a holy priesthood, we shall take part in His priestly work of pleading and prevailing with God for men. Yes, let us joyfully say, ignorant and feeble though we be, `Lord, teach us to pray:

Blessed Lord! who ever livest to pray, Thou canst teach me too to pray, me too to live ever to pray. In this Thou lovest to make me share Thy glory in heaven, that I should pray without ceasing, and ever stand as a priest in the presence of my God.

Lord Jesus! I ask Thee this day to enroll my name among those who confess that they know not how to pray as they ought, and specially ask Thee for a course of teaching in prayer. Lord! teach me to tarry with Thee in the school, and give Thee time to train me. May a deep sense of my ignorance, of the wonderful privilege and power of prayer, of the need of the Holy Spirit as the Spirit of prayer, lead me to cast away my thoughts of what I think I know, and make me kneel before Thee in true teachableness and poverty of spirit.

And fill me, Lord, with the confidence that with such a teacher as Thou art I shall learn to pray. In the assurance that I have as my teacher, Jesus, who is ever praying to the Father, and by His prayer rules the destinies of His Church and the world, I will not be afraid. As much as I need to know of the mysteries of the prayer-world, Thou wilt unfold for me. And when I may not know, Thou wilt teach me to be strong in faith, giving glory to God.

Blessed Lord! Thou wilt not put to shame Thy scholar who trusts Thee, nor, by Thy grace, would he Thee either. Amen.

In Spirit and Truth

The hour cometh, and now is, when the true Worshipers shall worship the Father in spirit and in truth: for such doth the Father seek to be Worshipers. God is a Spirit: and they that worship Him must worship Him in spirit and truth. John 4:23-24

These words of Jesus to the woman of Samaria are his first recorded teaching on the subject of prayer. They give us some wonderful first glimpses into the word prayer. The Father seeks Worshipers: our worship satisfies His loving heart and is a joy to Him. He seeks true Worshipers, but finds many not as He would have them. True worship is that which is in spirit and truth. The Son has come to open the way for this worship in spirit and truth, and teach it to us. And so one of our first lessons in the school of prayer must be to understand what it is to pray in spirit and in truth and to know how we can attain to it.

To the woman of Samaria our Lord spoke of a threefold worship. There is first, the ignorant worship of the Samaritans: 'Ye worship that which ye know not.' The second, intelligent worship of the Jew, having the true knowledge of God: ' We worship that which we know; for salvation is of the Jews. And then the new, the spiritual worship which He Himself has come to introduce: `The hour is coming, and is now, when the true Worshipers shall worship the Father in spirit and truth.' From the connection it is evident that the words `in spirit and truth do not mean, as is often thought, earnestly., from the heart, in sincerity. The Samaritans had the five books of Moses and some knowledge of God: there was doubtless more than one among them who honestly and earnestly sought God in prayer. The Jews had the true full revelation of God in His word, as thus given; there were among them godly men, who called upon God with their whole heart. And yet not `in spirit and truth,' in the full meaning of the words. Jesus says, `The hour is coming, and now is:' it is only in and through Him that the worship of God will be in spirit and truth.

Among Christians one still finds the three classes of Worshipers. Some who in their ignorance hardly know what they ask: they pray earnestly, and yet receive but little. Others there are, who have more correct knowledge, who try to pray with all their mind and heart, and often pray more earnestly, and yet do not attain to the full blessedness of worship in spirit and truth. It is into this third class we must ask our Lord Jesus to take us; we must be taught of them how to worship in spirit and truth. This alone is spiritual worship; this makes us Worshipers such as the Father seeks. In prayer everything will depend on our understanding well and practicing the worship in spirit and truth.

'God is a Spirit, and they that worship Him, must worship Him in spirit and truth.' The first thought suggested here by the Master is that there must be harmony between God and His worshipers; —such as God is; must His worship be. This is according to a principle which prevails throughout the universe: we look for correspondence between an object and the organ to which it reveals or yields itself. The eye has an inner fitness for the light, the ear for sound. The man who would truly worship God, who would find and know and possess and enjoy God, must be in harmony with Him, must have the capacity for receiving Him. Because God is Spirit, we must worship in spirit. As God is, so His worshiper.

And what does this mean? The woman had asked our Lord whether Samaria or Jerusalem was the true place of worship. He answers that henceforth worship is no longer to be limited to a certain place: `Woman, believe Me, the hour cometh, when neither in this mountain, nor in Jerusalem shall ye worship the Father.' As God is Spirit, not bound by space or time but in His infinite perfection always and everywhere the same, so His worship would henceforth no longer be confined by place or form, but importance. How much our Christianity suffers from this, that it is confined to certain times and places. A man, who seeks to pray earnestly in the church or in the closet, spends the greater part of the week or the day in a spirit entirely at variance with that in which he prayed. His worship was the work of a fixed place or hour, not of his whole being. God is a Spirit: He is the Everlasting and Unchangeable One; what He is, He is always and in truth. Our worship must even so be in spirit and truth: His worship must be the spirit of our life; our life must be worship in spirit as God is Spirit.

God is a Spirit: and they that worship Him must worship Him in spirit and truth.' The second thought comes to us is that this worship in the spirit must come from God Himself. God is Spirit: He alone has Spirit to give: It was for this He sent His Son, to fit us for spiritual worship, by giving us the Holy

Spirit. It is of His own work that Jesus speaks when He says twice, `The hour cometh,' and then adds, `and is now.' He came to baptize with the Holy Spirit; the Spirit could not stream forth until He was glorified (John 1.33, 7.37, 38, 16.7). It was when He had made an end of sin, and entering into the Holiest of all with His blood, had there on our behalf received the Holy Spirit (Acts 2.33), that He could send Him down to us as the Spirit of the Father. It was when Christ redeemed us, and we in Him had received the position of children, that the Father sent forth the Spirit of His Son into our hearts to cry, `Abba, Father.' The worship in spirit is the worship of the Father in the Spirit of Christ, the Spirit of Sonship.

This is the reason why Jesus here uses the name Father. We never find one of the Old Testament saints personally appropriate the name of child or call God Father. The worship of the Father is only possible to those to whom the Spirit of the Son has been given. The worship in spirit is only possible to those to whom Son has revealed the Father, and who have received the spirit of Sonship. It is only Christ who opens the way and, teaches the worship in spirit.

And in truth. That does not only mean, in sincerity. Nor does it only signify, in accordance with the truth of God's Word. The expression is one of deep and Divine meaning. Jesus is `the only-begotten of the Father, full of grace and truth: `The law was given by Moses, grace and truth came by Jesus Christ: Jesus says, `I am the truth and the life: In the Old Testament all was shadow and promise; Jesus brought and gives the reality, the substance, of things hoped for. In Him the blessings and powers of the eternal life are our actual possession and experience. Jesus is full of grace and truth; the Holy Spirit is the Spirit of truth; through Him the grace that is in Jesus is ours in deed and truth, a positive communication out of the Divine life. And so worship in spirit is worship in truth; actual living fellowship with God, a real correspondence and harmony—between the Father, who is a Spirit, and the child praying in the spirit.

What Jesus said to the woman of Samaria, she could not at once understand. Pentecost was needed to reveal its full meaning. We are hardly prepared at our first entrance into the school of prayer to grasp such teaching. We shall understand it better later on. Let us only begin and take the lesson as He gives it. We are carnal and cannot bring God the worship He seeks. But Jesus came to give the Spirit: He has given Him to us. Let the disposition in which we set ourselves to pray be what Christ's words have taught us. Let there be the deep confession of our inability to bring God the worship that is pleasing to Him; the childlike teachableness that waits on Him to instruct us;

the simple faith that yields itself to the breathing of the Spirit. Above all, let us hold fast the blessed truth—we shall find that the Lord has more to say to us about it—that the knowledge of the Fatherhood of God, the revelation of His infinite Fatherliness in our hearts, the faith in the infinite love that gives us His Son and His Spirit to make us children, is indeed the secret of prayer in spirit and truth. This is the new and living way Christ opened up for us. To have Christ the Son, and the Spirit of the Son, dwelling within us, and revealing the Father, this makes us true, spiritual Worshipers.

Blessed Lord! I adore the love with which Thou didst teach a woman, who had refused Thee a cup of water, what the worship of God must be. I rejoice in the assurance that Thou wilt no less now instruct Thy disciple, who comes to Thee with a heart that longs to pray in spirit and in truth. O my Holy Master! do teach me this blessed secret.

Teach me that the worship in spirit and truth is not of man, but only comes from Thee; that it is not only a thing of times and seasons, but the outflowing of a life in Thee. Teach me to draw near to God in prayer under the deep impression of my ignorance and my having nothing in myself to offer Him, and at the same time of the provision Thou my Savior, makest for the Spirit's breathing in my childlike stammerings. I do bless Thee that in Thee I am a child, and have a child's liberty of access; that in Thee I have the spirit of Sonship and of worship in truth. Teach me, above all, Blessed Son of the Father, how it is the revelation of the Father that gives confidence in prayer; and let the infinite Fatherliness of God's Heart be my joy and strength for a life of prayer and of worship. Amen.

Pray to Thy Father, Which Is in Secret or Alone with God

But thou, when thou prayest, enter into thine inner chamber, and having shut thy door, pray to thy Father which is in secret, and thy Father which seeth in secret shall recompense thee. —MATTHEW 6.6.

After Jesus had called His first disciples, He gave them their first public teaching in the Sermon on the Mount. He there expounded to them the kingdom of God, its laws and its life. In that kingdom God is not only King, but Father; He not only gives all, but is Himself all. In the knowledge and fellowship of Him alone is its blessedness. Hence it came as a matter of course that the revelation of prayer and the prayer-life was a part of His teaching concerning the New Kingdom He came to set up. Moses gave neither command nor regulation with regard to prayer: even the prophets say little directly of the duty of prayer; it is Christ who teaches to pray.

And the first thing the Lord teaches His disciples is that they must have a secret place for prayer ; every one must have some solitary spot where he can be alone with his God. Every teacher must have a schoolroom. We have learned to know and accept Jesus as our only teacher in the school of prayer. He has already taught us at Samaria that worship is no longer confined to times and places; that worship, spiritual true worship, is a thing of the spirit and the life; the whole man must in his whole life be worshiping in spirit and truth. And yet He wants each one to choose for himself the fixed spot where He can daily meet him. That inner chamber, that solitary place, is Jesus' schoolroom. That spot may be anywhere; that spot may change from day to day if we have to change our abode; but that secret place there must be, with the quiet time in which the pupil places himself in the Master's presence, to be by Him prepared to worship the Father. There alone, but there most surely, Jesus comes to us to teach us to pray.

A teacher is always anxious that his schoolroom should be bright and attractive, filled with the light and air of heaven, a place where pupils long to come, and love to stay. In His first words on prayer in the Sermon on the Mount, Jesus seeks to set the inner chamber before us in its most attractive light. If we listen carefully, we soon notice what the chief thing He has to tell us is of our tarrying there. Three times He uses the name of Father: `Pray to thy Father;' 'Thy Father shall recompense thee;' `Your Father knoweth what things ye have need of.' The first thing in closet-prayer is: I must meet my Father. The light that shines in the closet must be: the light of the Father's countenance. The fresh air from heaven with which Jesus would have it filled, the atmosphere in which I am to breathe and pray, is: God's Father-love, God's infinite Fatherliness. Thus each thought or petition we breathe out will be simple, hearty, childlike trust in the Father. This is how the Master teaches us to pray: He brings us into the Father's living presence. What we pray there must avail. Let us listen carefully to hear what the Lord has to say to us.

First `Pray to thy Father which is in secret.' God is a God who hides Himself to the carnal eye. As long as in our worship of God, we are chiefly occupied with our own thoughts and , exercises; we shall not meet Him who is a Spirit, the unseen One. But to the man who withdraws himself from all that is of the world and man, and prepares to wait upon God alone, the Father will reveal Himself. As he forsakes and gives up and shuts out the world, and the life of the world, and surrenders himself to be led of Christ into the secret of God's presence, the light of the Father's love will rise upon him. The secrecy of the inner chamber and the closed door, the entire separation from all around us, is an image of, and so a help to that inner spiritual sanctuary, the secret of God's tabernacle, within the veil, where our spirit truly comes into contact with the invisible One. And so we are taught, at the very outset of our search after the secret of effectual prayer, to remember that it is in the inner chamber; where we are alone with the Father, that we shall learn to pray aright. The Father is in secret: in these words Jesus teaches us where He is waiting for us, where He is always to be found. Christians often complain that private prayer is not what it should be. They feel weak and sinful, the heart is cold and dark; it is as if they have so little to pray, and in that little no faith or joy. They are discouraged and kept from prayer by the thought that they cannot come to the Father as they ought or as they wish. Child of God! listen to your Teacher. He tells you that when you go to private prayer your first thought must be: The Father is in secret, the Father awaits me there. Just because your heart is cold and prayerless, get into the presence of the loving Father. As a father pitieth his children so the Lord pitieth you. Do not be thinking of how little you have to bring God, but

of how much He wants to give you. Just place yourself before, and look up
into, His face; think of His love, His wonderful, tender, pitying love. Just tell
Him how sinful and cold and dark all is: it is the Father's loving heart that
will give light and warmth to yours. O do what Jesus says: Just shut the door,
and pray to thy Father which is in secret. Is it not wonderful? to be able to go
alone with God the infinite God, and then to look up and say: My Father!

`And thy Father, which seeth in secret, will recompense thee.' Here Jesus
assures us that secret prayer cannot be fruitless: its blessing will show itself in
our life. We have but in secret, alone with God, to entrust our life before men
to Him; He will reward us openly; He will see to it that the answer to prayer
be made manifest in His blessing upon us. Our Lord would thus teach us that
as infinite Fatherliness and Faithfulness is that with which God meets us in
secret, so on our part there should be the childlike simplicity of faith, the
confidence that our prayer does bring down a blessing. He that cometh to
God must believe that He is a rewarder of them that seek Him.' Not on the
strong or the fervent feeling with which I pray does the blessing of the closet
depend, but upon the love and the power of the Father to whom I there
entrust my needs. And therefore the Master has but one desire: Remember
your Father is, and sees and hears in secret; go there and stay there, and go
again from there in the confidence: He will recompense. Trust Him for it;
depend upon Him: prayer to the Father cannot be vain; He will reward you
openly.

Still further to confirm this faith in the Father-love of God, Christ speaks
a third word: `Your Father knoweth what things ye have need of before ye
ask Him.' At first sight it might appear as if this thought made prayer less
needful: God knows far better than we what we need. But as we get a deeper
insight into what prayer really is, this truth will help much to strengthen our
faith. It will teach us that we do not need, as the heathen, with the multitude
and urgency of our words, to compel an unwilling God to listen to us. It will
lead to a holy thoughtfulness and silence in prayer as it suggests the question:
Does my Father really know that I need this? It will, when once we have been
led by the Spirit to the certainty that our request is indeed something that,
according to the Word, we do need for God's glory, give us wonderful
confidence to say, My Father knows I need it and must have it. And if there
be any delay in the answer, it will teach us in quiet perseverance to hold on:
Father thou knowest I need it. O the blessed liberty and simplicity of a child
that Christ our Teacher would fain cultivate in us as we draw near to God:
let us look up to the Father until His Spirit works it in us. Let us sometimes
in our prayers, when we are in danger of being so occupied with our fervent,

urgent petitions, as to forget that the Father knows and hears, let us hold still and just quietly say: My Father sees, my Father hears, my Father knows; it will help our faith to take the answer, and to say: We know that we have the petitions we have asked of Him.

And now, all ye who have anew entered the school of Christ to be taught to pray, take these lessons, practice them, and trust Him to perfect you in them. Dwell much in the inner chamber, with the door shut—shut in from men, shut up with God; it is there the Father waits you, it is there Jesus will teach you to pray. To be alone in secret with *The Father*: this be your highest joy. To be assured that *The Father* will openly reward the secret prayer, so that it cannot remain unblessed: this be your strength day by day. And to know that the Father knows that you need what you ask: this be your liberty to bring every need, in the assurance that your God will supply it according to His riches in glory in Christ Jesus.

Blessed Savior! with my whole heart I do bless Thee for the appointment of the inner chamber, as the school where Thou meetest each of Thy pupils alone, and revealest to him the Father. O my Lord! strengthen my faith so in the Father's tender love and kindness, that as often as I feel sinful or troubled, the first instinctive thought may be to go where I know the Father wafts me, and where prayer never can go unblessed. Let the thought that He knows my need before I ask, bring me, in great restfulness Of faith, to trust that He will give what His child requires. O let the place of secret prayer become to me the most beloved spot of earth.

And, Lord! hear me as I pray that Thou wouldest everywhere bless the closets of Thy believing people. Let Thy wonderful revelation of a Father's tenderness free all young Christians from every thought of secret prayer as a duty or a burden, and lead them to regard it as the highest privilege of their life, a joy and a blessing. Bring back all who are discouraged, because they cannot find ought to bring Thee in prayer. O give them to understand that they have only to come with their emptiness to Him who has all to give, and delights to do it. Not, what they have to bring the Father, but what the Father waits to give them, be their one thought.

And bless especially the inner chamber of all Thy servants who are working for Thee, as the place where God's truth and God's grace are revealed to them, where they are daily anointed with fresh oil, where their strength is renewed, and the blessings are received in faith, with which they are to bless their fellow-men. Lord; draw us all in the closet nearer to Thyself and the Father. Amen.

After this Manner Pray

After this manner therefore pray ye: Our Father, which art in heaven.—MATTHEW 6.9.

Every teacher knows the power of example. He not only tells the child what to do and how to do it, but shows him how it really can be done. In condescension to our weakness, our Heavenly Teacher has given us the very words we are to take with us as we draw near to our Father. We have in them a form of prayer in which there breathe the freshness and fulness of the Eternal Life. So simple that the child can lisp it, so divinely rich that it comprehends all that God can give. A form of prayer that becomes the model and inspiration for all other prayer, and yet always draws us back to itself as the deepest utterance of our souls before our God.

`Our Father which art in heaven!' To appreciate this word of adoration aright, I must remember that none of the saints had in Scripture ever ventured to address God as their Father. The invocation places us at once in the center of the wonderful revelation the Son came to make of His Father as our Father too. It comprehends the mystery of redemption—Christ delivering us from the curse that we might become the children of God. The mystery of regeneration—the Spirit in the new birth giving us the new life. And the mystery of faith—ere yet the redemption is accomplished or understood the word is given on the lips of the disciples to prepare them for the blessed experience still to come. The words are the key to the whole prayer, to all prayer. It takes time, it takes life to study them; it will take eternity to understand them fully. The knowledge of God's Father-love is the first and simplest, but also the last and highest lesson in the school of prayer. It is in the personal relation to the living God, and the personal conscious fellowship of love with Himself, that prayer begins. It is in the knowledge of God's Fatherliness, revealed by the Holy Spirit, that the power of prayer will be found to root and grow. In the infinite tenderness and pity and patience of the infinite Father, in His loving readiness to hear and to help, the life of prayer has its joy. O let us take time, until the Spirit has made these words to

us spirit and truth, filling heart and life: Our Father which art in heaven.'
Then we are indeed within the veil, in the secret place of power where prayer
always prevails.

`Hallowed be Thy name.' There is something here that strikes us at once.
While we ordinarily first bring our own needs to God in prayer, and then
think of what belongs to God and His interests, the Master reverses the order.
First, Thy name, Thy kingdom, Thy will; then, give us, forgive us, lead us,
deliver us. The lesson is of more importance than we think. In true worship
the Father must be first, must be all. The sooner I learn to forget myself in the
desire that *He* may be glorified, the richer will the blessing be that prayer will
bring to myself. No one ever loses by what he sacrifices for the Father.

This must influence all our prayer. There are two sorts of prayer: personal
and intercessory. The latter ordinarily occupies the lesser part of our time and
energy. This may not be. Christ has opened the school of prayer specially to
train intercessors for the great work of bringing down, by their faith and
prayer, the blessings of His work and love on the world around. There can be
no deep growth in prayer unless this be made our aim. The little child may
ask of the father only what it needs for itself; and yet it soon learns to say,
give some for sister too. But the grownup son, who only lives for the father's
interest and takes charge of the father's business, asks more largely, and gets
all that is asked. And Jesus would train us to the blessed life of consecration
and service, in which our interests are all subordinate to the Name, and the
Kingdom, and the Will of the Father. O let us live for this and let, on each
act of adoration, Our Father! there follow in the same breath, Thy Name,
Thy Kingdom, Thy Will;—for this we look up and long.

Hallowed be Thy name.' What name? This new name of Father. The word
Holy is the central word of the Old Testament; the name Father of the New.
In this name of Love all the holiness and glory of God are now to be revealed.
And how is the name to be hallowed? By God Himself: `I will hallow My
great name which ye have profaned.' Our prayer must be that in ourselves in
all God's children, in presence of the world, God Himself would reveal the
holiness, the Divine power, the hidden glory of the name of Father. The
Spirit of the Father is the Holy Spirit: it is only when we yield ourselves to be
led of Him, that the name will be hallowed in our prayers and our lives. Let
us learn the prayer: `Our Father, hallowed be Thy name.'

'Thy kingdom come.' The Father is a King and has a kingdom. The son
and heir of a king has no higher ambition than the glory of his father's
kingdom. In time of war or danger this becomes his passion; he can think of
nothing else. The children of the Father are here in the enemy's territory,

where the kingdom, which is in heaven, is not yet fully manifested. What more natural than that, when they learn to hallow the Father-name, they should long and cry with deep enthusiasm: 'Thy kingdom come. The coming of the kingdom is the one great event on which the revelation of the Father's glory, the blessedness of His children, the salvation of the world depends. On our prayers too the coming of the kingdom waits. Shall we not join in the deep longing cry of the redeemed: 'Thy kingdom come'? Let us learn it in the school of Jesus.

'Thy will be done, as in heaven, so on earth.' This petition is too frequently applied alone to the suffering of the will of God. In heaven God's will is done, and the Master teaches the child to ask that the will may be done on earth just as in heaven: in the spirit of adoring submission and ready obedience. Because the will of God is the glory of heaven the doing of it is the blessedness of heaven. As the will is done,— the kingdom of heaven comes into the heart. And where ever faith has accepted the Father's love, obedience accepts the Father's will. The surrender to, and the prayer for a life of heaven—like obedience, is the spirit of childlike prayer.

`Give us this day our daily bread! When first the child has yielded himself to the Father in the care for His Name, His Kingdom, and His Will, he has full liberty to ask for his daily bread. A master cares for the food of his servant, a general of his soldiers, a father of his child. And will not the Father in heaven care for the child who has in prayer given himself up to His interests? We may indeed in full confidence say: Father, I live for Thy honor and Thy work; I know Thou carest for me. Consecration to God and His will gives wonderful liberty in prayer for temporal things: the whole earthly life is given to the Father's loving care.

`And forgive us our debts, as we also have forgiven our debtors. As bread is the first need of the body, so forgiveness for the soul, And the provision for the one is as sure as for the other. We are children, but sinners too; our right of access to the Father's presence we owe to the precious blood and the forgiveness it has won for us. Let us beware of the prayer for forgiveness becoming a formality: only what is really confessed is really forgiven. Let us in faith accept the forgiveness as promised: as a spiritual reality, an actual transaction between God and us, it is the entrance into all the Father's love and all the privileges of children. Such forgiveness, as a living experience, is impossible without a forgiving spirit to others: as forgiven expresses the heavenward, so forgiving the earthward, relation of God's child. In each prayer to the Father I must be able to say that I know of no one whom I do not heartily love.

`And lead us not into temptation, but deliver us from the evil one.' Our daily bread, the pardon of our sins, and then our being kept from all sin and the power of the evil one, in these three petitions all our personal need is comprehended. The prayer for bread and pardon must be accompanied by the surrender to live in all things in holy obedience to the Father's will, and the believing prayer in everything to be kept by the power of the indwelling Spirit from the power of the evil one.

Children of God! it is thus Jesus would have us to pray to the Father in heaven. O let His Name, and Kingdom, and Will, have the first place in our love; His providing, and pardoning, and keeping love will be our sure portion, So the prayer will lead us up to the true child-life: the Father all to the child, the Father all for the child. We shall understand how Father and child, the Thine and the our, are all one, and how the heart that begins its prayer with the God-devoted Thine, will have the power in faith to speak out the Our too. Such prayer will, indeed, be the fellowship and interchange of love, always bringing us back in trust and worship to Him who is not only the Beginning but the End:' For Thine is the Kingdom and the Power, and the Glory, for ever Amen.' Son of the Father, teach us to pray, 'Our Father'.

O Thou who art the only-begotten Son, teach us, we beseech Thee, to pray, 'Our *Father*.' We thank Thee, Lord, for these Living Blessed Words which Thou hast given us. We thank Thee for the millions who in them have learnt to know and worship the Father, and for what they have been to us. Lord! it is as if we needed days and weeks in Thy school with each separate petition; so deep and full are they. But we look to Thee to lead us deeper into their meaning: do it, we pray Thee, for Thy Name's sake; Thy name is Son of the Father.

Lord! Thou didst once say: `No man knoweth the Father save the Son, and he to whom the Son willeth to reveal Him.' And again: `I made known unto them Thy name, and will make it known, that the love wherewith Thou hast loved Me may be in them.' Lord Jesus! reveal to us the Father. Let His name, His infinite Father-love, the love with which He loved Thee, according to Thy prayer, *be in* us. Then shall we say aright, `OUR Father!'

Then shall we apprehend Thy teaching and the first spontaneous breathing of our heart will be: `Our Father, Thy Name, Thy Kingdom, Thy Will.' And we shall bring our needs and our sins and our temptations to Him in the confidence that the love of such a Father cares for all.

Blessed Lord! we are Thy scholars, we trust Thee; do teach us to pray, 'Our Father.' Amen.

Ask and it Shall Be Given You

' Ask, and it shall be given you; seek, and ye shall find; knock and it shall be opened unto you :for every one that asketh receiveth and he that seeketh findeth ; and to him that knocketh it shall opened.'—Matthew 7:7-8

Ye ask, and receive not, because ye ask amiss.'—James 4:3

Our Lord returns here in the Sermon the Mount a second time to speak of prayer. The first time He had spoken of the Father who is to be found in secret, and rewards openly, and has given us the pattern prayer (Matt. 6:5). Here He wants to teach us what in all Scripture is considered the chief thing in prayer: the assurance that prayer will be heard and answered. Observe how He uses words which mean almost the same thing, and each time repeats the promise distinctly: ` Ye shall receive, ye shall find, it shall be opened unto you;' and then gives us ground for such assurance the law of the kingdom: ` He that asketh receiveth ; he that seeketh, findeth to him that knocketh, it shall he opened. We cannot but feel how in this sixfold repetition He wants to impress deep on our minds this one truth, that we may and must most confidently expect an answer to our prayer. Next to the revelation of the Father's love, there is, in the whole course of the school of prayer, not a more important lesson than this: Every one that asketh, receiveth.

In the three words the Lord uses, ask, seek, knock, a difference in meaning has been sought. If such was indeed His purpose, then the first, *ask*, refers to the gifts we pray for. But I may ask and receive the gift without the Giver. Seek is the word Scripture uses of God Himself; Christ assures me that I can find Himself. But it is not enough to find God in time of need, without coming to abiding fellowship: *knock* speaks of admission to dwell with Him and in Him. Asking and receiving the gift would thus lead to seeking and finding the Giver, and this again to the knocking and opening of the door of the Father's home and love. One thing is sure : the Lord does want us to count most certainly on it that asking, seeking, knocking, cannot be in vain: receiving an answer, finding God, the opened heart and home of God, are the certain fruit of prayer.

That the Lord should have thought it needful in so many forms to repeat the truth, is a lesson of deep import. It proves that He knows our heart, how doubt and distrust toward God are natural to us, and how easily we are inclined to rest in prayer as a religious work without an answer. He knows too how even when we believe that God is the Hearer of prayer, believing prayer that lays hold of the promise, is something spiritual, too high and difficult for the halfhearted disciple. He therefore at the very outset of His instruction to those who would learn to pray, seeks to lodge this truth deep into their hearts: prayer does avail much; ask and ye shall receive; every one that asketh, receiveth. This is the fixed eternal law of the kingdom: if you ask and receive not, it must be because there is something amiss or wanting in the prayer. Hold on; let the word and Spirit teach you to pray aright, but do not let go the confidence He seeks to waken: Every one that asketh, receiveth.

'Ask, and it shall be given you.' Christ has no mightier stimulus to persevering prayer in His school than this. As a child has to prove a sum to be correct, so the proof that we have prayed aright is, the answer. If we ask and receive not, it is because we have not learned to pray aright. Let every learner in the school of Christ therefore take the Master's word in all simplicity: Every one that asketh, receiveth. He had good reasons for speaking so unconditionally. Let us beware of weakening the Word with our human wisdom. When He tells us heavenly things, let us believe Him. His Word will explain itself to him who believes it fully. If questions and difficulties arise, let us not seek to have them settled before we accept the Word. No; let us entrust them all to Him: it is His to solve them: our work is first and fully to accept and hold fast His promise. Let in our inner chamber, in the inner chamber of our heart too, the Word be inscribed in letters of light, Every one that asketh, receiveth.

According to this teaching of the Master, prayer consists of two parts, has two sides, a human and a Divine. The human is the asking, the Divine is the giving. Or, to look at both from the human side, there is the asking and the receiving—the two halves that make up a whole. It is as if He would tell us that we are not to rest without an answer, because it is the will of God, the rule in the Father's family : every childlike believing petition is granted. If no answer comes, we are not to sit down in the cloth that calls itself resignation, and suppose that it is not God's will to give an answer. No; there must be something in the prayer that is not as God would have it, childlike and believing; we must seek for grace to pray so that the answer may come. It is far easier to the flesh to submit without the answer than to yield itself to be searched and purified by the Spirit, until it has learnt to pray the prayer of faith.

It is one of the terrible marks of the diseased state of Christian life in these days, that there are so many who rest content without the distinct experience of answer to prayer. They pray daily, they ask many things, and trust that some of them will be heard, but know little of direct definite answer to prayer as the rule of daily life. And it is this the Father wills ; He seeks daily intercourse with His children in listening to and granting their petitions. He wills that I should come to Him day by day with distinct requests; He wills day by day to do for me what I ask. It was in His answer to prayer that the saints of old learned to know God as the Living One, and were stirred to praise and love (Psalm 34, Psalm 66:19, Psalm 116:1) Our Teacher waits to imprint this upon our minds; prayer and its answer, the child asking and the father giving, belong to each other.

There may be cases in which the answer is a refusals, because the request is not according to God's Word, as when Moses asked to enter Canaan. But still there was an answer: God did not leave His servant in uncertainty as to His will. The gods of the heathen are dumb and cannot speak. Our Father lets His child know when He cannot give him what he asks, and he withdraws his petition, even as the Son did in Gethsemane. Both Moses the servant and Christ the Son knew that what they asked was not according to what 'the Lord had spoken: their prayer was the humble supplication whether it was not possible for the decision to be changed. God will teach those who are teach able and give Him time, by His Word and Spirit, whether their request be according to His will or not. Let us withdraw the request, if it be not according God's mind, or persevere till the answer come. Prayer is appointed to obtain the answer. It is in prayer and its answer that the interchange of love between .the Father and His child takes place.

How deep the estrangement of our heart from God must be, that we find it so difficult to grasp such promises, even while we accept the words and believe their truth, the faith of the heart, that fully has them and rejoices in them, comes so slowly. It is because our spiritual life is still so weak, and the capacity for taking God's thoughts is so feeble. But let us look to Jesus to teach us as none but He can teach. If we take His words in simplicity, and trust Him by his Spirit to make them within us life and power, they will so enter into our inner being, to the spiritual Divine reality of the truth they contain will indeed take possession of us, and we shall not rest content until every petition we offer is borne heavenward on Jesus' own words ` Ask, and it shall be given you.'

Beloved fellow-disciples in the school of Jesus, let us set ourselves to learn this lesson well. Let us take these words just as they were spoken. Let us not suffer human reason to weaken their force. Let us take these words as Jesus gives them, and believe them. He will teach us in due time how to understand them fully: let us begin by implicitly believing them. Let us take time, often as we pray, to listen to His voice: Every one that asketh, receiveth. Let. us not make the feeble experiences of our unbelief the measure of what our faith may expect. Let us seek, not only just in our seasons of prayer, but at all times, to hold fast the joyful assurance: man's prayer on earth and God's answer in heaven are meant for each other. Let us trust Jesus to teach us so too pray, that the answer can come. He will do it, if we hold fast the word He gives today : ` Ask, and ye shall receive.'

Lord, Teach up to Pray!

0 Lord Jesus! teach me to understand and believe what Thou hast now promised me. It is not hid from Thee, 0 my Lord, with what reasonings my heart seeks to satisfy itself, when no answer comes. There is the thought that my prayer is not in harmony with the Father's secret counsel ; that there is perhaps something better Thou wouldest give me; or that prayer as fellowship with God is blessing enough without an answer And yet, my blessed Lord, I find in Thy teaching on prayer that Thou didst not speak of these things, but didst say so plainly, that prayer may and must expect an answer. Thou doth assure us that this is the fellowship of a child with the Father; the child asks and the Father gives.

Blessed Lord ! Thy words are faithful and true. It must be, because I pray amiss, that my experience of answered prayer is not clearer. It must be, because I live too little in the Spirit, that my prayer is too little in the Spirit, and that the power for the prayer of faith is wanting.

Lord ! teach me to pray. Lord Jesus! I trust Thee for it; teach me to pray in faith. Lord teach me this lesson of to-day! Every one that asketh, receiveth. Amen.

How Much More?

'Or what man is there of you, who, if his son ask him for a loaf, will give him a stone; or if he shall ask for a fish, will give him a serpent! If ye then, being evil, know how to give good gifts unto your children, how much more shall your Father which is in Heaven give good things to them that ask Him!' Matthew 7:9-11

In these words our Lord proceeds further to confirm what He said of the certainty of an answer to prayer. To remove all doubt, and show us on what sure ground His promise rests, He appeals to what every one has seen and experienced here on earth. We are all children, and know what we expected of our fathers. We are fathers, or continually see them ; and everywhere we look upon it as the most natural thing there can be, for a father to hear his child. And the Lord asks us to look up from earthly parents, of whom the best are but evil, and to calculate How much more the heavenly Father will give good gifts to them that ask Him. Jesus would lead us up to see, that as much greater as God is than sinful man, so much greater our assurance ought to be that He will more surely than any earthly father grant our childlike petitions. As much greater as God is than man, so much surer is that prayer will be heard with the Father in heaven than with a father on earth.

As simple and intelligible as this parable is, so deep and spiritual is the teaching it contains. The Lord would remind us that the prayer of a child owes its influence entirely to the relation in which he stands to the parent. The prayer can exert that influence only when the child is really living in that relationship, in the home, in the love, in the service of the Father. The power of the promise, 'Ask, and it shall be given you,' lies in the loving relationship between us as children and the Father in heaven; when we live and walk in that relationship, the prayer of faith and its answer will be the natural result. And so the lesson we have today in the school of prayer is this : Live as a child of God, then you will be able to pray as a child, and as a child you will most assuredly be heard.

And what is the true child-life ? The answer can be found in any home. The child that by preference forsakes the father's house, that finds no pleasure in the presence and love and obedience of the father, and still thinks to ask and obtain what he will, will surely be disappointed. On the contrary, he to whom the intercourse and will and honor and love of the father are the joy of his life, will find that it is the father's joy to grant his requests. Scripture says, ' As many as are led by the Spirit of God, they are the children of God:' the childlike privilege of asking all is inseparable from the childlike life under the leading of the Spirit. He that gives himself to be led by the Spirit in his life, will be led by Him in his prayers too. And he will find that Fatherlike giving is the Divine response to childlike living.

To see what this childlike living is, in which childlike asking and believing have their ground, we have only to notice what our Lord teaches in the Sermon on the Mount of the Father and His children. In it the prayer-promises are imbedded in the life-precepts; the two are inseparable. They form one whole; and He alone can count on the fulfilment of the promise, who accepts too all that the Lord has connected with it. It is as if in speaking the word, `.Ask, and ye shall receive,' He says: I give these promises to those whom in the beatitudes I have pictured in their childlike poverty and purity, and of whom I have said, 'They shall be called the children of God' (Matt. 5: 3-9): to children, who 'let your light shine before men, so that they may glorify your Father in heaven:' to those who walk in love, 'that ye may be children of your Father which is in heaven,' and who seek to be perfect ` even as your Father in heaven is perfect' (v. 45) : to those whose fasting and praying and almsgiving (6: 1-18) is not before men, but ' before your Father which seeth in secret;' who forgive even as your Father forgiveth you' (6:15);who trust the heavenly Father in righteousness (6:26-32); who not only say, Lord,

Lord, but do the will of my Father which is in heaven (7:21). Such are the children of the Father, and such is the life in the Father's love and service; in such a child-life, answered prayers are certain and abundant.

But will not such teaching discourage the feeble one? If we are first to answer to this portrait of a child, must not many give up all hope of answers to prayer? The difficulty is removed if we think again of the blessed name of father and child. A child is weak; there is a great difference among children in age and gift. The Lord does not demand of us a perfect fulfilment of the law; no, but only the childlike and whole-hearted surrender to live as a child with Him in obedience and truth. Nothing more. But also, nothing less. The Father must have the whole heart. When this is given, and He sees the child with honest purpose and steady will seeking in everything to be and live as a child, then our prayer will count with Him as the prayer of a child. Let any one simply and honestly begin to study the sermon on the Mount and take it as his guide in life, and he will find, notwithstanding weakness and failure, an ever-growing liberty to claim the fulfilment of its promises in regard to prayer. In the names of father and child he has the pledge that his petitions will be granted.

This is the one chief thought on which Jesus dwells here, and which He would have all His scholars take in. He would have us see that the secret of effectual prayer is: to have the heart filled with the Father—love of God. It is not enough for us to know that God is a Father: He would have us take time to come under the full impression of what that name implies. We must take the best earthly father we know; we must think of the tenderness and love with which he regards the request of his child, the love and joy with which he grants every reasonable desire; we must then, as we think in adoring worship of the infinite Love and Fatherliness of God, consider with how much more tenderness and joy He sees us come to Him, and gives us what we ask aright. And then, when we see how much this Divine arithmetic is beyond our comprehension, and feel how impossible it is for us to apprehend God's readiness to hear us, then He would have us come and open our heart for the Holy Spirit to shed abroad God's Father-love there. Let us do this not only when we want to pray, but let us yield heart and life to dwell in that love. The child who only wants to know the love of the father when he has something to ask, will be disappointed. But he who lets God be Father always and in everything, who would fain live his whole life in the Father's presence and love, who allows God in all the greatness of His love to be a Father to him, oh! he will experience most gloriously that a life in God's infinite Fatherliness and continual answers to prayer are inseparable.

Beloved fellow-disciple! we begin to see what the reason is that we know so little of daily answers to prayer, and what the chief lesson is which the Lord has for us in His school. It is all in the name of Father. We thought of new and deeper insight into some of the mysteries of the prayer-world as what we should get in Christ's school; He tells us the first is the highest lesson; we must learn to say well, ' Abba, Father!' 'Our Father which art in heaven.' He that can say this, has the key to all prayer. In all the compassion with which a father listens to his weak or sickly child, in all the joy with which he hears his stammering child, in all the gentle patience with which he bears with a thoughtless child, we must, as in so many mirrors, study the heart of our Father, until every prayer be borne upward on the faith of this Divine word: ' How much more shall your heavenly Father give good gifts to them that ask Him.'

' Lord, Teach Us to Pray.'

Blessed Lord! Thou knowest that this, though it be one of the first and simplest and most glorious lessons in Thy school, is to our hearts one of the hardest to learn: we know so little of the love of the Father. Lord! teach us so to live with the Father that His love may be to us nearer, clearer, dearer, than the love of any earthly father. And let the assurance of His hearing our prayer be as much greater than the confidence in an earthly parent, as the heavens are higher than earth, as God is infinitely greater than man. Lord! show us that it is only our unchild-like distance from the Father that hinders the answer to prayer, and lead us on to the true life of God's children. Lord Jesus ! it is fatherlike love that wakens childlike trust. O reveal to us the Father, and His tender, pitying love, that we may become childlike, and experience how in the child-life lies the power of prayer.

Blessed Son of God! the Father loveth Thee and hath given Thee all things. And Thou lovest the Father, and hast done all things He commanded Thee, and therefore hast the power to ask all things. Lord! give us Thine own Spirit, the Spirit of the Son. Make us childlike, as Thou wert on earth. And let every prayer be breathed in the faith that as the heaven is higher than the earth, so God's Father-love, and His readiness to give us what we ask, surpasses all we can think or conceive. Amen,

How Much More the Holy Spirit

If ye then, being evil, know how to give good gifts unto your children, how much more shall the heavenly Father give the Holy Spirit to them that ask Him.! Luke 11:13

In the Sermon on the Mount, the Lord had already given utterance to His wonderful How much more? Here in Luke, where He repeats the question, there is a difference. Instead of speaking, as then, of giving good gifts, He says, `How much more shall the heavenly Father give *the Holy Spirit* ?' He thus teaches us that the chief and the best of these gifts is the Holy Spirit, or rather, that in this gift all others are comprised. The Holy Spirit is the first of the Father's gifts, and the one He delights most to bestow. The Holy Spirit is therefore the gift we ought first and chiefly to seek.

The unspeakable worth of this gift we can easily understand. Jesus spoke of the Spirit as `the promise of the Father;' the one promise in which God's Fatherhood revealed itself. The best gift a good and wise father can bestow on a child on earth is his own spirit. This is the great object of a father in education—.to reproduce in his child his own disposition and character. If the child is to know and understand his father; if, as he grows up, he is to enter into all his will and plans; if he is to have his highest joy in the father, and the father in him,—he must be of one mind and spirit with him. And so it is impossible to conceive of God bestowing any higher gift on His child than this, His own Spirit. God is what He is through His Spirit; the Spirit is the very life of God. Just think what it means—God giving His own Spirit to His child on earth.

Or was not this the glory of Jesus as a Son upon earth, that the Spirit of the Father was in Him ? At His baptism in Jordan the two things were united,— the voice, proclaiming Him the Beloved Son, and the Spirit, descending upon Him, And so the apostle says of us, ` Because ye are sons, God sent forth the Spirit of His Son into your hearts, crying, Abba, Father.' A king seeks in the whole education of his son to call forth in him a kingly spirit. Our Father in heaven desires to educate us as His children for the holy, heavenly life in which He dwells, and for this gives us, from the depths of His heart, His own Spirit. It was this which was the whole aim of Jesus when, after having made atonement with His own blood, He entered for us into God's presence. that He might obtain for us, and send down to dwell in us, the Holy Spirit. As the Spirit of the Father, and the Son, the whole life and love of the Father and the Son are in Him ; and coming down into us, He lifts us up into their fellowship. As Spirit of the Father, He sheds abroad the Father's love, with which He loved the Son, in our hearts, and teaches us to live in it. As Spirit of the Son, He breaths in us the childlike liberty, and devotion, and obedience in which the Son lived upon earth. The Father can bestow no higher or more wonderful gift than this: His own Holy Spirit, the Spirit of sonship.

This truth naturally suggests the thought that this first and chief gift of God must be the first and chief object of all prayer. For every need of the spiritual life this is the one thing needful: the Holy Spirit. All the fulness is in Jesus; the fulness of grace and truth, out of which we receive, grace for grace. The Holy Spirit is the appointed conveyancer, whose special work it is to make Jesus and all there is in Him for us ours in personal appropriation, in blessed experience. He is the Spirit of life in Christ Jesus; as wonderful as the life is, so wonderful is the provision by which such an agent is provided to communicate it to us. If we but yield ourselves entirely to the disposal of the Spirit, and let Him have His way with us, He will manifest the life of Christ within us. He will do this with a Divine power, maintaining the life of Christ in us in uninterrupted continuity. Surely, if there is one prayer that should draw us to the Father's throne and keep us there, it is this: for the Holy Spirit, whom we as children have received, to stream into us and out from us in greater fulness.

In the variety of the gifts which the Spirit has to dispense, He meets the believer's every need: Just think of the names He bears. The Spirit of grace, to reveal and impart all of grace there is in Jesus. The Spirit of faith, teaching us to begin, and go on and increase in ever believing. The Spirit of adoption and assurance, who witnesses that we are God's children, and inspires the confiding and confident Abba Father! The Spirit of truth, to lead into all truth, to make each word of God ours in deed and in truth. The Spirit of prayer, through whom we speak with the Father; prayer that must be heard. The Spirit of judgment and burning, to search the heart, and convince of sin. The Spirit of holiness, manifesting and communicating the Father's holy presence within us. The Spirit of power, through whom we are strong to testify boldly and work effectually in the Father's service. The Spirit of glory, the pledge of our inheritance, the preparation and the foretaste of the glory to come. Surely the child of God needs but one thing to be able really to live as a child: it is, to be filled with this Spirit.

And now, the lesson Jesus teaches us today in His school is this: That the Father is just longing to give Him to us if we will but ask in the childlike dependence on what He says: ' If ye know to give good gifts unto your children, *How Much More* shall your heavenly Father gave the holy Spirit to them that ask Him.' In the words of God's promise, 'I will pour out my Spirit abundantly; 'and of His command, ' Be ye filled with the Spirit,' we have the measure of what God is ready to give, and what we may obtain. As God's children, we have already received the Spirit. But we still need to ask and pray for His special gifts and operations as we require them. And not only this, but for Himself to take complete and entire possession; for His unceasing momentary guidance. Just as the branch, already filled with the sap of the vine, is ever crying for the continued and increasing flow of that sap, that it may bring its fruit to perfection, so the believer, rejoicing in the possession of the Spirit, ever thirsts and cries for more. And what the great Teacher would have us learn is, that nothing less than God's promise and God's command may be the measure of our expectation and our prayer; we must be filled abundantly. He would have us ask this in the assurance that the wonderful How much more of God's Father-love is the pledge that, when we ask, we do most certainly receive.

Let us now believe this. As we pray to be filled with the Spirit, let us not seek for the answer in our feelings. All spiritual blessings must be received, that is, accepted or taken in faith.' Let me believe, the Father gives the Holy Spirit to His praying child. Even now, while I pray, I must say in faith: I have what I ask, the fulness of the Spirit is mine. Let us continue steadfast in this faith. On the strength of God's Word we know that we have what we ask. Let us, with thanksgiving that we have been heard, with thanksgiving for what we have received and taken and now hold as ours, continue steadfast in believing prayer that the blessing, which has already been given us, and which we hold in faith, may break through and fill our whole being. It is in such believing thanksgiving and prayer, that our soul opens up for the Spirit to take entire and undisturbed possession. It is such prayer that not only asks and hopes, but takes and holds, that inherits the full blessing. In all our prayer let us remember the lesson the Savior would teach us this day; that, if there is one thing on earth we can be sure of, it is this, that the Father desires to have us filled' with His Spirit, that He delights to give us His Spirit.

And when once we have learned thus to believe for ourselves, and each day to take out of the treasure, we hold in heaven, what liberty and power to pray for the outpouring of the Spirit on the Church of God, on all flesh, on individuals, or on special efforts! He that has once learned to know the Father in prayer for himself, learns to pray most confidently for others too. The Father gives the Holy Spirit to them that asks Him, not least, but most, when they ask for others.

Lord, Teach Us to Pray!

Father in heaven ! Thou didst send Thy Son to reveal Thyself to us, Thy Father-love, and all that that love has for us. And He has taught us, that the gift above all gifts which Thou wouldest bestow in answer to prayer is, the Holy Spirit.

O my Father! I come to Thee with this prayer; there is nothing I would—may I not say, I do— desire so much as to be filled with the Spirit, the Holy Spirit. The blessings He brings are so unspeakable and just what I need. He sheds abroad Thy love in the heart, and fills it with Thyself. I long for this. He breathes the mind and life of Christ in me, so that I live as He did, in and for the Father's love. I long for this. He endues with power from on high for all my walk and work. I long for this, O Father ! I beseech Thee, give me this day the fulness of Thy Spirit.

Father! I ask this, resting on the words of my Lord : ` How much more the Holy Spirit!' I do believe that Thou hearest my prayer; I receive now what I ask; Father! I claim and I take it: the fulness of Thy Spirit as mine. I receive the gift this day again as a faith gift; in faith I reckon my Father works through the Spirit all He has promised. The Father delights to breathe His Spirit into His waiting child as He tarries in fellowship with Himself. Amen

Because of His Importunity

And He said unto them, Which of you shall have a friend, and shall go to him at midnight, and say to him, Friend, lend me three loaves; for a friend of mine is come to me from a journey, and I have nothing to set before him; and he from within shall answer and say, Trouble me not: the door is now shut, and my children are with me in bed; I cannot rise and give thee. 1 say unto you though he will not rise and give him because he is his friend, yet because of his importunity he will rise and give him as many as he needeth: —LUKE 11.5-8.

The first teaching to his disciples was given by our lord in the sermon on the Mount. It was nearly a year later that the disciples asked Jesus to teach them to pray. In answer He gave them a second time the Lord's prayer, so teaching them what to pray. He then speaks of how they ought to pray, and repeats what he formerly said of God's Fatherliness and the certainty of an answer. But in between He adds the beautiful parable of the friend at midnight, to teach them the twofold lesson, that God does not only want us to pray for ourselves, but for the perishing around us, and that in such intercession great boldness of entreaty is often needful, and always lawful yea, pleasing to God.

The parable is a perfect storehouse of instruction in regard to true intercession. There is, first, the love which seeks to help the needy around us: `my friend is come to me.' Then the need which urges to the cry: I have nothing to set before him.' Then follows the confidence that help is to be had: `which of you shall ask a friend and say, Friend, lend me three loaves.' Then comes the unexpected refusal; `I cannot rise and give thee.' Then again the Perseverance that takes no refusal: `because of his importunity. And lastly, the reward of such prayer: `he will give him as many as he needeth.' A wonderful setting forth of the way of prayer and faith in which the blessing of God has so often been sought and found.

Let us confine ourselves to the chief thought: prayer as an appeal to the friendship of God; and we shall find that two lessons are specially suggested. The one, that if we are God's friends and come as such to Him we must prove ourselves the friends of the needy; God's friendship to us and ours to others go hand in hand. The other, that when we come thus we may use the utmost liberty in claiming an answer.

There is a twofold use of prayer: the one, to obtain strength and blessing for our own life; the other, the higher, the true glory of prayer, for which Christ has taken us into His fellowship and teaching, is intercession, where prayer is the royal power a child of God exercises in heaven on behalf of others and even of the kingdom. We see it in Scripture how it was in intercession for others that Abraham and Moses, Samuel and Elijah, with all the holy men of old, proved that they had power with God and prevailed. It is when we give ourselves to be a blessing that we can specially count on the blessing of God. It is when we draw near to God as the friend of the poor and the perishing that we may count on His friendliness; the righteous man who is the friend of the poor is very specially the friend of God. This gives wonderful liberty in prayer. Lord! I have a needy friend whom I must help. As a friend I have undertaken to help him. In Thee I have a Friend, whose kindness and riches I know to be infinite: I am sure Thou wilt give me what I ask. If I, being evil, am ready to do for my friend what I can, how much more wilt Thou, O my heavenly Friend, now do for Thy friend what he asks?

The question might suggest itself, whether the Fatherhood of God does not give such confidence in prayer, that the thought of His Friendship can hardly teach us anything more: a father is more than a friend. And yet, if we consider it, this pleading the friendship of God opens new wonders to us. That a child obtains what he asks of his father looks so perfectly natural, we almost count it the father's duty to give. But with a friend it is as if the kindness is more free, dependent, not on nature, but on sympathy and character. And then the relation of a child is more that of perfect dependence; two friends are more nearly on a level. And so our Lord, in seeking to unfold to us the spiritual mystery of prayer, would fain have us approach God in this relation too, as those whom He has acknowledged as His friends, whose mind and life are in sympathy with His.

But then we must be living as His friends. I am still a child even when a wanderer; but friendship depends upon the conduct. 'Ye are my friends if ye do whatsoever I command you.' 'Thou seest that faith wrought with his works, and by works was faith made perfect; and the scripture was fulfilled which saith, And Abraham believed God and he was called the friend of God.' It is the Spirit, `the same Spirit,' that leads us that also bears witness to our acceptance With God; `likewise, also,' the same Spirit helpeth us in prayer. It is a life as the friend of God that gives the wonderful liberty to say:

I have a friend to whom I can go even at midnight. And how much more when I go in the very spirit of that friendliness, manifesting myself the very kindness I look for in God, seeking to help my friend as I want God to help me. When I come to God in prayer, He always looks to what the aim is of my petition. If it be merely for my own comfort or joy I seek His grace, I do not receive. But if I can say that it is that He may be glorified in my dispensing His blessings to others, I shall not ask in vain. Or if I ask for others, but want to wait until God has made me so rich, that it is no sacrifice or act of faith to aid them, I shall not obtain. But if I can say that I have already undertaken for my needy friend, that in my poverty I have already begun the work of love, because I know I had a friend Who would help me, my prayer will be heard. Oh, we know not how much the plea avails: the friendship of earth looking in its need to the friendship of heaven: `He will give him as much as he needeth.'

But not always at once. The one thing by which man can honor and enjoy his God is faith. Intercession is part of faith's training-school. There our friendship with men and with God is tested. There it is seen whether my friendship with the needy is so real, that I will take time and sacrifice my rest, will go even at midnight and not cease until I have obtained for them what I need. There it is seen whether my friendship with God is so clear, that I can depend on Him not to turn me away and therefore pray on until He gives.

O what a deep heavenly mystery this is of perseverance prayer. The God who has promised, who longs, whose fixed purpose it is to give the blessing, holds it back. It is to Him a matter of such deep importance that His friends on earth should know and fully trust their rich Friend in heaven, that He trains them, in the school of answer delayed, to find out how their perseverance really does prevail, and what the mighty power is they can wield in heaven, if they do but set themselves to it. There is a faith that sees the promise, and embraces it, and yet does not receive it (Hebrews 11:13,39). It is when the answer to prayer does not come, and the promise we are most firmly trusting appears to be of none effect, that the trial of faith, more precious than of gold, takes place. It is in this trial that the faith that has embraced the promise is purified and strengthened and prepared in personal, holy fellowship with the living God, to see the glory of God. It takes and holds the promise until it has received the fulfilment of what it had claimed in a living truth in the unseen but living God.

Let each child of God who is seeking to work the work of love in his Father's service take courage. The parent with his child, the teacher with his class, the visitor with his district, the Bible reader with his circle, the preacher with his hearers, each one who, in his little circle, has accepted and is bearing the burden of hungry, perishing souls—let them all take courage. Nothing is at first so strange to us as that God should really require persevering prayer, that there should be a real spiritual needs—be for importunity. To teach it us, the Master uses this almost strange parable. If the unfriendliness of a selfish earthly friend can be conquered by importunity, how much more will it avail with the heavenly Friend, who does so love to give, but is held back by our spiritual unfitness, our incapacity to possess what He has to give. O let us thank Him that in delaying His answer He is educating us up to our true position and the exercise of all our power with Him, training us to live with Him in the fellowship of undoubting faith and trust, to be indeed the friends of God. And let us hold fast the threefold cord that cannot be broken: the hungry friend needing the help, and the praying friend seeking the help, and the Mighty Friend, loving to give as much as he needeth.

O my Blessed Lord and Teacher! I must come to Thee in prayer. Thy teaching is so glorious, and yet too high for me to grasp. I must confess that my heart is too little to take in these thoughts of the wonderful boldness I may use with Thy Father as my Friend. Lord Jesus I trust Thee to give me Thy Spirit with Thy Word, and to make the Word quick and powerful in my heart. I desire to keep Thy Word of this day: `Because of his importunity he will give him as many as he needeth.'

Lord! teach me more to know the power of persevering prayer. I know that in it the Father suits Himself to our need of time for the inner life to attain its growth and ripeness, so that His grace may indeed be assimilated and made our very own. I know that He would fain thus train us to the exercise of that strong faith that does not let Him go even in the face of seeming disappointment. I know He wants to lift us to that wonderful liberty, in which we understand how really He has made the dispensing of His gift dependent on our prayer. Lord! I know this: O teach me to see it in spirit and truth.

And may it now be the joy of my life to become the almoner of my Rich Friend in heaven, to care for all the angry and perishing, even at midnight, because I know my friend who always gives to him who perseveres, because of his importunity, as many as he needeth. Amen.

Prayer Provides Laborers

"Then saith he unto his disciples, The harvest truly is 'plenteous, but the laborers are few. Pray ye therefore the Lord of the harvest, that he will send forth laborers into his harvest" (Matthew 9:37-38).

The Lord frequently taught His disciples that they must pray and how they should pray. But He seldom told them what to pray. This He left to their sense of need and the leading of the Spirit. But in the above scripture He expressly directs them to remember one thing. In view of the abundant harvest, and the need for reapers, they must cry to the Lord of the harvest to send laborers. Just as in the parable of the friend at midnight, He wants them to understand that prayer is not to be selfish; it is the power through which blessing can come to others. The Father is Lord of the harvest. When we pray for the Holy Spirit, we must pray for Him to prepare and send laborers for the work.

Why does He ask His disciples to pray for this? Could He not pray Himself? Would not one prayer of His achieve more than a thousand of theirs? Is God, the Lord of the harvest, not aware of the need? And would He not, in His own good time, send laborers without the disciples' prayers? Such questions lead us into the deepest mysteries of prayer and its power in the Kingdom of God. The answer to such questions will convince us that prayer is indeed a power on which the gathering of the harvest and the coming of the Kingdom do in very truth depend.

Prayer is no form or show. The Lord Jesus was Himself the truth; everything He spoke was the truth. It was when "He saw the multitude, and was moved with compassion on them, because they were scattered abroad, as sheep having no shepherd," that He called on the disciples to pray for laborers to be sent to them (see Matthew 9:36). He did so because He really believed that their prayer was needed and would help.

The veil which hides the invisible world from us was wonderfully transparent to the holy human soul of Jesus. He had looked long and deep and far into the hidden connection of cause and effect in the spiritual world.

He had marked in God's Word how God called men like Abraham, Moses, Joshua, Samuel, and Daniel, giving them authority over men in His Name. God also gave these men the authority to call the powers of heaven to their aid as they needed them. Jesus knew that the work of God had been entrusted to these men of old and to Himself for a time here upon earth. Now it was about to pass over into the hands of His disciples. He knew that where they were given responsibility for this work, it would not be a mere matter of form or show. The success of the work would actual depend on them and their faithfulness.

As a single individual, within the limitations of a human body and a human life, Jesus feels how little a short visit can accomplish among these wandering sheep He sees around Him. He longs for help to have them properly cared for. He therefore tells His disciples to begin to pray. When they have taken over the work from Him on earth, they are to make this one of their chief petitions in prayer: that the Lord of the harvest Himself would send laborer into His harvest. But since He entrusted them with the work and made it to a large extent dependent on them, He gives them authority to apply to Him for laborers and makes the supply dependent on their prayer.

How little Christians really feel and mourn the need of laborers in the fields of the world, so ripe for the harvest. How little they believe that our labor supply depends on prayer and that prayer will really provide "as many as he needeth." The dearth of labor is known and discussed. Efforts are sometimes made to supply the need. But how little the burden of the sheep wandering without a Shepherd is really assumed in the faith that the Lord of the harvest will send forth the laborers in answer to prayer. Without this prayer, fields ready for reaping will be left to perish. And yet it is so. The Lord has surrendered His work to His Church. He has made Himself dependent on them as His Body, through whom His work must be done. The power which the Lord gives His people to exercise in heaven and earth is real; the number of laborers and the measure of the harvest does actually depend on their prayer.

Why don't we obey the Master's instruction more heartily and cry more earnestly for laborers? There are two reasons. The one is: We miss the compassion of Jesus which gave rise to this request for prayer. Believers must learn to love their neighbors as themselves and to live entirely for God's glory in their relationships with fellow-men. The Father's first commandment to His redeemed ones is that they accept those who are perishing as the charge entrusted to them by their Lord. Accept them not only as a field of labor, but as the objects of loving care and interest. Soon, compassion towards the hopelessly perishing will touch your heart, and the cry will ascend with a new sincerity.

The other reason for the neglect of the command is: We believe too little in the power of prayer to bring about definite results. We do not live close enough to God to be capable of the confidence that He will answer. We have not surrendered entirely to His service and Kingdom. But our lack of faith will be overcome as we plead for help. Let us pray for a life in union with Christ, so that His compassion streams into us and His Spirit assures us that our prayer is heard.

Such prayer will obtain a twofold blessing. There will first be a desire for an increase in the number of men entirely given up to the service of God. That there are times when men actually cannot be found for the service of the Master as ministers, missionaries, or teachers of God's Word is a terrible blot upon the Church of Christ. As God's children make this a matter of supplication in their own circles or churches, it will be given. The Lord Jesus is now Lord of the harvest. He has been exalted to bestow the gifts of the Spirit. He wants to make gifts of men filled with the Spirit. But His supply and distribution of these gifts depend on the cooperation of the members with Him. Prayer will lead to such cooperation and will stir those praying to believe that they will find the men and the means for the work.

The other blessing will be equally great. Every believer is a laborer. As God's children, we have been redeemed for service and have our work waiting. It must be our prayer that the Lord would fill all His people with the spirit of devotion, so that no one may be found standing idle in the vineyard. Wherever there is a complaint about the lack of fit helpers for God's work, prayer has the promise of a supply. God is always ready and able to provide. It may take time and importunity, but Christ's command to ask the Lord of the harvest is the pledge that the prayer will be heard. "I say unto you, he will arise and give him as many as he needeth."

This power to provide for the needs of the world and secure the servants for God's work has been given to us in prayer. The Lord of the harvest will hear. Christ Who taught us to pray this way will support the prayers offered ire His Name and interest. Let us set apart time and give all of ourselves to this part of our intercessory work. It will lead us into the fellowship of that compassionate heart of His that led Him to call for our prayers. It will give us the insight of our royal position as children of the King whose will counts for something with the great God in the advancement of His Kingdom. We will feel that we really are God's fellow-worker on earth, that we have earnestly been entrusted with a share in His work. We will become partakers in the work of the soul. But we will also share in the satisfaction of the soul as we learn how, in answer to prayer, blessing has been given that otherwise would not have come.

Lord, Teach Us to Pray.

Blessed Lord! Once again You have given us another wondrous lesson to learn. We humbly ask that you let us see these spiritual realities. There is a large harvest which is perishing as it waits for sleepy disciples to give the signal for laborers to come. Lord, teach us to view it with a heart full of compassion and pity. There are so few laborers, Lord. Show us what terrible sin the lack of prayer and faith is, considering there is a Lord of the harvest so able and ready to send them forth. Show us how He does indeed wait for the prayer to which He has promised an answer. We are the disciples to whom the commission to pray has been given. Lord, show us how You can breathe Your Spirit into us, so that Your compassion and the faith in Your promise will rouse us to unceasing, prevailing prayer.

O Lord! We cannot understand how You can entrust such work and give such power to men so slothful and unfaithful. We thank You for all those whom You are teaching day and night to cry for laborers to be sent. Lord, breathe Your Spirit into all Your children. Let them learn to live only for the Kingdom and glory of their Lord and become fully awake to the faith in what their prayer can accomplish. And let our hearts be filled with the assurance that prayer offered in living faith in the living God will bring certain and abundant answer. Amen.

Prayer Must Be Definite

"And Jesus answered and said unto him, What would thou that I should do unto thee?" (Mark 10:51; Luke 18:41).

The blind man had been crying out loud repeatedly, "Thou Son of David, have mercy on me." The cry had reached the ear of the Lord. He knew what the man wanted and was ready to grant it to him. But before He did it, He asked him, "What wilt thou that I should do unto thee?" He wanted to hear not only the general petition for mercy, but the distinct expression of what the man's desire was that day. Until he verbalized it, he was not healed.

There are still petitioners to whom the Lord puts the same question who cannot get the aid they need until they answer that question. Our prayers must be a distinct expression of definite need, not a vague appeal to His mercy or an indefinite cry for blessing. It isn't that His loving heart does not understand or is not ready to hear our cry. Rather, Jesus desires such definite prayer for our own sakes because it teaches us to know our own needs better. Time, thought, and self-scrutiny are required to find out what our greatest need really is. Our desires are put to the test to see whether they are honest and real and are according to God's Word. We also consider whether we really believe we will receive the things we ask. Such reflective prayer helps us to wait for the special answer and to mark it when it comes.

So much of our prayer is vague and pointless. Some cry for mercy, but do not take the trouble to know exactly why they want it. Others ask to be delivered from sin, but do not name any sin from which a deliverance can be claimed. Still others pray for God's blessing on those around them—for the outpouring of God's Spirit on their land or on the world—and yet have no special field where they can wait and expect to see the answer. To everyone the Lord says, "What do you really want, and what do you expect Me to do?"

Every Christian has only limited power. Just as he must have his own specific field of labor in which to serve God, he must also make his prayers specific. Each believer has his own circle, family, friends, and neighbors. If he were to take one or more of these by name, he would find himself entering the training school of faith which leads to personal dealing with his God. When we have faithfully claimed and received answers in such distinct matters, our more general prayers will be believing and effectual. Not many prayers will reach the mark if we just pour out our hearts in a multitude of petitions, without taking time to see whether every petition is sent with the purpose and expectation of getting an answer.

Bow before the Lord with silence in your soul and ask such questions as these:

What is really my desire?

Do I desire it in faith, expecting to receive an answer?

Am I ready to present it to the Father and leave it there in His bosom?

Is there agreement between God and me that I will get an answer?

We should learn to pray in such a way that God will see, and we will know what we really expect.

The Lord warns us against the vain repetitions of the Gentiles, who expect to be heard because they pray so much. We often hear prayers of great earnestness and fervor, in which a multitude of petitions are poured forth. The Savior would undoubtedly have to respond to some of them by asking: "What do you want?"

If I am in a foreign country on business for my father, I would certainly write two different sorts of letters home. There will be family letters with typical affectionate expressions in them, and there will be business letters containing orders for what I need. There may also be letters in which both are found. The answers will correspond to the letters. To each sentence of the letters containing the family news I do not expect a special answer. But for each order I send I am confident of an answer regarding the forwarding of the desired article. In our dealings with God, the business element must be present. Our expressions of need, sin, love, faith, and consecration must be accompanied by an explicit statement of what we are asking for and what we expect to receive. In response, the Father loves to give us a token of His approval and acceptance.

But the word of the Master teaches us more. He does not say, "What dost thou wish?" but, "What dost thou will?" One often wishes for a thing without willing it. I wish to have a certain article but the price is too high, so I decide not take it. I wish, but do not will to have it. The lazy man wishes to be rich, but does not will it: Many people wish to be saved, but perish because they do not will it.

The will rules the whole heart and life. If I really will to have something that is within my reach, I do not rest until I have it. When Jesus asks us,

"What wilt thou?" He asks whether it is our intention to get what we ask for at any price, however great the sacrifice. Do you really will to have it enough to pray continuously until He hears you, no matter how long it takes? How many prayers are wishes sent up for a short time and then forgotten! And how many are sent up year after year as a matter of duty, while we complacently wait without the answer.

One may ask if it wouldn't be better to make our wishes known to God, leaving it to Him to decide what is best, without our seeking to assert our wills. The answer is: by no means. The prayer of faith which Jesus sought to teach His disciples does not simply proclaim its desire and then leave the decision to God. That would be the prayer of submission for cases in which we cannot know God's will. But the prayer of faith, finding God's will in some promise of the Word, pleads for that promise until it comes.

In Matthew 9:28, Jesus said to the blind man, "Believe ye that I can do this?" In Mark He said, "What wilt thou that I should do?"(Mark 10:51). In both cases He said that faith had saved them. And He said to the Syrophenician woman, too, "Great is thy faith: be it unto thee even as thou wilt." Faith is nothing but the purpose of the will resting on God's Word and saying, "I must have it." To believe truly is to will firmly.

Such a will is not at variance with our dependence on God and our submission to Him. Rather, it is the true submission that honors God. It is only when the child has yielded his own will in entire surrender to the Father that he receives from the Father the liberty and power to will what he desires. Once the believer has accepted the will of God, as revealed through the Word and the Spirit, as his will, too, then it is the desire of God that His child use this renewed will in His service. The will is the highest power of the soul. Grace desires above everything to sanctify and restore this will to full and free exercise because it is one of the chief traits of God's image. God's child is like a son who lives only for his father's interests, seeks his father's will rather than his own, and is trusted by the father with his business. God speaks to that child in all truth, "What wilt thou?"

It is often spiritual sloth that, under the appearance of humility, professes to have no will. It fears the trouble of searching for the will of God, or, when found, the struggle of claiming it in faith. True humility is always accompanied by strong faith. Seeking to know only the will of God, that faith then boldly claims the fulfillment of the promise, "Ye shall ask what ye will, and it shall be done unto you."

Lord, Teach Us to Pray.

Lord Jesus! Teach me to pray with all my heart and strength that there may be no doubt with You or with me about what I have asked. I want to know what I desire so well that as my petitions are being recorded in heaven, I can also record them here on earth and note each answer as it comes. Make my faith in what Your Word has promised so clear that the Spirit may work within me the liberty to will that it will come. Lord! Renew, strengthen, and sanctify my entire will for the work of effectual prayer.

Blessed Savior! I pray that You reveal to me the wonderful grace You show us, the grace that asks us to say what we desire and then promises to do it. Son of God! I cannot fully understand it. I can only believe that You have indeed redeemed us wholly for Yourself, and that You want to mold our wills, making them Your most efficient servant. Lord! I unreservedly yield my will to You as the channel through which Your Spirit is to rule my whole being. Let Him take possession of it, lead it into the truth of Your promises, and make it so strong in prayer that I may always hear Your voice saying, "Great is thy faith: be it unto thee even as thou wilt." Amen.

The Faith That Takes

"Therefore I say unto you, All things whatsoever ye pray and ask for, believe that ye have received them, and ye shall have them" (Mark 11:24).

What a promise! It is so large, so Divine, that our little hearts cannot comprehend it. In every possible way we seek to limit it to what we think is safe or probable. We don't allow it to come in just as He gave it to us with its quickening power and energy. If we would allow it, that promise would enlarge our hearts to receive all of what His love and power are really ready to do for us.

Faith is very far from being a mere conviction of the truth of God's Word or a conclusion drawn from certain premises. It is the ear which has heard God say what He will do and the eye which has seen Him doing it. Therefore, where there is true faith it is impossible for the answer not to come. We must do this one thing that He asks of us as we pray: "Believe that ye have received. "He will see to it that He does the thing He has promised: "Ye shall have them. "

The essence of Solomon's prayer (2 Chronicles 6:4) is, "Blessed be the Lord God of Israel, who hath with His hands fulfilled that which He spake with His mouth to my father David." This should be the essence of all true prayer. It is the joyful adoration of a God whose hand always secures the fulfillment of what His mouth has spoken. Let us in this spirit listen to the promise Jesus gives because each part of it has a Divine message.

"All things whatsoever. "From the first word our human wisdom begins to doubt and say, "This can't possibly be literally true." But if it isn't, why did the Master say it? He used the very strongest expression He could find: "All things whatsoever." And He said it more than once: "If thou canst believe, all things are possible to him that believeth" (Mark 9:23); "If ye have faith as a grain of mustard seed... nothing shall be impossible to you" (Matthew 17:20). Faith is completely the work of God's Spirit through His Word in the prepared heart of the believing disciple. It is impossible for the fulfillment not to come, because faith is the pledge and forerunner of the coming answer.

"All things whatsoever ye shall ask in prayer believing, ye receive. " The tendency of human reason is to intervene here with certain qualifiers, such as "if expedient," "if according to God's will," to break the force of a statement which appears dangerous. Beware of dealing this way with the Master's words. His promise is most literally true. He wants His frequently repeated "all things" to enter our hearts and reveal how mighty the power of faith is. The Head truly calls the members of His Body to share His power with Him. Our Father places His power at the disposal of the child who completely trusts Him. Faith gets its food and strength from the "all things" of Christ's promise. As we weaken it, we weaken faith.

The whatsoever is unconditional except for what is implied in the believing. Before we can believe, we must find out and know what God's will is. Believing is the exercise of a soul surrendered to the influence of the Word and the Spirit. Once we do believe, nothing is impossible. Let us pray that we do not limit Christ's "all things" with what we think is possible. Rather, His "whatsoever" should determine the boundaries of our hope and faith. It is seed-word which we should take just as He gives it and keep it in our hearts. It will germinate and take root, filling our lives with its fullness and bearing abundant fruit.

"All things whatsoever ye pray and ask for." It is in prayer that these" all things" are to be brought to God. The faith that receives them is the fruit of the prayer. There must be a certain amount of faith before there can be prayer, but greater faith is the result of prayer. In the personal presence of the Savior and in conversation with Him, faith rises to grasp what at first appeared too high. Through prayer we hold up our desires to the light of God's Holy Will, our motives are tested, and proof is given whether we are indeed asking in the Name of Jesus and only for the glory of God. The leading of the Spirit shows us whether we are asking for the right thing and in the right spirit. The weakness of our faith becomes obvious as we pray. But we are encouraged to say to the Father that we do believe and that we prove the reality of our faith by the confidence with which we persevere. It is in prayer that Jesus teaches and inspires faith. Whoever waits to pray, or loses heart in prayer because he doesn't feel the faith needed to get an answer, will never learn that faith. Whoever begins to pray and ask will find the Spirit of faith is given nowhere so surely as at the foot of the throne.

"Believe that ye have received." Clearly we are to believe that we receive the very things we ask. The Savior does not say that the Father may give us something else because He knows what is best. The very mountain that faith wants to remove is cast into the sea.

There is one kind of prayer in which we make known our request in everything, and the reward is the sweet peace of God in our hearts and minds. This is the prayer of trust. It makes reference to the countless desires of daily life which we cannot find out if God will give. We leave it to Him to decide whether or not to give, as He knows best.

But the prayer of faith of which Jesus speaks is something higher and different. Nothing honors the Father like the faith that is assured that He will do what He has said in giving us whatever we ask. Such faith takes its stand on the promise delivered by the Spirit. It knows most certainly that it receives exactly what it asks, whether in the greater interest of the Master's work or in the lesser concerns of daily life. Notice how clearly the Lord states this in Mark 11:23: "Whosoever shall not doubt in his heart, but shall believe that what he saith cometh to pass, he shall have it." This is the blessing of the prayer of faith of which Jesus speaks.

"Believe that ye have received." This word of central importance is too often misunderstood. Believe that you have received what you're asking for now, while praying! You may not actually see it manifested until later. But now, without seeing it, you are to believe that it has already been given to you by the Father in heaven. Receiving or accepting an answer to prayer is just like receiving or accepting Jesus. It is a spiritual thing, an act of faith separate from all feeling. When I go to Jesus, asking Him for forgiveness for a sin, I believe He is in heaven for just that purpose, and I accept His forgiveness. In the same way, when I go to God asking for any special gift which is according to His Word, I must believe that what I desire is mine. I believe that I have it; I hold it in faith; and I thank God that it's mine. "If we know that He hear us, whatsoever we ask, we know that we have the petitions that we desired of Him" (I John 5:15).

"And ye shall have them. "The gift which we first hold in faith as ours from heaven will become ours in personal experience. But will it be necessary to pray longer once we know we have been heard and have received what we asked? Additional prayer will not be necessary when the blessing is on its way. In these cases we should maintain our confidence, proving our faith by praising God for what we have received, even though we haven't experienced it yet.

There are other cases in which faith needs to be further tried and strengthened in persevering prayer. Only God knows when everything is fully ripe for the manifestation of the blessing that has been given to faith. Elijah knew for certain that rain would come. God had promised it. And yet he had to pray the seven times. That prayer was not just for show. It was an intense spiritual reality both in the heart of Elijah as he lay there pleading and in heaven where it has its effectual work to do. It is through faith and patience we inherit the promises (Hebrews 6:12). Faith says most confidently, "I have received it." Patience perseveres in prayer until the gift bestowed in heaven is seen on earth. "Believe that ye have received, and ye shall have. " Between the have received in heaven, and the shall have of earth, the key word is believe. Believing praise and prayer is the link. Remember that it is Jesus Who said this. As we see heaven opened to us and the Father on the throne offering to give us whatever we ask for in faith, we are ashamed that we have so little availed ourselves of the privilege. We feel afraid that our feeble faith will still not be able to grasp what is so clearly placed within our reach. One thing must make us strong and full of hope: It is Jesus Who brought us this message from the Father. He Himself lived the life of faith and prayer when He was on earth. When the disciples expressed their surprise at what He had done to the fig tree, He told them that the very same life He led could be theirs. They could command not only the fig tree, but the very mountain, and they would obey.

Jesus is our life. In us He is everything now that He was on earth. He really gives everything He teaches. He is the Author and the Perfecter of our faith. He gives the spirit of faith. Don't be afraid that such faith isn't meant for us. Meant for every child of the Father, it is within the reach of anyone who will be childlike, yielding himself to the Father's will and love and trusting the Father's Word and power. Dear fellow Christian! Have courage! This word comes through Jesus, Who is God's Son and our Brother. Let our answer be, "Yes, blessed Lord, we do believe Your Word that we receive whatever we ask."

Lord, Teach Us to Pray.

Blessed Lord! The Father sent You to show us all His Love and all the treasures of blessing that Love is waiting to bestow. Lord! You've given us such abundant promises concerning our liberty in prayer. We are ashamed that our poor hearts have accepted so little of it. It has simply seemed too much for us to believe.

Lord! Teach us to take and keep and use Your precious Word: "All things whatsoever ye ask, believe that ye have received." Blessed Jesus! It is in You that our faith must be rooted if it is to grow strong. Your work has completely freed us from the power of sin and has opened the way to the Father. Your love is longing to bring us into the full fellowship of Your glory and power. Your Spirit is constantly drawing us into a life of perfect faith and confidence.

We are sure that through Your teaching we will learn to pray the prayer of faith. You will train us to pray so that we will believe that we really have what we ask for. Lord! Teach me to know and trust and love You in such a way that I live and dwell in You. Through You, may all my prayers rise up and go before God, and may my soul have the assurance that I am heard. Amen.

The Secret of Believing Prayer

"Jesus, answering, saith unto them, Have faith in God. For verily I say unto you,... Whosoever shall not doubt in his heart, but shall believe that those things which he saith shall come to pass; he shall have whatsoever he saith"(Mark 11:22-23).

Answer to prayer is one of the most wonderful lessons in all Scripture. In many hearts it must raise the question, "How can I ever attain the faith that knows it receives everything it asks for?" It is this question our Lord will answer today.

Before He gave that wonderful promise to His disciples, Christ shows where faith in the answer to prayer originates and finds its strength. Have faith in God. This faith precedes the faith in the promise of an answer to prayer. The power to believe a promise depends entirely on faith in the promiser. Trust in the person engenders trust in what he says. We must live and associate with God in personal, loving communication. God Himself should be everything to us. His Holy Presence is revealed where our whole being is opened and exposed to His mighty influence. There the capacity for believing His promises will be developed.

The connection between faith in God and faith in His promise will become clear to us if we consider what faith really is. It is often compared to the hand or the mouth, by which we take and use what is given to us. But it is important that we understand that faith is also the ear by which we hear what is promised and the eye by which we see what is offered. The power to take depends on this. I must hear the person who gives me the promise because the very tone of his voice gives me courage to believe. I must see him because the light of his face melts all my qualms about my right to take. The value of the promise depends on the promiser. It is on my knowledge of what the promiser is that faith in the promise depends.

For this reason Jesus says, "Have faith in God, " before He gives the wonderful prayer-promise. Let your eye be open to the living God. Through this eye we yield ourselves to God's influence. Just allow it to enter and leave its impression on our minds. Believing God is simply looking at God and what He is, allowing Him to reveal His presence to us. Give Him time and completely yield to Him, receiving and rejoicing in His love. Faith is the eye through which the light of God's presence and the vigor of His power stream into the soul. As that which I see lives in me, so by faith God lives in me, too.

Faith is also the ear through which the voice of God is always heard. The Father speaks to us through the Holy Spirit. The Son is the Word—the substance of what God says—and the Spirit is the living voice. The child of God needs this secret voice from heaven to guide him, and teach him, as it taught Jesus, what to say and what to do. An ear opened towards God is a believing heart that waits to hear what He says.

The words of God will be not only the words of a book, they will be spirit, truth, life, and power. They will make mere thoughts come to life. Through this opened ear, the soul abides under the influence of the life and power of God Himself. As His words enter the mind, dwelling and working there, through faith God enters the heart, dwelling and working there.

When faith is in full use as eye and ear—the faculties of the soul by which we see and hear God—then it will be able to exercise its full power as hand and mouth—the faculties by which we take God and His blessings. The power of reception will depend entirely on the power of spiritual perception. For this reason, before Jesus gave the promise that God would answer believing prayer, He said, "Have faith in God." Faith is simply surrender. I yield myself to the suggestions I hear. By faith I yield myself to the living God. His glory and love fill my heart and have mastery over my life.

Faith is fellowship. I give myself up to the influence of the friend who makes me a promise and become linked to him by it. When we enter into living fellowship with God Himself, in a faith that always sees and hears Him, it becomes easy and natural to believe His promise regarding prayer. Faith in the promise is the fruit of faith in the promiser. The prayer of faith is rooted in the life of faith. And in this way the faith that prays effectively is indeed a gift of God. It is not something He bestows or infuses all at once, but is far deeper and truer. It is the blessed disposition or habit of soul which grows up in us through a life of communion with Him. Surely for one who knows his Father well and lives in constant close communion with Him, it is a simple thing to believe the promise that He will do what His child wishes.

Because very many of God's children do not understand this connection between the life of faith and the prayer of faith, their experience of the power of prayer is limited. Sincerely desiring to obtain an answer from God, they concentrate wholeheartedly on the promise and try their utmost to grasp that promise in faith. When they do not succeed, they are ready to give up hope. The promise is true, but it is beyond their power to accept it in faith.

Listen to the lesson Jesus teaches us: Have faith in God, the Living God. Let faith focus on God more than on the thing promised, because it is His love, His power, His living presence that will awaken and work the faith. To someone asking to develop more strength in his hands and arms, a physician would say that his whole constitution must be built up. So the cure of feeble faith can be found only in the invigoration of our whole spiritual lives through communication with God. Learn to believe in God, hold on to God, and to let God take possession of our life. It will become easy to grasp the promise. Whoever knows and trusts God finds it easy to also trust the promise.

Note how distinctly this comes out in former saints. Every exhibition of the power of faith was the fruit of a special revelation from God. We see it in Abraham: "And the word of the Lord came unto Abram in a vision, saying, Fear not, Abram; I am thy shield .... And He brought him forth abroad, and said.....And he believed the Lord" (Genesis 15:1,5,6). And later again: "The Lord appeared to Abram, and said unto him, I am the Almighty God ....And Abram fell on his face, and God talked with him, saying, As for me, behold my covenant is with thee" (Genesis 17:1,3,4). It was the revelation of God Himself that gave the promise its living power to enter the heart and cultivate the faith. Because they knew God, these men of faith could not do anything but trust His promise. God's promise will be to us what God Himself is. The man who walks before the Lord and falls on his face to listen while the living God speaks to him will receive the promise. We have God's promises in the Bible with full liberty to claim them. Our spiritual power depends on God Himself speaking those promises to us. He speaks to those who walk and live with Him.

Therefore, have faith in God. Let faith be all eyes and ears. Surrender to God and let Him make His full impression on you, revealing Himself fully in your soul. Consider it a blessing of prayer that you can exercise faith in God as the living mighty God Who is waiting to give us the good pleasure of His will and faith with power. Regard Him as the God of love, Whose delight it is to bless and impart His love. In such faithful worship of God, the power will speedily come to believe the promise, too. "What things soever ye desire, when ye pray, believe that ye receive." Make God your own through faith; the promise will become yours, also.

Jesus is teaching us a precious lesson today. We seek God's gifts, but God wants to give us Himself first. We think of prayer as the means of extracting good gifts from heaven, and we think of Jesus as the means to draw ourselves up to God. We want to stand at the door and cry. Jesus wants us to enter in and realize that we are friends and children. Accept His teaching. Let every experience of the weakness of our faith in prayer incite us to have and exercise more faith in the living God, and in such faith to yield ourselves to Him. A heart full of God has power for the prayer of faith. Faith in God fosters faith in the promise, including the promise of an answer to prayer.

Therefore, child of God, take time to bow before Him and wait for Him to reveal Himself. Take time to let your soul exercise and express its faith in the Infinite One in holy worship. As He shares Himself with and takes possession of you, the prayer of faith will crown your faith in God.

Lord, Teach Us to Pray.

O my God! I do believe in You. I believe You are the Father, infinite in Your love and power. As the Son, You are my redeemer and my life. And as the Holy Spirit, You are my comforter, my guide, and my strength. I have faith that You will share everything You are with me and that You will do everything You promise.

Lord Jesus! Increase my faith! Teach me to take time to wait and worship in God's Holy presence until my faith absorbs everything there is in Him for me. Let my faith see Him as the fountain of all life, working with almighty strength to accomplish His will in the world and in me. Let me see Him in His love longing to meet and fulfill my desires. Let faith take possession of my heart and life to the extent that through it God may dwell there. Lord Jesus, help me! I want with my whole heart to believe in God. Fill me every moment with faith in God.

O my Blessed Savior! How can Your Church glorify You and fulfill the work of intercession through which Your Kingdom will come unless our whole lives consist of faith in God. Blessed Lord! Speak Your Word, "Have faith in God," into the depths of our souls. Amen.

Prayer and Fasting

"Then came the disciples to Jesus apart, and said Why could not we cast him out? And Jesus said unto them, Because of your unbelief. For verily I say unto you, If ye have faith as a grain of mustard seed, ye shall say unto this mountain, Remove hence to yonder place, and it shall remove; and nothing shall be impossible unto you. How-be-it this kind goeth nor out but by prayer and fasting"(Matthew 17:19-21).

When the disciples saw Jesus cast the evil spirit out of the epileptic whom they could not cure, they asked the Master why they had failed. He had given them "power and authority over all devils, and to cure all diseases." They had often exercised that power, and joyfully told how the devils were subject to them. And yet now, while He was on the Mount, they had utterly failed. Christ's casting the evil spirit out proved that there had been nothing in the will of God or in the nature of the case to make the miracle impossible. From their expression, "Why could we not?", it is evident that the disciples had wanted and tried to cast the spirit out. They had probably called upon it, using the Master's Name. But their efforts had been in vain. They had been put to shame in front of the crowd.

Christ's answer was direct and plain: "Because of your unbelief." Christ's success was not a result of His having a special power to which the disciples had no access. He had so often taught them that there is one power—the power of faith—to which, in the kingdom of darkness as in the Kingdom of God, everything must bow. In the spiritual world failure has only one cause: lack of faith. Faith is the one condition on which all Divine power can enter man and work through him. It is the sensitivity of man's will yielded to and molded by the will of God.

The power the disciples had received to cast out devils did not belong to them as a permanent gift or possession. The power was in Christ, to be received, held, and used by faith alone, living faith in Himself. Had they been full of faith in Him as Lord and Conqueror in the spirit world, had they been full of faith in Him as having given them authority to cast out in His Name, their faith would have given them the victory. "Because of your unbelief" was, for all time, the Master's explanation and reproof of impotence and failure in His Church.

Such a deficiency of faith must have a cause. The disciples may have asked, "Why couldn't we believe? Our faith has cast out devils before this. Why did we fail in believing this time?" The Master answers them before they can ask, "This kind goeth not out but by prayer and fasting."

Though faith is the simplest exercise of the spiritual life, it is also the highest. The spirit must yield itself in perfect receptivity to God's Spirit and become strengthened for this activity. Such faith depends entirely on the state of the spiritual life. Only when this is strong and in good health when the Spirit of God has total influence in our lives does faith have the power to do its mighty deeds.

Therefore Jesus adds, "How-be-it this kind goeth not out but by prayer and fasting." The faith than can overcome stubborn resistance such as you have just seen in this evil spirit, Jesus tells them, is not possible except for men living in very close fellowship with God and in very special separation from the world—in prayer and fasting. And so He teaches us two lessons in regard to prayer of deep importance. The one is that faith needs a life of prayer in which to grow and keep strong. The other is that prayer needs fasting for its full and perfect development.

Faith needs a life of prayer for its full growth. In all the different parts of the spiritual life there is a close union between unceasing action and reaction, so that each may be both cause and effect. Thus it is with faith. There can be no true prayer without faith; some measure of faith must precede prayer. And yet prayer is also the way to more faith: There can be no higher degrees of faith except through much prayer. This is the lesson Jesus teaches here.

Nothing needs to grow as much as our faith. "Your faith groweth exceedingly" is said of one church. When Jesus spoke the words,"According to your faith be it unto you" (Matthew 9:29), He announced the law of the Kingdom, which tells us that different people have different degrees of faith, that one person may have varying degrees, and that the amount of faith will always determine the amount of one's power and blessing. If we want to know where and how our faith is to grow, the Master points us to the throne of God. It is in prayer, exercising one's faith in fellowship with the living God, that faith can increase. Faith can only live by feeding on what is Divine, on God Himself.

It is in the adoring worship of God—the waiting on Him and for Him in the deep silence of soul that yields itself for God to reveal Himself—that the capacity for knowing and trusting God will be developed. As we take His

Word from the Blessed Book and ask Him to speak it to us with His living, loving voice, the power to believe and receive the Word as God's own word to us will emerge in us. It is in prayer, in living contact with God in living faith, that faith will become strong in us. Many Christians cannot understand, nor do they feel the need, of spending hours with God. But the Master says (and the experience of His people has confirmed) that men of strong faith are men of much prayer.

This brings us back again to the lesson we learned when Jesus, before telling us to believe that we receive what we ask for, first said,"Have faith in God." It is God—the living God—into Whom our faith must strike its roots deeply and broadly. Then it will be strong enough to remove mountains and cast out devils. "If ye have faith, nothing shall be impossible to you." If we could only give ourselves up to the work God has for us in the world! As we came into contact with the mountains and the devils that are to be cast away and cast out, we would soon comprehend how much we need great faith and prayer. They alone are the soil in which faith can be cultivated. Christ Jesus is our life and the life of our faith. It is His life in us that makes us strong and ready to believe. The dying to self which much prayer implies allows a closer union to Jesus in which the spirit of faith will come in power. Faith needs prayer for its full growth.

The second lesson is that prayer needs fasting for its full growth. Prayer is the one hand with which we grasp the invisible. Fasting is the other hand, the one with which we let go of the visible. In nothing is man more closely connected with the world of sense than in his need for, and enjoyment of, food. It was the fruit with which man was tempted and fell in Paradise. It was with bread that Jesus was tempted in the wilderness. But He triumphed in fasting.

The body has been redeemed to be a temple of the Holy Spirit. In body as well as spirit, Scripture says, we are to glorify God in eating and drinking. There are many Christians to whom this eating for the glory of God has not yet become a spiritual reality. The first thought suggested by Jesus' words in regard to fasting and prayer is that only in a life of moderation and self-denial will there be sufficient heart and strength to pray much.

There is also a more literal meaning to His words. Sorrow and anxiety cannot eat, but joy celebrates its feasts with eating and drinking. There may come times of intense desire, when it is strongly felt how the body and its appetites still hinder the spirit in its battle with the powers of darkness. The need is felt of keeping it subdued. We are creatures of the senses. Our minds are helped by what comes to us in concrete form. Fasting helps to express, to deepen, and to confirm the resolution that we are ready to sacrifice anything, even ourselves, to attain the Kingdom of God. And Jesus, Who Himself fasted and sacrificed, knows to value, accept, and reward with spiritual power the soul that is thus ready to give up everything for Him and His Kingdom.

There is still a wider application of Christ's words. Prayer is reaching out for God and the unseen. Fasting is letting go of everything that can be seen and touched. Some Christians imagine that everything that isn't positively forbidden and sinful is permissible to them. So they try to retain as much as possible of this world with its property, its literature, and its enjoyments. The truly consecrated soul, however, is like a soldier who carries only what he needs for battle. Because he frees himself of all unnecessary weight, he is easily capable of combating sin. Afraid of entangling himself with the affairs of a worldly life, he tries to lead a Nazarite life as one specially set apart for the Lord and His service. Without such voluntary separation, even from what is lawful, no one will attain power in prayer. Such power comes only through fasting and prayer.

Disciples of Jesus!—You have asked the Master to teach you to pray, so come now and accept His lessons! He tells you that prayer is the path to faith—strong faith that can cast out devils. He tells you: "If ye have faith, nothing shall be impossible to you." Let this glorious promise encourage you to pray much. Isn't the prize worth the price? Give up everything to follow Jesus in the path He opens to us! Fast if you need to! Do anything you must so that neither the body nor the world can hinder us in our great life-work—talking to God in prayer, so that we may become men of faith whom He can use in His work of saving the world.

Lord, Teach Us to Pray.

O Lord Jesus! How continually You must reprimand us for our unbelief. Our terrible inability to trust our Father and His promises must appear quite strange to You. Lord! Let Your words, "Because of your unbelief," sink into the very depths of our hearts and reveal how much of the sin and suffering around us is our fault. Then teach us, Blessed Lord, that faith can be gained and learned in the prayer and fasting that brings us into living fellowship with Yourself and the Father.

O Savior! You are the Author and the Perfecter of our faith. Teach us what it means to let You live in us by Your Holy Spirit. Lord! Our efforts and prayers for grace to believe have been so ineffective. We know it is because we want You to give us strength in ourselves. Holy Jesus! Teach us the mystery of Your life in us—how You, by Your Spirit, live the life of faith in us, insuring that our faith will not fail. Make our faith a part of that wonderful prayer-life which You give to those who expect their training for the ministry of intercession to come from not only words and thoughts, but from the Spirit of Your own life. And teach us how, in fasting and prayer, we can mature in the faith for which nothing will be impossible. Amen.

Prayer and Love

"And when ye stand praying, forgive, if ye have ought against any; that your Father also which is in heaven may forgive you your trespasses" (Mark 11:25).

These words immediately follow the great prayer promise, "What things soever ye desire, when ye pray, believe that ye receive them, and ye shall have them" (Mark 11:24). We have already seen how the words that preceded that promise, `Have faith in God,' taught us that, in prayer, everything depends: on the clarity of our relationship with God. These words that follow it remind us that our relationships: with our fellow-men must be clear, too. Love of God and love of our neighbor are inseparable. The prayer from a heart that is not right with God or with men will not succeed.

Faith and love are essential to each other. This is thought to which our Lord frequently gave expression. In the Sermon on the Mount, when speaking of the sixth commandment, He taught His disciples that acceptable worship of the Father was impossible if everything was not right with one's brother: "If thou art offering thy gift at the altar, and there rememberest that thy brother hath aught against thee, leave there thy gift before the altar, and go thy way; first be reconciled to thy brother, and then come and offer thy gift" (Matthew 5:23-24). After having taught us to pray, "Forgive us our debts, as we also have forgiven our debtors," Christ added, "If you forgive not men their trespasses, neither will your Father forgive your trespasses." At the close of the parable of the unmerciful servant, He applies His teaching in the words, "So likewise shall my heavenly Father do also unto you, if ye from your hearts forgive not every one his brother their trespasses" (Matthew 18:35).

Here, in Mark 11, beside the dried—up fig tree, as Jesus speaks of the power and the prayer of faith, He abruptly introduces the thought, "When ye stand praying, forgive, if ye have aught against any; that your Father also which is in heaven may forgive you your trespasses" (Mark 11:25). Perhaps the Lord had learned during His life that disobedience to the law of brotherly love was the great sin of even praying people, and the great cause of the ineffectiveness of their prayer. It is as if He wanted to lead us into His own blessed experience that nothing strengthens faith as much as the consciousness that we have given ourselves in love and compassion for those whom God loves.

The first lesson we are taught here is to have a forgiving disposition. We should pray, "Forgive us just as we have forgiven others." Scripture says, "Forgive one another, even as God also in Christ forgave you." God's full and free forgiveness should be the model of our forgiveness of men. Otherwise our reluctant, half-hearted forgiveness, which is not forgiveness at all, will be God's rule with us. All of our prayers depend on our faith in God's pardoning grace. If God dealt with us while keeping our sins in mind, not one prayer would be heard. Pardon open the door to all God's love and blessing. Because God has pardoned all our sins, our prayers can go through to obtain all we need.

The deep sure ground of answer to prayer is God's forgiving love. When it has taken possession of our hearts, we pray in faith. But also, when it has taken possession of our hearts, we live in love. God's forgiving nature, revealed to us in His love, becomes our nature. With the power of His forgiving love dwelling in us, we forgive just as He forgives.

If great injury or injustice occurs, try first of all to assume a Godlike disposition. Avoid the sense of wounded honor, the desire to maintain your rights, and the need to punish the offender. In the little annoyances of daily life, never excuse a hasty temper, a sharp word, or a quick judgment with the thought that we mean no harm, or that it is too much to expect feeble human nature to really forgive the way God and Christ do. Take the command literally: "Even as Christ forgave, so also do ye." The blood cleanses selfishness from the conscience. The love it reveals is a pardoning love that takes possession of us and flows through us to others. Our forgiving love toward men is the evidence of God's forgiving love in us. It is a necessary condition of the prayer of faith.

There is a second, more general lesson: Our daily life in the world is the test of our communication with God in prayer. How often the Christian, when he comes to pray, does his utmost to cultivate certain frames of mind which he thinks will be pleasing. He doesn't understand (or he forgets) that life does not consist of a lot of loose pieces which can be picked up at random and then be discarded. Life is a whole. The hour of prayer is only a small part of daily life. God's opinion of what I really am and desire is not based on the feeling I conjure up, but on the tone of my life during the day.

My relationship with God is part of my relationships with men. Failure in one will cause failure in the other. It isn't necessary that it be a distinct consciousness of something wrong between my neighbor and myself. An ordinary current of thinking and judging—the unloving thoughts and words I allow to pass unnoticed—can hinder my prayer. The effective prayer of faith comes from a life given up to the will and the love of God. Not as a result of what I try to be when praying, but because of what I am when I'm not praying, is my prayer answered by God.

All these thoughts can be gathered into a third lesson: In life among human beings, the one thing on which everything depends is love. The spirit of forgiveness is the spirit of love. Because God is love, He forgives. It is only when we are dwelling in love that we can forgive as God forgives. In love for our brothers we have the evidence of love for the Father, the basis for our confidence before God, and the assurance that our prayer will be heard. "Let us love in deed and truth; hereby shall we assure our heart before Him. If our heart condemn us not, we have boldness toward God, and whatever we ask, we receive of Him" (1 John 4:20; 3:18-22,23). Neither faith nor work will profit if we don't have love. Love unites us with God; it proves the reality of faith. "Have faith in God" and "Have love to men" are both essential commandments. The right relationships with the living God above me and the living men around me are the conditions for effective prayer.

This love is of special consequence when we are praying for our fellow men. We sometimes commit ourselves to work for Christ out of zeal for His cause or for our own spiritual health, without giving ourselves in personal self-sacrificing love for those whose souls we seek. No wonder our faith is powerless and without victory! View each wretched one, however unlovable he is, in the light of the tender love of Jesus the Shepherd searching for the lost. Look for Jesus Christ in him and take him into a heart that really loves, for Jesus' sake. This is the secret of believing prayer and successful effort. Jesus speaks of love as the root of forgiveness. It is also the root of believing prayer.

There is nothing as heart-searching as believing prayer, or even the honest effort to pray in faith. Don't deflect that self-examination by the thought that God does not hear your prayer. "Ye ask and receive not, because ye ask amiss" (James 4:3). Let that Word of God search us. Ask whether our prayer is indeed the expression of a life completely given over to the will of God and the love of man. Love is the only soil in which faith can take root and thrive. Only in the love of fixed purpose and sincere obedience can faith obtain the blessing. Whoever gives himself to let the love of God dwell in him, whoever in daily life loves as God loves, will have the power to believe in the love that hears his every prayer. That almighty love is the Lamb Who is in the midst of the throne. It is suffering and enduring love that exists with God in prayer. The merciful shall obtain mercy; the meek shall inherit the earth.

Lord, Teach Us to Pray.

Blessed Father! You are love, and only he who dwells in love can come into fellowship with You. Your blessed Son has taught me again how deeply true this. O my God! Let the Holy Spirit flood my heart with Your love. Be a fountain of love inside me that flows out to everyone around me. Let the power of believing prayer spring out of this life of love. O my Father! Grant by the Holy Spirit that this love may be the gate through which I find life in Your love. Let the joy with which I daily forgive whom ever might offend me be the proof that Your forgiveness is my power and life.

Lord Jesus! Blessed Teacher! Teach me how to forgive and to love. Let the power of Your blood make the pardon of my sins a reality, so that Your forgiveness of me and my forgiveness of others may be the very joy of heaven. Point out the weaknesses in my relationships with others that might hinder my fellowship with God. May my daily life at home and in society be the school in which strength and confidence are gathered for the prayer of faith. Amen.

The Power of United Prayer

"Again I say unto you, That if two of you shall agree on earth as touching any thing that they shall risk, it shall be done for them of my Father which is in heaven. For where two or three are gathered together in my name, there am I in the midst of them" (Matthew 18:19-20).

One of the first lessons of our Lord in His school of prayer was not to pray visibly. Go into your closet and be alone with the Father. When He has taught us that the meaning of prayer is personal, individual contact with God, He gives us a second lesson: You also need public, united prayer. He gives us a very special promise for the united prayer of two or three who agree in what they ask. As a tree has its root hidden in the ground and its stem growing up into the sunlight, so prayer needs secrecy in which the soul meets God alone and public fellowship with those who find their common meeting place in the Name of Jesus.

The reason why this must be so is plain. The bond that unites a man with his fellow-men is no less real and close than that which unites him to God: He one with them. Grace renews not only our relationship with God, but our relationships with our fellow human beings, too. We not only learn to say "My Father." It would be unnatural for the children of family to always meet their father separately, never expressing their desires or their love jointly. Believers are not only members of one family, but of one Body. Just as each member of the Body depends on the other, the extent to which the Spirit can dwell in the Body depends on the union and cooperation of everyone. Christians cannot reach the full blessing God is ready to bestow through His Spirit until they seek and receive it in fellowship with each other. It was to the hundred and twenty praying together in total agreement under the same roof that the Spirit came from the throne of the glorified Lord. In the same way, it is in the union and fellowship of believers that the Spirit can manifest His full power.

The elements of true, united prayer are given to us in these words of our Lord. The first is agreement as to the thing asked. It isn't enough to generally;

consent to agree with anything another may ask. The object prayed for must be some special thing, a matter of distinct, united desire. The agreement must be, as in all prayer, in spirit and in truth. In such agreement exactly what we are asking for becomes very clear. We find out whether we can confidently ask for it according to God's will, and whether we are ready to believe that we have received it.

The second element is the gathering in the Name of Jesus. Later, we will learn much more about the necessity and the power of the Name of Jesus in prayer. Here our Lord teaches us that His Name must be the center and the bond of the union that makes them one, just as a home contains and unites all who are in it. "The Name of the Lord is a strong tower: the righteous runneth into it, and is safe" (Proverbs 18:10). That Name is such a reality to those who understand and believe in it, that to meet within it is to have Him present. Jesus is powerfully attracted by the love and unity of His disciples: "Where two or three are gathered in my Name, there am I in the midst of them" (Matthew 18:20). The presence of Jesus, alive in the fellowship of His loving, praying disciples, gives united prayer its power.

The third element is the sure answer: "It shall be done for them of my Father." Although a prayer meeting for maintaining religious fellowship, or for our own edification, may have its use, this was not the Savior's reason for recommending it. He meant it as a means of securing special answer to prayer. A prayer meeting without recognized answer to prayer ought to be the exception to the rule. When we feel too weak to exercise the faith necessary to attain a distinct desire, we ought to seek strength in the help of others. In the unity of faith, love, and the Spirit, the power of the Name and the presence of Jesus acts more freely, and the answer comes more surely. The evidence that there has been true, united prayer is the fruit—the answer, the receiving of the thing for which we have asked. "I say unto you, It shall be done for them of my Father which is in heaven."

What an extraordinary privilege united prayer is! What a potential power it has! Who can say why blessing might be gained:

if the believing husband and wife knew they were joined together in the Name of Jesus to experience His presence and power in united prayer (I Peter 33);

if friends were aware of the mighty help two or three praying in concert could give each other;

if in every prayer meeting the coming together in the Name, the faith in His presence, and the expectation of the answer stood in the foreground;

if in every church united, effective prayer were regarded as one of the chief purposes for which they are banded together;

if in the universal Church the coming of the Kingdom and of the King Himself were really matter of unceasing, united crying to God!

The Apostle Paul had great faith in the power of united prayer. To the Romans he writes, "I beseech you, brethren, by the love of the Spirit, that ye strive together with me in your prayer to God for me (Romans 15:30). He expects in answer to be delivered from his enemies and to prosper in his work. To the Corinthians he declares, "God will still deliver us, ye also helping together on our behalf by your supplications" (2 Corinthians 1:11). He expects their prayer to have a real share in his deliverance. To the Ephesians he writes, "With all prayer and supplication, praying at all seasons in the Spirit for all the saints and on my behalf, that utterance may be given unto me" (Ephesians 6:18-19). He makes the power and success in his ministry dependent on their prayers. With the Philippians he expects that his trials will become his salvation and increase the progress of the gospel, "through your supplications and the supply of the Spirit of Jesus Christ" (Philippians 1:19). When telling the Colossians to continue praying constantly, he adds, "Withal praying for us too, that God may open unto us a door for the word" (Colossians 4:3). And to the Thessalonians he writes, "Finally, brethren, pray for us, that the word of the Lord may run and be glorified, and that we may be delivered from unreasonable men" (2 Thessalonians 3:1-2).

It is quite evident that Paul perceived himself as the member of a Body whose sympathy and cooperation he depended on. He counted on the prayers of these churches to gain for him what otherwise might not be given. The prayers of the Church were to him as real a factor in the work of the Kingdom as the power of God.

Who can say what power a church could develop and exercise if it would assume the work of praying day and night for the coming of the Kingdom, for God's power, or for the salvation of souls? Most churches think their members gather simply to take care of and edify each other. They don't know that God rules the world by the prayers of His saints, that prayer is the power by which Satan is conquered, and that through prayer the Church on earth has access to the powers of the heavenly world. They do not remember that Jesus has, by His promise, made every assembly in His Name a gate to heaven, where His presence is to be felt, and His power experience by the Father fulfilling their desires.

We cannot sufficiently thank God for the blessed work of united prayer, with which Christendom, in our days, opens every year. It is of unspeakable value as proof of our unity and our faith in the power of united prayer, as a training school for the enlargement of our hearts to take in all the needs of the Church, and as a help to united persevering prayer. But it has been a special blessing as stimulus to continued union in prayer in the smaller circles. When God's people realize what it means to meet as one in the Name of Jesus, with His presence in the midst of a Body united in the Holy Spirit, they will boldly claim the promise that the Father will do what they agree to request.

Lord, Teach Us to Pray.

Blessed Lord! You ask so earnestly for the unity of Your people. Teach us how to encourage our unity with Your precious promise regarding united prayer. Show us how to join together in love any desire, so that Your presence is in our faith in the Father's answer.

O Father! We pray for those smaller circles of people who meet together so that they may become one. Remove all selfishness and self-interest, all narrowness of heart and estrangement that hinders their unity. Cast out the spirit of the world and the flesh through which Your promise loses all its power. Let the thought of Your presence and the Father's favor draw us all nearer to each other.

Grant especially, blessed Lord, that Your Church may believe that it is by the power of united prayer that she can bind and loose in heaven, cast out Satan, save souls, remove mountains, and hasten the coming of the Kingdom. And grant, good Lord, that my prayer circle may indeed pray with the power through which Your Name and Word are glorified. Amen.

The Power of Persevering Prayer

"And he spake a parable unto them to this end, that men ought always to pray, and not to faint; saying there was in a city a judge, which feared not God neither regarded man: And there was a widow in that city; and she came unto him, saying, Avenge me of mine adversary. And he would not for a while but afterward he said within himself, Though I fear not God, nor regard man; Yet because this widow troubleth me, I will avenge her, lest by her continual coming she weary me. And the Lord said, Hear what the unjust judge saith. And shall not God avenge his own elect, which cry day and night unto him, though he bear long with them? I tell you that he will avenge them speedily. Nevertheless, when the Son of may cometh, shall he find faith on the earth?" (Luke 18:1-8).

Of all the mysteries of the prayer world, the need for persevering prayer is one of the greatest. We cannot easily understand why the Lord, Who is so loving and longing to bless us, should have to be petitioned time after time, sometimes year after year, before the answer comes. It is also one of the greatest practical difficulties in the exercise of believing prayer. When our repeated prayers remain unanswered, it is easy for our lazy flesh maintaining the appearance of pious submission—to think that we must stop praying because God may have a secret reason for withholding His answer to our request. Faith alone can overcome difficulty. Once faith has taken its stand on God's Word and the Name of Jesus, and has yielded itself to the leading of the Spirit to seek only God's will and honor in its prayer, it need not be discouraged by delay. It knows from Scripture that the power of believing, prayer is considerable; real faith can never be disappointed. It knows that to exercise its power, it must he gathered up, just like water, until the stream carp come down in full force. Prayer must often be "heaped up" until God sees that its measure is full. Then the answer comes. Just as each of ten thousand seeds is a part of the final harvest, frequently be repeated, persevering prayer is necessary to acquire a desired blessing. Every single believing prayer has its influence. It is stored up toward an answer which comes in due time to whomever perseveres to the end. Human thoughts and possibilities have nothing to do with it; only the Word of the living God matters. Abraham for so long "in hope believed against hope" and then "through faith and patience inherited the promise." Wait and pray often for the coming of the Lord to fulfill His promise.

When the answer to our prayer does not come at once we should combine quiet patience and joyful as confidence in our persevering prayer. To enable us to do this, we must try to understand two words in which our Lord describes the character and conduct of our God and Father towards those who cry day and night to Him: "He is long-suffering over them. He will avenge them speedily."

The Master uses the word speedily. The blessing is all prepared. The Father is not only willing, but most anxious to give them what they ask. His everlasting love burns with His longing desire to reveal itself fully to His beloved and to satisfy their need. God will not delay one moment longer than is absolutely necessary. He will do everything in His power to hasten the answer.

But why if this is true and God's power is infinite does it often take so long to get an answer to prayer? And why must God's own elect so often, in the midst of suffering and conflict, cry day an night? "He is long-suffering over them." "Behold! the husbandman waiteth for the precious fruit of the earth, being long-suffering over it, till he receive the early and the latter rain" (James 5:7). Of course the husbandman longs for his harvest. But he knows it must have its full term of sunshine and rain, so he has plenty of patience. A child so often wants to pick the half-ripe fruit, while the farmer knows to wait until the proper time.

In his spiritual nature, man, too, is under the law of gradual growth that reigns in all created life. Only on the path of development can he reach his divine destiny. And only the Father, Who determines the times and seasons, knows the moment when the soul , or the Church is ripened to that fullness of faith in which it can really take and keep a blessing . As a father who longs to have his only child home from school, and yet waits patiently until the time of , training is completed, so it is with God and His children.

Insight into this truth should lead the believer to cultivate the corresponding attitudes of patience, faith, waiting, and praise, which are the secret of his perseverance. By faith in the promise of God, we know that we have the petitions we have asked of Him. Faith holds the answer in the promise as an unseen spiritual possession. It rejoices in it and praises God for it. But there is a difference between this kind of faith and the clearer, fuller, riper faith that obtains the promise as a present experience. It is in persevering, confident, and praising prayer that the soul grows up into full union with its Lord in which it can possess the blessing in Him.

There may be things around us that have to be corrected through prayer before the answer can fully happen. The faith that has, according to the command, believed that it has received, can allow God to take His time. It knows it has and must succeed. In quiet, persistent, and determined perseverance it continues in prayer and thanksgiving until the blessing comes. And so we see a combination of what at first sight appears to be so contradictory: the faith that rejoices in God's answer as a present possession combined with the patience that cries day and night until that answer comes. The waiting child meets God triumphantly with his patient faith.

The great danger in this school is the temptation to think that it may not be God's will to give us what we desire. If our prayer agrees with God's Word and is led by the Spirit, don't give way to these fears.

Learn to give God time. He needs time with us. In daily fellowship with Him, we must give Him time to exercise the full influence of His presence in us. Day by day, as we are kept waiting, it is necessary that faith be given time to prove its reality and fill our beings entirely. God will lead us from faith to vision; we will see His glory.

Don't let delay shake your faith, for it is faith that will provide the answer in time. Each believing prayer is a step nearer to the final victory! It ripens the fruit, conquers hindrances in the unseen world, and hastens the end. Child of God! Give the Father time! He is long-suffering over you. He wants your blessing to be rich, full, and sure. Give Him time, but continue praying day and night. And above all, remember the promise: "I say unto you, He will avenge them speedily."

The blessing of such persevering prayer is indescribable. There is nothing that examines the heart more closely than the prayer of faith. It teaches you to discover, confess, and give up everything that hinders the coming of the blessing everything that is not in accordance with the Father's will. It leads to closer fellowship with Him, Who alone can teach you to pray. Complete surrender becomes possible under the covering of the blood and the Spirit. Christian! Give God time! He will perfect whatever concerns you!

Let your attitude be the same whether you are praying for yourself or for others. All labor, bodily or mental, needs time and effort. We must give ourselves up to it. Nature reveals her secrets and yields her treasures only to diligent and thoughtful labor. However little we can understand it, spiritual husbandry is always the same: The seed we sow in the soil of heaven, the efforts we put forth, and the influence we seek to exert in the world above all require our complete surrender in prayer. Maintain great confidence that when the time is right, we will reap abundantly if we don't give up (Galatians 6:9).

Let us especially learn this lesson as we pray for the Church of Christ. She is indeed like a poor widow in the absence of her Lord, apparently at the mercy of her adversary and helpless to correct the situation. When we pray for His Church or any portion of it that is under the power of the world, let us ask Him to visit her with mighty workings of His Spirit to prepare her for His coming. Pray in the assured faith that prayer does help. Unceasing prayer will bring the answer. Just give God time. And remember this day and night: "Hear what the unrighteous judge saith. And shall not God avenge His own elect, which cry to Him day and night, and He is longsuffering over them. I say unto you, He will avenge them speedily."

Lord, Teach Us to Pray.

O Lord my God! Teach me how to know Your way and in faith to learn what Your beloved Son has taught: "He will avenge them speedily." Let Your tender love, and the delight You have in hearing and blessing Your children, lead me implicitly to accept the promise that we may have whatever we ask for, and that the answer will be seen in due time. Lord! We understand nature's seasons; we know how to wait for the fruit we long for. Fill us with the assurance that You won't delay one moment longer than is necessary, and that our faith will hasten the answer.

Blessed Master! You have said that God's elect appeal to Him day and night. Please teach us to understand this. You know how quickly we become tired. Perhaps we feel that the Divine Majesty of the Father is so far beyond the reach of our continued prayer that is isn't becoming for us to plead with Him too much. O Lord! Teach me how real the labor of prayer is! I know that here on earth, when I fail at something, I can often succeed by renewed and more continuous effort, and by taking more time and thought. Show me how, by giving myself more entirely to prayer—by actually living in prayer I can obtain what I have asked for.

Above all, O blessed Teacher, Author and Perfecter of my faith, let my whole life be one of faith in the Son of God Who loved me and gave Himself for me! In You my prayer gains acceptance and I have the assurance of the answer. Lord Jesus! In such faith I will pray always, ceasing never. Amen.

Author's Note

The need of persevering prayer appears to be at variance with the faith which knows that it has received what it asks (Mark 11:24). One of the mysteries of the Divine life is the harmony between sudden, complete possession and slow, imperfect appropriation. Here persevering prayer appears to be the school in which the soul is strengthened for the boldness of faith. Considering the diversity of operations of the Spirit, there may be some in whom faith takes the form of persistent waiting. For others, triumphant thanksgiving appears the only proper expression of the assurance of having been heard.

Prayer in Harmony with God

"Father, I thank thee that thou hast heard me. And I knew that thou hearest me always" (John 11:41-42).

"Thou art my Son; this day have I begotten thee. Ask of me, and I shall give thee" (Psalm 2:7-8).

In the New Testament we find a distinction made between faith and knowledge. "To one is given, through the Spirit, the word of wisdom; to another the word of knowledge, according to the same Spirit; to another faith, in the same Spirit" (1 Corinthians 12:8-9). In a child or an uninformed Christian there may be much faith with little knowledge. Childlike simplicity accepts the truth without difficulty, and often cares little to give any reason for its faith but this: God said it. But it is the will of God that we should love and serve Him, not only with all the heart but also with all the mind. He wants us to develop an insight into the Divine wisdom and beauty of all His ways, words, and works. Only in this way will the believer be able to fully approach and rightly adore the glory of God's grace. And only thus can our hearts intelligently understand the treasures of wisdom and knowledge, that exist in redemption, preparing us to join in the, highest note of the song that rises before the throne: "O the depth of the riches both of the wisdom and knowledge of God!"

This truth has its full application in our prayer life. While prayer and faith are so simple that the newborn convert can pray with power, more mature Christians may find in the doctrine of prayer some of their deepest questions. How extensive is the power of prayer? How can God grant to prayer such mighty power? How can prayer be harmonized with the will of God? How can God's sovereignty and our will God's liberty and ours—be reconciled? These and similar questions are appropriate subjects for Christian meditation and inquiry. The more earnestly and reverently we approach such mysteries, the more we will fall down in adoring wonder to praise Him Who has in prayer given such power to man.

One of the difficulties with regard to prayer is the result of the perfection of God. He is absolutely independent of everything outside of Himself. He is an infinite being Who owes what He is to Himself alone. With His wise and holy will, He has determined Himself and everything that is to be. How can our prayer influence Him? How can He be moved by prayer to do what He otherwise would not do? Isn't the promise of an answer to prayer simply a condescension to our weakness? Is the power of prayer anything more than an accommodation of our mode of thought, because the accomplishments of Deity are never dependent of any outside action? And isn't the real blessing of prayer simply the influence it exerts on us?

Seeking answers to such questions provides the key to the very being of God in the mystery of the Holy Trinity. If God were only one Person, shut up within Himself, there could be no thought of nearness to Him or influence on Him. But in God there are three Persons: Father and Son, Who have in the Holy Spirit their living bond of unity and fellowship. When the Father gave the Son a place next to Himself as His equal and His counselor, He opened a way for prayer and its influence into the very inmost life of Deity itself.

On earth, just as in heaven, the whole relationship between Father and Son is that of giving and taking. If the taking is to be as voluntary and self-determined as the giving, the Son must ask and receive. "Thou art my Son; this day I have begotten thee. Ask of me, and I shall give thee" (Psalm 2:7-8). The Father gave the Son the place and the power to influence Him. The Son's asking wasn't just for show. It was one of those life-movements in which the love of the Father and the Son met and completed each other. The Father had determined that He would not be alone in His counsels. Their fulfillment would depend on the Son's asking and receiving. Thus asking was in the very Being and Life of God. Prayer on earth was to be the reflection and the outflow of this.

Jesus said, "I knew that Thou hearest me always" (John 11:42). Just as the Sonship of Jesus on earth cannot be separated from His Sonship in heaven, His prayer on earth is the continuation and the counterpart of His asking in heaven. His prayer is the link between the eternal asking of the only begotten Son in the bosom of the Father and the prayer of men on earth. Prayer has its rise and its deepest source in the very Being of God. In the bosom of Deity nothing is ever done without prayer—the asking of the Son and the giving of the Father.

This may help us to understand how the prayer of man, coming through the Son, can have an effect on God. God's decrees are not made without reference to the Son, His petition, or a petition sent up through Him. The

Lord Jesus is the first-begotten, the Head and Heir of all things. As the Representative of all creation, He always has a voice in the Father's decisions. In the decrees of the eternal purpose, room was always left for the liberty of the Son as Mediator and Intercessor. The same holds true for the petitions of all who draw near to the Father through the Son.

If Christ's liberty and power to influence the Father seems to be at variance with the immutability of the Divine decrees, remember that God doesn't leave a past, as man does, to which He is irrevocably bound. The distinctions of time have no meaning to Him Who inhabits eternity. Eternity is an ever-present now, in which the past never passes and the future is always present. To meet our human comprehension of time, Scripture must speak of past decrees and a coming future.

In reality, the unchanging nature of God's plan is still in perfect harmony with His liberty to do whatever He wills. The prayers of the Son and His people weren't included in the eternal decrees simply for show. Rather, the Father listens with His heart to every prayer that rises through the Son. God really does allow Himself to be moved by prayer to do what He otherwise would not have done.

This perfect, harmonious union of Divine sovereignty and human liberty is an unfathomable mystery because God as the Eternal One transcends all our thoughts. But let it be our comfort and strength to know that in the eternal fellowship of the Father and the Son, the power of prayer has its origin and certainty. Through our union with the Son, our prayer is taken up and can have its influence in the inner life of the Blessed Trinity. God's decrees are no iron framework against which man's liberty struggles vainly. God Himself is living love, Who in His Son as man has entered into the tenderest relationship with all that is human. Through the Holy Spirit, He takes up everything human into the Divine life of love, leaving Himself free to give every human prayer its place in His government of the world.

In the light of such thoughts, the doctrine of the Blessed Trinity is no longer an abstract speculation, but the living manifestation of how man is taken up into the fellowship of God, his prayer becoming a real factor in God's rule of this earth. We can catch a glimpse of the light shining out from the eternal world in words such as these: "Through Him, we have access by one Spirit unto the Father."

Lord, Teach Us to Pray.

Everlasting God! In deep reverence I worship before the holy mystery of Your Divine being. If it pleases You, most glorious God, to reveal some of that mystery to me, I would bow with fear and trembling rather than sin against You as I meditated on Your glory.

Father! I thank You for being not only the Father of Your children here on earth, but the Father of Jesus Christ through eternity. Thank You for hearing our prayers and for having given Christ's asking a place in Your eternal plan. Thank You also for sending Christ to earth and for His blessed communication with You in heaven. There has always been room in Your counsel for His prayers and the answers to those prayers. And I thank You above all that through Christ's true human nature on Your throne above, and through Your Holy Spirit in our human nature here below, a way has been opened by which every human cry of need can be received into the life and love of God, always obtaining an answer.

Blessed Jesus! As the Son, You have opened this path of prayer and assured us of an answer. We beseech You to teach us how to pray. Let our prayers be the sign of our sonship, so that we, like You, know that the Father always hears us. Amen.

Prayer in Harmony with the Destiny of Man

"And he saith unto them, Whose is this image and superscription?" (Matthew 22:20).

"And God said, Let us make man in our image, after our likeness" (Genesis 1:26).

"Whose is this image?" It was with this question that Jesus foiled His enemies when they tried to trick Him, settling the matter of responsibility in regard to paying taxes. The question and the principle it involves are universally applicable, particularly to man himself. Bearing God's image decides man's destiny. He belongs to God and prayer to God is what he was created for. Prayer is part of the wondrous likeness he bears to His Divine original. It is the earthly likeness of the deep mystery of the fellowship of love in which the Trinity has its blessedness.

The more we meditate on what prayer is and on the wonderful power it has with God, the more we have to ask how man is so special, that such a place in God's plan has been allotted to him. Sin has so degraded him that we can't conceive of what he was meant to be based on what he is now. We must turn back to God's own record of man's creation to find what God's purpose was, and what capacities man was given to fulfill that purpose.

Man's destiny appears clearly in God's language at creation. It was to fill, to subdue, and to have dominion over the earth and everything in it. These three expressions show us that man was intended, as God's representative, to rule here on earth. As God's deputy, he was to fill God's place, keeping everything in subjection to Him. It was the will of God that everything done on earth should be done through man, i.e., the history of the earth was to be entirely in his hands.

In accordance with such a destiny was the position he was to occupy and the power at his disposal. When an earthly sovereign sends a representative to a distant province, that representative advises the sovereign as to the policy to be adopted there. The sovereign follows that advice, doing whatever is necessary to enact the policy and maintain the dignity of his empire. If the sovereign, however, doesn't approve of the policy, he replaces the representative with someone who better understands his desires for the empire. But as long as the representative is trusted, his advice is carried out.

As God's representative, man was to have ruled. Everything was to have been done according to his will. On his advice and at his request, heaven was to have bestowed its blessing on earth. His prayer was to have been the natural channel through which the Lord in heaven and man, as lord of this world, communicated. The destinies of the world were given into the power of the wishes, the will, and the prayers of man.

With the advent of sin, all this underwent a terrible change: Man's fall brought all creation under the curse. Redemption brought the beginning of a glorious restoration. In Abraham, God began to make Himself a people from whom kings (not to mention the Great King) would emerge. We see how Abraham's prayer power affected the destinies of those who came into contact with him. In Abraham we see how prayer is not only the means of obtaining blessing for ourselves. It is the exercise of a royal prerogative to influence the destinies of men and the will of God which rules them. We do not once find Abraham praying for himself. His prayers for Sodom and Lot, for Abimelech, and for Ishmael prove that a man who is God's friend has the power to control the history of those around him.

This had been man's destiny from the first. But Scripture tells us more: God could entrust man with such a high calling because He had created him in His own image and likeness. The external responsibility was not committed to him without the inner fitness. The root of man's inner resemblance to God was in his nature to have dominion, to be lord of all. There was an inner agreement and harmony between God and man, an embryonic Godlikeness, which gave man a real fitness for being the mediator between God and His world.

Man was to be prophet, priest, and king, to interpret God's will, to represent nature's needs, to receive and dispense God's bounty. It was in bearing God's image that he could bear God's rule. He was indeed so much like God—so capable of entering into God's purposes and carrying out His plans that God could trust him with the wonderful privilege of asking for and obtaining what the world might need.

Although sin has for a time frustrated God's plans, prayer still remains what it would have been if man had never fallen: the proof of man's Godlikeness, the vehicle of his communication with the Father, and the power that is allowed to hold the hand that holds the destinies of the universe. Man is of Divine origin, created for and capable of possessing kinglike liberty. His prayer is not merely a cry for mercy. It is the greatest execution of his will.

What sin destroyed, grace has restored. What the first Adam lost, the second has won back. In Christ, man regains his original position, and the Church, abiding in Christ, inherits the promise: "Ask what ye will, and it shall be done unto you."

To begin with, such a promise does by no means refer to the grace or blessing we need for ourselves. It has reference to our position as the fruit-bearing branches of the heavenly Vine, who, like Him, only live for the work and glory of the Father. It is for those who abide in Him, who have forsaken themselves for a life of obedience and self-sacrifice in Him, who have completely surrendered to the interests of the Father and His Kingdom. They understand how their redemption through Christ has brought them back to their original destiny, restoring God's image and the power to have dominion.

Such men indeed have the power—each in his own area—to obtain and dispense the powers of heaven here on earth. With holy boldness they may make known what they will. They live as priests in God's presence. They are kings possessing the powers of the world to come. "God is seeking priests among the sons of men. A human priesthood is one of the essential parts of His eternal plan. To rule creation by man is His design. They enter upon the fulfillment of the promise: "Ask whatsoever ye will, and it shall be done unto you."

Church of the living God! Your calling is higher and holier than you know! God wants to rule the world through your members. He wants you to be His kings and priests. Your prayers can bestow and withhold the blessings of heaven. In His elect who are not content just to be saved, but who surrender themselves completely, the Father will fulfill all His glorious counsel through them just as He does through the Son. In His elect, who cry day and night to Him, God wants to prove how wonderful man's original destiny was. Man was the image-bearer of God on earth, which was indeed given to him to rule. When he fell, everything fell with him. Now the whole creation groans and travails in pain together.

But now man is redeemed. The restoration of the original dignity has begun. It is God's purpose that the fulfillment of His eternal purpose and the coming of His Kingdom should depend on His people. They abide in Christ and are ready to accept Him as their Head, their great Priest-King. In their prayers they boldly say what they desire God to do for them. As God's image-bearer and representative on earth, redeemed man has the power to determine the history of this earth through his prayers. Man was created and then redeemed to pray, and by his prayer to have dominion.

"Priesthood is the appointed link between heaven and earth, the channel of communication between the sinner and God. Such a priesthood, insofar as expiation is concerned, is in the hands of the Son of God alone; insofar as it is to be the medium of communication between Creator and creature, is also in the hands of redeemed men of the Church of God.

"God is seeking kings. Not out of the ranks of angels. Fallen man must furnish Him with the rulers of His universe. Human hands must wield the scepter, human heads must wear the crown." (The Rent Veil, by Dr. H. Bonar.)

Lord, Teach Us to Pray.

"Lord! What is man, that thou art mindful of him? and the son of man, that thou visitest him? for thou hast made him a little lower than the angels, and hast crowned him with glory and honor. Thou madest him to have dominion over the works of thy lands; thou hast put all things under his feet .... 0 Lord our Lord, how excellent is thy name in all the earth!" (Psalm 8:4-6,9).

Lord God! Man has sunk so low because of sin. And how terribly it has darkened his mind. He doesn't even know his Divine destiny: to be Your servant and representative. How sad it is that, even when their eyes are opened, men are so unready to accept their calling! They could have such power with God and with men, too!

Lord Jesus! Through You, the Father has again crowned man with glory and honor; opening the way for us to be what He wants us to be. O Lord! Have mercy on Your people—Your heritage! Work mightily with us in Your Church! Teach Your believing disciples to accept and to go forth in their royal priesthood. Teach us to use the power of prayer to which You have given such wonderful promises, to serve Your Kingdom, to have rule over the nations, and to make the Name of God glorious on the earth. Amen.

Power for Praying and Working

"Verily, verily, I say unto you, He that believeth on me, the works that I do shall he do also; and greater works than these shall he do; because I go unto my Father. And whatsoever ye shall ask in my name, that will l do, that the Father may be glorified in the Son. If ye shall ask any thing in my name, I will do it" (John 14:12-14).

The Savior opened His public ministry in the Sermon on the Mount with the same subject He uses here in His parting address from the Gospel of John: prayer. But there is a difference. The Sermon on the Mount is directed to disciples who have just entered His school, scarcely knowing that God is their Father, whose prayers have reference chiefly to their personal needs. In His closing address, He speaks to disciples whose training time is coming to an end, who are ready as His messengers to take over His place and His work.

Christ's first lesson had been: Be childlike, pray believingly, and trust the Father to give you everything good. Here He points to something higher. The disciples are now His friends. He has told then everything He knows about the Father. They are His messengers into whose hands the care of His work and Kingdom on earth is to be entrusted. Now they must assume that role, performing even greater works than Christ in the power of His approaching exaltation. Prayer is to be the channel through which that power is received. With Christ's ascension to the Father, a new epoch for both their working and their praying commences.

This connection comes out clearly in our text from John, chapter fourteen. As His Body here of earth, as those who are one with Him in heaven, the disciples are now to do greater works than He had done. Their successes and their victories are to be greater than His. Christ mentions two reasons for this. One is that He was going to the Father to receive all power; the other is that they could now ask for and expect that power in His Name "Because I go to the Father, and' (notice this and "and whatever ye shall ask, I will do." His going to the Father brings a double blessing: The disciple; could ask for and receive everything in His Name and as a consequence, would do the greater works This first mention of prayer in our Savior's parting words teaches us two most important lessons. Whoever wants to do the works of Jesus must pray in His Name. Whoever prays in His Name must work in His Name.

In prayer the power for work is obtained. When Jesus was here on earth, He did the greatest works Himself. Devils that the disciples could not cast out fled at His word. When He went to be with the Father, He was no longer here in body to work directly. The disciples were now His Body. All His work from the throne in heaven must and could be done here on earth through them.

Now that Christ was leaving the scene and could only work through commissioners, it might have been expected that the works would be fewer and weaker. He assures us of the contrary: "Verily, verily I say unto you, He that believeth on me, the works that I do shall he do also; and greater works than these shall he do; because I go unto my Father" (John 14:12). His approaching death was to be a breaking down of the power of sin. With the resurrection, the powers of the eternal life were to take possession of the human body and obtain supremacy over human life. With His ascension, Christ was to receive the power to communicate the Holy Spirit completely to His Body. The union—the oneness between Himself on the throne and those on earth was to be so intensely and divinely perfect, that He meant it as the literal truth: "Greater works than these shall he do, because I go to the Father."

And how true it was! Jesus, during three years of personal labor on earth, gathered little more than five hundred disciples, most of whom were so powerless that they weren't much help to His cause. Men like Peter and Paul did much greater things than He had done. From the throne He could do through them what He Himself in His humiliation could not yet do. He could ask the Father, receiving and bestowing new power for the greater works. And what was true for the disciples is true for us: As we believe and ask in His Name, the power comes and takes possession of us also to do the greater works.

Alas! There is little or nothing to be seen of the power to do anything like Christ's works, not to mention anything greater. There can only be one reason: the belief in Him and the believing prayer in His Name are absent. Every child of God must learn this lesson: Prayer in the Name of Jesus is the only way to share in the mighty power which Jesus has received from the Father for His people. It is in this power alone that the believer can do greater works. To every complaint about difficulties or lack of success, Jesus gives this one answer: "He that believeth on me shall do greater works, because I go to the Father, and whatsoever ye shall ask in my Name, that will I do." If you want to do the work of Jesus, believe and become linked to Him, the Almighty One. Then pray the prayer of faith in His Name. Without this our work is just human and carnal. It may have some use in restraining sin or in preparing the way for a blessing, but the real power is missing. Effective working first needs effective praying.

The second lesson is this: Whoever prays must work. It is for power to work that prayer has such great promises. Power for the effective prayer of faith is gained through working. Our blessed Lord repeats no less than six times (John 14:13-14; 15:7,16; 16:23-24) those unlimited prayer-promises which evoke anxious questions as to their real meaning: "whatsoever," "anything," "what ye will," "ask and ye shall receive."Many a believer has read these with joy and hope, and in deep earnestness of soul has attempted to plead them for his own need, arid has come out disappointed. The simple reason was that he separated the promise from its context.

The Lord gave the wonderful promise of the free case of His Name with the Father in conjunction with doing His works. The disciple who lives only for Jesus' work and Kingdom, for His will and honor, vain be given the power to appropriate the promise. Anyone grasping the promise only when he wants something very special for himself will be disappointed, because he is making Jesus the servant of his own comfort. But whoever wants to pray the effective prayer of faith because he needs it for the work of the Master will learn it, because he has made himself the servant of his Lord's interests. Prayer not only teaches and strengthens one for work, work teaches and strengthens one for prayer.

This is true in both the natural and the spiritual worlds. "Unto every one which hath (more) shall be given" (Luke 19:26). Whoever is "faithful over a few things, I will make ....ruler over many things" (Matthew 25:21). With the small amount of grace we have already received, let us give ourselves to the Master for His work! It will be to us a real school of prayer. When Moses had to take full charge of a rebellious people, he felt the need, but also the courage, to speak boldly to God and to ask great things of Him (Exodus 33:12,15,18). As you give yourself entirely to God for His work, you will feel that these great promises are exactly what you need and that you may most confidently expect nothing less.

Believer in Jesus! You are called—you are appointed —to do the works of Jesus, and even greater works He has gone to the Father to get the power to do them in and through you. Remember His promise "Whatsoever ye shall ask in my Name, that will I do. "Give yourself and live to do the works of Christ and you will learn how to obtain wonderful answers to prayer. You will learn to do not only what He did but much more. With disciples full of faith in Himself, boldly asking great things in prayer, Christ can conquer the world.

Lord, Teach Us to Pray.

O my Lord! Once again, I am hearing You say things that are beyond my comprehension. I can do nothing but accept them and keep them in simple childlike faith as Your gift to me. You have said than because of Your going to be with the Father, anyone who believes in You can do not only the things You have done, but greater things as well.

Lord! I worship You as the Glorified One and eagerly await the fulfillment of Your promise. May my whole life be one of continued believing in You. Purify and sanctify my heart. Make it so tenderly susceptible to Yourself and Your love that believing in You will become its very breath.

You have said that because You went to the Father, You will do whatever we ask You to do. You want Your people to share Your power. From Your throne, You want to work through them, as members of Your Body, in response to their believing prayer in Your Name. You have promised us power in our prayers to You and power in our work here on earth.

Blessed Lord! Forgive us for not believing You and Your promise more. Because of our lack of faith, we have failed to demonstrate how You are faithful to fulfill that promise. Please forgive us for so little honoring Your all-prevailing Name in heaven or on earth.

Lord! Teach me to pray so that I can prove Your Name is all powerful with God, with men, and with devils. Teach me to work and to pray in a way that glorifies You, and do Your great works through me. Amen.

The Chief End of Prayer

"I go unto my Father. And whatsoever ye shall ask in my name, that will I do, that the Father may be glorified in the Son" (John 14:12-13).

"That the Father may be glorified in the Son': It is to this end that Jesus on His throne in glory will do everything we ask in His Name. Every answer to prayer He gives will have this as its object. When there is no prospect of this object being obtained, He will not answer. It follows as a matter of course that with us, as with Jesus, this must be the essential element in our petitions. The glory of the Father must be the aim—the very soul and life—of our prayer.

This was Jesus' goal when He was on earth: "I seek not mine own honor: I seek the honor of Him that sent me." In such words we have the keynote of His life. The first words of His High-Priestly prayer voice it: "Father glorify Thy Son, that Thy Son may glorify Thee. I have glorified Thee on earth: glorify me with Thyself" (John 17:1,4). His reason for asking to be taken up into the glory He had with the Father is a twofold one: He has glorified Him on earth; He will still glorify Him in heaven. All He asks is to be able to glorify the Father more.

As we begin to share Jesus' feeling on this point, ratifying Him by making the Father's glory our chief object in prayer, too, our prayer cannot fail to get an answer. The Beloved Son has said that nothing glorifies the Father more than His doing what we ask. Therefore, Jesus won't miss any opportunity to do what we request. Let us make His aim ours! Let the glory of the Father be the link between our asking and His doing!

Jesus' words come indeed as a sharp two-edged word, dividing the soul and the spirit, and quickly discerning the thoughts and intents of the heart. In His prayers on earth, His intercession in heaven, and His promise of an answer to our prayers, Jesus makes His first object the glory of His Father. Is this our object, too? Or are self-interest and self-will the strongest motives urging us to pray? A distinct, conscious longing for the glory of the Father must animate our prayers.

The believer does at times desire it. But he doesn't desire it enough. The reason for this failure is that the separation between the spirit of his daily life and the spirit of his hour of prayer is too wide. Desire for the glory of the Father is not something we can arouse and present to our Lord when we prepare ourselves to pray. Only when the whole life in all its parts is given up to God's glory can we really pray to Christ's glory, too. "Do all to the glory of God," and "Ask all to the glory of God." These twin commands are inseparable. Obedience to the former is the secret of grace for the latter. Living for the glory of God is the condition of the prayers that Jesus can answer.

This demand that prayer be to the glory of God is quite right and natural. Only the Lord is glorious. There is no glory but His, and what He allots to His creations. Creation exists to show forth His glory. Everything that doesn't glorify Him is sinful, dark, and dead. It is only in the glorifying of God that creatures can find glory. What the Son of Man did—giving Himself wholly to glorify the Father—is nothing but the simple duty of every redeemed one. He will also receive Christ's reward.

We cannot attain a life with God's glory as our only aim by any effort of our own. It is only in the man Christ Jesus that such a life can be found. Yes, blessed be God! His life is our life. He gave Himself for us. He is now our life. It is essential to discover, confess, and deny the self because it takes God's place. Only the presence and rule of the Lord Jesus in our hearts can cast out all self-glorification, replacing it with His own God—glorifying life and Spirit. It is Jesus, Who longs to glorify the Father in hearing our prayers, Who will teach us to live and to pray to the glory of God.

What power is there that can urge our slothful hearts to yield themselves to our Lord to work this in us? Surely nothing more is needed than a glimpse of how worthy of glory the Father is. Our faith should learn to bow before Him in adoring worship, ascribing to Him alone the Kingdom, the power, and the glory, yielding ourselves to life in His light. Surely we will be stirred to say, "To Him alone be glory." And we will look to our Lord Jesus with new intensity of desire for a life that refuses to recognize anything but the glory of God. When there isn't enough prayer to be answered, the Father is not glorified. It is our duty to live and pray so that our prayer can be answered. For the sake of God's glory, let us learn to pray well.

What a humbling thought it is, that so often there is earnest prayer in which the desire for our own joy or pleasure is far stronger than many desire for God's glory. No wonder there are so many unanswered prayers! Here we have the secret. God cannot be glorified when that glory is not the object of our prayers. Whoever wants to pray the prayer of faith must give himself to live literally so that the Father in all things is glorified in him. This must be his aim; without it there cannot be a prayer of faith.

"How can ye believe," said Jesus, "which receive honor of one another, and seek not the honor that cometh from God only?" (John 5:44). When we seek our own glory among men, we make faith impossible. Only the deep, intense self-sacrifice that gives up its own glory and seeks the glory of God wakens in the soul that spiritual susceptibility to Divine faith. The surrender to God and the expectation that He will show His glory in hearing us are essential. Only he who seeks God's glory will see it in the answer to his prayer.

How do we accomplish this? Let us begin with a confession. The glory of God hasn't really been an all—absorbing passion in our lives and our prayers. How little we have lived in the likeness of the Son and in sympathy with Him for God and His glory alone. Take time to allow the Holy Spirit to reveal how deficient we have been in this. True knowledge and confession of sin are the sure path to deliverance.

And then let us look to Jesus. In death He glorified God; through death He was glorified with Him. It is by dying-being dead to self and living for God—that we can glorify Him. This death to self, this life to the glory of God, is what Jesus gives and lives in each one who can trust Him for it. Let the spirit of our daily lives consist of the decision to live only for the glory of the Father as Christ did, the acceptance of Him with His life and strength working it in us, and the joyful assurance that we can live for the glory of God because Christ lives in us. Jesus helps us to live this way. The Holy Spirit is waiting to make it our experience, if we will only trust and let Him. Don't hold back through unbelief! Confidently do everything for the glory of God! Our obedience will please the Father. The Holy Spirit will seal us within with the consciousness that we are living for God and His glory.

What quiet peace and power will be in our prayers when we know that we are in perfect harmony with Christ, Who promises to do what we ask, "That the Father may be glorified in the Son." With our whole beings consciously yielded to the inspiration of the Word and Spirit, our desires will no longer be ours. They will be His, and their main purpose will be the glory of God. With increasing liberty we will be able in prayer to say, "Father! You know we ask it only for Your glory. Answers to prayer, instead of being mountains we cannot climb, will give us greater confidence that we are heard. And the privilege of prayer will become doubly precious because it brings us into perfect unison with the Beloved Son in the wonderful partnership He proposes: "You ask, and I do, that the father may be glorified in the Son."

Lord, Teach Us to Pray.

Blessed Lord Jesus! Once again I am coming to You. Every lesson you give me convinces me all the more deeply that I don't know hove to pray properly. But every lesson also inspires me with hope that You are going to teach me What prayer should be. O my Lord! I look to You with courage. You are the Great Intercessor. You alone pray and hear prayer for the sole purpose of glorifying the Father. Teach me to pray as You do.

Savior! I want to be nothing, yielding my totally to You. I am giving myself to be crucified with You. Through the Spirit the works of self will be made dead. Let your life and Your love of the Father take Possession of me. A new longing is filling my soul that every day and every hour prayer to the glory of the Father will become everything to me. O my Lord! Please teach me this!

My God and my Father! Accept the desire of Your child who has seen that Your glory is alone worth living for. Show me Your glory. Let it overshadow me and fill my heart! May I dwell in it as Christ did. Tell me what pleases You, fulfill in me Your own good pleasure, so that I may find my glory in seeking the glory of my Father. Amen.

The All-Inclusive Condition

"If ye abide in me, and my words abide in you, ye shall ask what ye will, and it shall be done unto you" (John 15:7).

In all God's relations with us, the promise and its conditions are inseparable. If we fulfill the conditions He fulfills the promise. What He is to be to us depends on what we are willing to be to Him: "Draw near to God, and He will draw near to you." Therefore, in prayer the unlimited promise, "Ask what ye will, " has one simple and natural condition, "if ye abide in me." It is Christ Whom the Father always hears. God is in Christ. To reach God, we must be in Christ, too. Fully abiding in Him, we have the right to ask whatever we want and the promise that we will get an answer.

There is a terrible discrepancy between this promise and the experience of most believers. How many prayers bring no answer? The cause must be either that we do not fulfill the condition, or God does not fulfill the promise. Believers are not willing to admit either, and therefore have devised a way of escape from the dilemma. They put a qualifying clause into the promise that our Savior did not put there—if it be God's will. This maintains both God's integrity and their own. If they could only accept it and hold fast to it as it stands, trusting Christ to make it true! And if only they would confess their failure in fulfilling the condition as the one explanation for unanswered prayer. God's Spirit would then lead them to see how appropriate such a promise is to those who really believe that Christ means it. The Holy Spirit would then make our weakness in prayer a mighty motivation for us to discover the secret and obtain the blessing of fully abiding in Christ.

"If ye abide in me. "As a Christian grows in grace and knowledge of the Lord Jesus, he is often surprised to find how God's words grow, too, into new and deeper meaning. He can look back to the day when some word of God was opened up to him, and he rejoiced in the blessing he had found in it. After a time, some deeper experience gave it a new meaning, and it was as if he never had seen what it contained. And yet once again, as he advanced in the Christian life, the same word stood before him as a great mystery, until the Holy Spirit led him still more deeply into its Divine fullness.

The Master's precious "Abide in me" is one of these ever growing, never-exhausted words. Step by step, it opens the fullness of the Divine life to us. As the union of the branch with the vine is one of never-ceasing growth, so our abiding in Christ is a life process in which the Divine life takes more and more complete possession of us. The young believer may really be abiding in Christ to the limited extent which is possible for him. If he reaches onward to attain what the Master means by full abiding, he will inherit all the promises connected with it.

In the growing life of abiding in Christ, the first stage is that of faith. As the believer sees that Christ's command is really meant for him, his great aim is simply to believe that abiding in Christ is his immediate duty and a blessing within his reach. He is especially occupied with the love, power, and faithfulness of the Savior. He feels his one basic need is to believe.

It isn't long before he sees something more is needed. Obedience and faith must go together. But faith can't simply be added to obedience; it must be revealed in obedience. Faith is obedience at home, looking to the Master; obedience is faith going out to do His will.

The privilege and the blessings of this abiding are often of more interest than its duties and its fruit. Much self-will passes unnoticed. The peace which a young disciple enjoys in believing leaves him. In practical obedience the abiding must be maintained: "If ye keep my commands, ye shall abide in my love." Before, the truth that the mind believed was enough to let the heart rest on Christ and His promises. Now, in this stage, his chief effort is to get his will united with the will of his Lord, with his heart and life brought entirely under Christ's rule.

And yet there still seems to be something missing The will and the heart are on Christ's side; the disciple obeys and loves his Lord. But why does the fleshly nature still have so much power? Why aren't his spontaneous actions and emotions what they should be? Where is the beauty of holiness, the zeal of love, and the conformity with Jesus and His death, in which the life of self is lost? There must surely be something which he has not yet experienced through abiding in Christ.

Faith and obedience are just the pathway to blessing. Before giving us the parable of the vine and the branches, Jesus had very distinctly told what that full blessing is. Three times over He said, "If ye love me, keep my commandments," promising threefold blessing with which He would crown such obedient love: the indwelling of the Holy Spirit, the manifestation of the Son, the Father and Son coming to make Their abode within us.

As our faith grows into obedience, and in obedience and love our whole being reaches out and clings to Christ, our inner life opens up. The capacity is formed within us of receiving the life and the Spirit of the glorified Jesus, through a distinct and conscious union with Christ and with the Father. The word is fulfilled in us: "In that day ye shall know that I am in my Father and ye in me, and I in you" (John 14:20) God and Christ exist in each other, not only in will and in love, but in identity of nature and life. We come to understand that because of this union between the Father and the Son, so we are in Christ and Christ is in us in exactly the same way.

After Jesus had spoken thus, He said, "Abide in me, and I in you. Accept, consent to receive that Divine life of union with myself, in virtue of which, as you abide in me, I also abide in you, even as I abide in the Father. So that your life is mine and mine is yours." True abiding consists of two parts: occupying a position into which Christ can come and abide, and abiding in Him so that the soul lets Him take the place of the self to become our life. Like little children who have no cares, we find happiness in trusting and obeying the love that has done everything for us.

To those who thus abide, the promise, "Ask whatsoever ye will," comes as their rightful heritage. It cannot be otherwise. Christ has full possession of them. He dwells in their love, their wills, and their lives. Not only have their wills been given up, Christ has entered them, dwelling and breathing there by His Spirit. These people pray in Him. He prays in them, and the Father always hears Him. What they ask will be done for them.

Beloved fellow-believer! Let us confess that because we do not abide in Christ as He would like us to, the Church is impotent in the face of infidelity, worldliness, and heathendom. In the midst of such enemies, the Lord could make her more than a conqueror. We must believe that He means what He promises, and accept the conviction the confession implies.

But don't be discouraged. The abiding of the branch in the Vine is a life of never-ceasing growth. The abiding (as the Master meant it) is within our reach, for He lives to give it to us. Let us but be ready to count all things as loss and to say, "What I have attained so far is hardly anything. I want to learn to perceive Christ the same way He perceives me." It is not be occupied so much with the abiding as with Him to Whom the abiding links us and His fullness. Let it be Christ—the whole Christ, in His obedience and humiliation, in His exaltation and power, Whom our soul moves and acts. He Himself will fulfill His promise in us.

As we abide and grow into fuller and fuller abiding, let us exercise our right—the will to enter into God's will. Obeying what that will commands, let us claim what it promises. Let us yield to the teaching of the Holy Spirit. He will show each of us what the will of God is so that we may claim it prayer. And let us be content with nothing less than the personal experience of what Jesus gave when said, "If ye abide in me, ye shall ask what ye will, and it shall be done unto you."

Lord, Teach Us to Pray.

Beloved Lord! Make Your promise in all simplicity new to men. Teach me to accept it, letting the only limitation on Your holy giving be my own willingness. Lord! Let each word of Your promise be, in a new way, made quick and powerful in soul.

You say, "Abide it? me!" O my Master, my Life my All—I do abide in You. Allow me to grow up in all your fullness. It is not the effort of faith, trying to cling to You and trusting You to protect me; nor my will, obeying You and keeping Your commandments, that alone can satisfy me. Only You Yourself, living in me as You do in the Father, can satisfy me. It is You, my Lord, no longer before me and above me, but united with me, that I need. I trust You for this.

You say, "Ask whatever you will." Lord! I know that a life of complete, deep abiding will renew, sanctify, and strengthen my will in such a way that I will have the desire and the liberty to ask for great things. Lord! Let my will—dead in Your death, living in Your life—be bold and large in its petitions.

You say, "It shall be done. "O Jesus! You are the Amen, the Faithful and True Witness. Give me in Yourself the joyous confidence that You will make this promise even more wonderfully true to me than ever before, because it has not entered into the heart of man to conceive what God has prepared for those who love Him. Amen.

Author's Note

Many books and sermons on prayer emphasize the blessing of prayer as a spiritual exercise, even if there is no answer. God's fellowship ought to be more important to us than the gift we ask for. But a careful examination of what Christ said about prayer reveals that He wanted us to think of prayer more as the means to an end. The answer was to be the proof that we and our prayer are acceptable to the Father in heaven. It is not that Christ would have us consider the gifts of higher value than the fellowship and favor of the

Father. By no means. But the Father intends the answer to be a token of His favor and of the reality of our fellowship with Him.

Daily answer to prayer is the proof of our spiritual maturity. It shows that we have attained the true abiding in Christ, that our will is truly one with God's will. It also reveals that our faith is strong enough to see and take what God has prepared for us, that the Name of Christ and His nature have taken full possession of us, and that we have been found fit to take a place among those whom God admits to His counsels, according to whose prayer He rules the world. Prayer is very blessed; the answer is more blessed still. It is the response from the Father that our prayer, our faith, and our will are indeed as He would wish them to be.

I make these remarks with the one desire of leading my readers to put together for themselves everything that Christ has said about prayer. Accept the truth that when prayer is what it should be, or rather when we are what we should be, the answer must be expected. It will bring us out from those refuges where we have comforted ourselves with unanswered prayer. It will show us the place of power to which Christ has appointed His Church, that place which it occupies so little. It will reveal the terrible weakness of our spiritual life as the cause of our not praying boldly in Christ's Name. It will urge us mightily to rise to a life in full union with Christ and in the fullness of the Spirit as the secret of effective prayer. And it will so lead us to realize our destiny: "At that day: Verily, verily I say unto you, If ye shall ask anything of the Father, He will give it you in my Name: ask, and ye shall receive, that your joy may be fulfilled." Prayer that is really, spiritually, in union with Jesus is always answered.

The Word and Prayer

"If ye abide in me, and my words abide in you, ye shall ask what ye will, and it shall be done unto you " (John 15:7).

The vital connection between the Word and prayer is one of the simplest and earliest lessons of the Christian life. As that newly-converted heathen put it: "I pray—I speak to my Father; I read—my Father speaks to me." Before prayer, God's Word strengthens me by giving my faith its justification and its petition. And after prayer, God's Word prepares me by revealing what the Father wants me to ask. In prayer, God's Word brings me the answer, for in it the Spirit allows me to hear the Father's voice.

Prayer is not monologue, but dialogue. Its most essential part is God's voice in response to mine. Listening to God's voice is the secret of the assurance that He will listen to mine. "Incline thine ear and hear," "Give ear to me," and "Hearken to my voice," are words which God speaks to man as well as man to God. His hearkening will depend on ours. My willingness to accept His words will determine the power my words have with Him. What God's words are to me is the test of what He Himself is to me. It shows the uprightness of my desire to meet Him in prayer.

It is this connection between His Word and our prayer that Jesus points to when He says, "If ye abide in me, and my words abide in you, ye shall ask what ye will, and it shall be done unto you." The deep importance of this truth becomes clear if we notice the expression which this one replaces. More than once Jesus had said, "Abide in me and I in you. "His abiding in us was the complement and the crown of our abiding in Him. But here, instead of "Ye in me and I in you, "He says, "Ye in me and my words in you." The abiding of His words is the equivalent of Himself abiding.

What a view this opens up to us of the place the words of God in Christ are to have in our spiritual lives, especially in our prayer. A man's words reveal himself. In his promises, he gives himself away, binding himself to the one who receives his promises. In his commands, he proclaims his will, seeking to make himself master of those whose obedience he claims, to guide and use them as if they were part of himself. Through our words, spirit holds fellowship with spirit. If a man's words are heard, accepted, held fast, and obeyed, he can impart himself to someone else through them. But with human beings, this can happen only in a limited sense.

God, however, is the infinite Being in Whom everything is life, power, spirit, and truth, in the very deepest meaning of the words. When God reveals Himself in His words, He does indeed give Himself— love and His life, His will and His power to those who receive these words, in a reality passing comprehension. In every promise, He gives us the power to grasp and possess Himself. In every command, He allows us to share His will, His holiness, and His perfection. God's Word gives us God Himself. That Word is nothing less than the Eternal Son, Christ Jesus. Therefore, all of Christ's words are God's words, full of a Divine, quickening life and power. "The words that I speak unto you, they are spirit and they are life."

Those who study the deaf and mute tell us how much the power of speaking depends on that of hearing, and how the loss of hearing in children is followed by a loss of speaking, too. This is also true in a broader sense: Our speech is based on what we hear. In the highest sense, this is true of our conversation with God. To offer a prayer—to utter certain wishes and appeal to certain promises—is an easy thing that man can learn with human intelligence. But to pray in the Spirit—to speak words that reach and touch God, affecting and influencing the powers of the unseen world—depends entirely on our hearing God's voice. We must listen to the voice and language that God uses and, through the words of God, receive His thoughts, His mind, and His life into our hearts. The extent to which we listen will determine the extent to which we learn to speak in the voice and the language that God hears. The ear of the learner, wakened morning by morning, prepares him to speak to God. (Isaiah 1:4).

This hearing the voice of God is something more than the thoughtful study of the Word. One can study and gain knowledge of the Word having little real fellowship with the living God. But there is also a reading of the Word, in the very presence of the Father and under the leading of the Spirit, in which the Word comes to us in living power from God Himself. It is to us the very voice of the Father, a real, personal fellowship with Himself. The living voice of God enters the heart, bringing blessing and strength, and awakening the response of a living faith that reaches back to the heart of God.

The power both to obey and believe depends on hearing God's voice this way. The chief thing isn't knowing what God has said we must do, but that God Himself says it to us. Neither the law nor the book nor the knowledge of what is right works obedience. This can be accomplished only by the personal influence of God through His living fellowship. The presence of God Himself as the Promiser, not the knowledge of what He has promised, awakens faith and trust in prayer. It is only in the full presence of God that disobedience and unbelief become impossible.

"If ye abide in me, and my words abide in you, ye shall ask what ye will, and it shall be done unto you." In these words, the Savior gives Himself. We must have the words in us taken up into our wills and lives, reproduced in our inner natures and conduct. They must abide in us. Our lives must be one continuous display of the words that fill us. The words reveal Christ inside and our lives reveal Him outside. As the words of Christ enter our very hearts, becoming and influencing our lives, our words will enter His heart and influence Him. My prayer will depend on my life: Whatever God's words are to me and in me will determine what my words will be to God and in God. If I do what God says, God will do what I say.

The Old Testament saints understood this connection between God's words and ours quite well. Their prayer really was a loving response to what they had heard God speak. If the word were a promise, they counted on God to do as He had spoken. "Do as Thou hast said"; "For Thou, Lord, hast spoken it"; "According to Thy promise"; "According to Thy word": In such expressions they showed that what God spoke in promise was the root and the life of what they spoke in prayer. If the word was a command, they simply did as the Lord had spoken: "So Abram departed as the Lord had spoken." Their lives were fellowship with God, the exchange of word and thought. What God spoke they heard and did; what they spoke God heard and did. In each word, He speaks to us, and the whole Christ gives Himself to fulfill it. For each word, He asks no less than that we give the whole man to keep that word and to receive its fulfillment."If my words abide in you." The condition is simple and clear. In His words His will is revealed. As the words abide in me, His will rules me. My will becomes the empty vessel which His will fills, and the willing instrument which His will rules. He fills my inner being. In the exercise of obedience and faith, my will becomes stronger and is brought into deeper inner harmony with Him. Because He can fully trust it to will nothing but what He wills, He is not afraid to give the promise, "If my words abide in you, ye shall ask what ye will, and it shall be done unto you." To all who believe it and act upon it, He will make it literally true. Disciples of Christ! While we have been excusing our unanswered prayers with a fancied submission to God's wisdom and will, the real reason has been that our own feeble lives have been the cause of our feeble prayers! Nothing can make men strong but the word coming from God's mouth. By that we must live. The word of Christ makes us one with Him and fits us spiritually for touching and taking hold of God. We must love and live in that Word, letting it abide in and become part of us. All that is of the world passes away. Whoever does God's will lives forever. Let us yield heart and life to the words of Christ, the words in which He gives Himself, the personal living Savior. His promise will become our rich experience: "If ye abide in me, and my words abide in you, ye shall ask what ye will, and it shall be done unto you."

Lord, Teach Us to Pray.

Blessed Lord! I see why my prayer has not been more believing and effective. I was more occupied with my speaking to You than with Your speaking to me. I did not understand that the secret of faith is this: There can be only as much faith as there is of the living Word dwelling in the soul.

Your Word taught me so clearly to be swift to hear and slow to speak, and not to be hasty to say just anything to God. Lord, teach me that it is only when I take Your Word into my life that my words can be taken into Your heart. Teach me that if Your Word is a living power within me, it will be a living power with You, also. Show me that what Your mouth has spoken Your hand will perform.

Lord Jesus! Deliver me from the uncircumcised ear! Give me the opened ear of the learner, wakened morning by morning to hear the Father's voice. Just as You speak only what You hear from the Father, may my speaking be the echo of Your speaking to me. "When Moses went into the tabernacle to speak with Him, he heard the voice of One speaking unto him from off the mercy seat." Lord, may it be so with me, too. Let my life and character reveal that Your words abide and are seen in me. May this be my preparation for the complete blessing: "Ye shall ask what ye will, and it shall be done unto you." Amen.

Obedience: the Path to Power in Prayer

"Ye have not chosen me, but I have chosen you, and ordained you, that ye should go and bring forth fruit, and that your fruit should remain; that whatsoever ye shall ask of the father in my name, he may give it you" (John 15:16).

"The effectual fervent prayer of a righteous man availeth much" (James 5:16).

The promise of the Father's giving whatsoever we ask is here once again renewed, showing us to whom such wonderful influence in the council chamber of the Most High is to be granted. "I chose you," the Master says, "and appointed you that ye should go and bear fruit, and that your fruit should remain." He then adds, to the end "that whatsoever ye," (the fruit bearing ones) "shall ask of the Father in my name, He may give it you." This is nothing but a fuller expression of what He meant by the words, "If ye abide in me." He had spoken of the object of this abiding as the bearing of "fruit," "more fruit," and "much fruit." In this, God would be glorified and the mark of discipleship would be seen. He now adds that the reality of the abiding, as seen in fruit abounding and abiding, is the qualification for our praying so as to obtain what we ask. Entire dedication to the fulfillment of our calling is the key to effective prayer and the unlimited blessings of Christ's wonderful prayer-promises.

There are Christians who fear that such a statement is at variance with the doctrine of free grace. But surely it doesn't disagree with free grace rightly understood or the many express statements of God's blessed Word. Take the words of St. John, "Let us love in deed and truth; hereby shall we assure our heart before Him. And whatsoever we ask, we receive of Him because we keep His commandments, and do the things that are pleasing in His sight" (1 John 3:18-19,22). Or take the often-quoted words of James:"The effectual fervent prayer of a righteous man availeth much" (James 5:16). This describes a man of whom, according to the definition of the Holy Spirit, it can be said,

"He that doeth righteousness, is righteous even as He is righteous." Mark the spirit of so many of the Psalms, with their confident appeal to the integrity and righteousness of the supplicant. In Psalm 18 David says: "The Lord rewarded me according to my righteousness; according to the cleanness of my hands hath he recompensed me... I was also upright before him, and I kept myself from mine iniquity. Therefore hath the Lord recompensed me according to my righteousness" (Psalm 18:20,23). See also Psalms 7:3-5; 15:1-2; 17:3,6; 26:16; 119:121, 153). If we carefully consider these scriptures in the light of the New Testament, we find them in perfect harmony with the explicit teaching of the Savior's parting words: "If ye keep my commandments, ye shall abide in my love"; "Ye are my friends if ye do what I command you." The words are indeed meant literally: "I appointed you that ye should go and bear fruit, that, "then, "whatsoever ye shall ask of the Father in my name, He may give it you."

Let us seek to enter into the spirit of what the Savior teaches us here. There is a danger in our evangelical religion of looking too much at what it offers from one side, as a certain experience obtained in prayer and faith. There is another side which God's Word puts very strongly, that of obedience as the only path to blessing. What we need to realize is that in our relationship to God He is the Infinite Being Who created and redeemed us. The first sentiment that ought to motivate us is that of subjection ,surrender to His supremacy, His glory, His will, and His pleasure. This ought to be the first and uppermost thought of our lives.

The question is not, however, how we are to obtain and enjoy His favor, for in this the main thing may still be self. What this Being in the very nature of things rightfully claims, and is infinitely and unspeakably worthy of, is that His glory and pleasure should be my only object. Surrender to His perfect and blessed will—a life of service and obedience—is the beauty and the charm of heaven. Service and obedience were the thoughts that were uppermost in the mind of the Son when He was on earth. Service and obedience must become the chief objects of our desires and aims, even more so than rest, light, joy, or strength. In them we will find the path to all the higher blessedness that awaits us.

Note what a prominent place the Master gives it, not only in this fifteenth chapter, in connection with the abiding, but in the fourteenth, where He speaks of the indwelling of the Trinity. John 14:15 says: "If ye love me, keep my commandments," and the Spirit will be given to you by the Father. Then verse 21:"He that hath my commandments and keepeth them, he it is that loveth me." He will have the special love of the Father and the special manifestation of Christ. Verse 23 is one of the highest of all the great and precious promises: "If a man loves me he will keep my words, and the Father and I will come and take up our abode with him." Could words put it more clearly that obedience is the way to the indwelling of the Spirit, to His revealing the Son within us, and to His preparing us to be the abode, the home of the Father? The indwelling of the Trinity is the heritage of those who obey.

Obedience and faith are simply two parts of one act—surrender to God and His will. As faith strengthens itself in order to be obedient, it is in turn strengthened by obedience. Faith is made perfect by works. Often our efforts to believe are unsuccessful because we don't assume the only position in which a large faith is legitimate or possible—that of entire surrender to the honor and the will of God. The man who is entirely consecrated to God and His will finds the power to claim everything that His God has promised to be for him.

The application of this in the school of prayer is very simple but very solemn. "I chose you, " the Master says, "and appointed you that ye should go and bear fruit, " much fruit (verses 5,8), "and that your fruit should abide, "that your life might be one of abiding fruit and abiding fruitfulness, "that" as fruitful branches abiding in me, "whatsoever ye shall ask of the Father in my name, He may give it you. "

How often we've tried to pray an effective prayer for grace to bear fruit and have wondered why the answer didn't come. It was because we were reversing the Master's order. We wanted to have the comfort, the joy, and the strength first, so we could do the work easily and without any feeling of difficulty or self-sacrifice. But He wanted us to do what He said in the obedience of faith, without worrying about whether we felt weak or strong, or whether the work was hard or easy. The path of fruit-bearing leads us to the place and the power of successful prayer.

Obedience is the only path that leads to the glory of God. Obedience doesn't replace faith or supply its shortcomings. But faith's obedience gives access to all the blessings our God has for us. In the Gospel of John, the baptism of the Spirit (John 14:16), the manifestation of the Son (14:21), the indwelling of the Father (14:23), the abiding in Christ's love (15:10), the privilege of His holy friendship (15:14), and the power of effective prayer (15:16), all wait for the obedient.

Now we know the great reason why we have not had power in faith to pray successfully. Our lives weren't as they should have been. Simple obedience—abiding fruitfulness—was not its chief mark. We whole-heartedly approve of the Divine appointment of men to whom God gives the power to rule the world. At their request, He does what otherwise would not have taken place. Their will guides the path in which God's will is to work. These men must have learned obedience themselves. Their loyalty and submission to authority must be above all suspicion. If we approve the law, that obedience and fruit-bearing are the path to prevailing prayer, we must with shame acknowledge how little our lives have exemplified this.

Let us yield ourselves to take up the appointment the Savior gives us. If we concentrate on our relationship to Him as our Master, we should no longer begin each new day with thoughts of comfort, joy, or blessing. Our first thought should be: "I belong to the Master." Every moment I must act as His property, as a part of Himself, as one who only seeks to know and do His will. I am a servant, a slave of Jesus Christ. Let this be the spirit that animates me. If He says, "No longer do I call you servants, but I have called you friends," let us accept the place of friends, because, "Ye are my friends if ye do the things which I command you."

The one thing He commands us as His branches is to bear fruit. Live to bless others, to testify of the life and the love there is in Jesus. In faith and obedience give your whole life to that which Jesus chose us for and appointed us to—fruit-bearing. Think of His electing us to this, accepting your appointment as coming from Him Who always gives us everything He demands of us. We will grow strong in the confidence that a life of fruit-bearing and abiding is within our reach. And we will understand why this fruit-bearing alone can be the path to the place of all effective prayer. The man who, in obedience to Christ, proves that he is doing what his Lord wills, will receive whatever he desires from the Father. "Whatsoever we ask we receive, because we keep His commandments, and do the things that are pleasing in His sight."

Lord, Teach Us to Pray.

Blessed Master! Teach me to understand fully what I only partly realize, that only by obeying the will of God can we obtain His promises and use them effectively in our prayers. Show me how bearing fruit perfects the deeper growth of the branch into the Vine, allowing us to experience that perfect union with— God in which we can ask for whatever we want.

O Lord! Reveal to us how with all the hosts of heaven, with all the saints here on earth, and even with Yourself on earth, that obedience to God is the highest privilege. It gives access to oneness with the Father Himself in that which is His highest glory—His all—perfect will. And show us how, if we keep Your commandments and bear fruit according to Your will, our spiritual natures will grow to the full stature of a perfect man, having power to ask and receive anything.

O Lord Jesus! Reveal Yourself to us! Through Your purpose and power, make Your wonderful promises the daily experience of everyone who completely yields himself to You and Your words. Amen.

The All-Prevailing Plea

"And whatsoever ye shall ask in my name, that will I do ....If ye shall ask anything in my name, I will do it....that whatsoever ye shall ask of the Father in my name, he may give it to you .... Verily, verily, I say unto you, Whatsoever ye shall ask the Father in my name, he will give it to you ....Hitherto have ye asked nothing in my name: ask, and ye shall receive ....At that day ye shall ask in my name" (John 14:13-14;15:16; 16:23-24,26).

Until now the disciples had not asked in the Name of Christ, nor had He Himself ever used the expression. Here in His parting words, He repeats the word unceasingly in connection with those promises of unlimited meaning: "Whatsoever," "Anything," "What ye will. "He wanted to teach them and us that His Name is our only, but also our completely sufficient, plea. The power of prayer and its answer depend on the right use of the Name.

What is a person's name? It is a word or expression in which a person is represented to us. When I mention, or hear a name, it brings to mind the whole man, what I know of him, and also the impression he has made on me. The name of a king includes his honor, his power, and his kingdom. His name is the symbol of his power. And so each name of God embodies and represents some part of the glory of the Unseen One. The Name of Christ is the expression of everything He has done and everything He is and lives to do as our Mediator.

What does it mean to do a thing in the name of another? It is to come with his power and authority, as his representative and substitute. Using another's name always presupposes a common interest. No one would give another the free use of his name without first being assured that his honor and interests were as safe with that other person as with himself.

What does it mean when Jesus gives us power over His Name—the free use of it—with the assurance that whatever we ask in it will be given to us? The ordinary comparison of one person giving another, on some special occasion, the liberty to ask something in his name, comes altogether short here. Jesus solemnly gives to all His disciples a general and unlimited power to use His Name at all times for everything they desire. He could not do this if He did not know that He could trust us with His interests and that His honor would be safe in our hands.

The free use of someone else's name is always a token of great confidence and close union. Someone who gives his name to another stands aside to let that person act for him. Someone who takes the name of another gives up his own as of no value. When I go in the name of another, I deny myself. I take not only his name, but himself and what he is, instead of myself and what I am.

Such use of a person's name may be the result of a legal union. A merchant leaving his home and business gives his chief clerk a general power by which he can withdraw thousands of dollars in the merchant's name. The clerk does this, not for himself, but only in the interests of the business. Because the merchant knows and trusts him as wholly devoted to his interests and business, he dares put his name and property at his command.

When the Lord Jesus went to heaven, He left His work—the management of His Kingdom on earth in the hands of His servants. He also gave them His Name to draw all the supplies they needed for the due conduct of His business. Christ's servants have the spiritual power to use the Name of Jesus only insofar as they yield themselves to live only for the interests and the work of the Master. The use of the Name always supposes the surrender of our interests to Him Whom we represent.

Another use of a name may be because of a life union. (In the case of the merchant and his clerk, the union is temporary.) Oneness of life on earth gives oneness of name: A child has the father's name because he has his life. Often the child of a good father is honored or helped by others for the sake of the name he bears. But this would not last long if it were found that it was only a name, and that the father's character wasn't present in it. The name and the character or spirit must be in harmony. When such is the case, the child will have a double claim on the father's friends. The character secures and increases the love and esteem extended at first for the name's sake.

It is the same with Jesus and the believer: We are one; we have one life and one Spirit with Him. For this reason we may proceed in His Name. Our power in using that Name, whether with God, men, or devils, depends on the measure of our spiritual life union with Christ. Our use of His Name rests on the unity of our lives with Him.

The Name and the Spirit of Jesus are one. "Whatsoever ye shall ask in my Name" means "in my nature." With God, things are requested according to their nature. Asking in Christ's Name doesn't mean that at the end of some request we say, "This I ask in the Name of Jesus Christ." It means we are praying according to His nature, which is love that doesn't seek its own will, but only the will of God and the good of all creatures. Such asking is the cry of Christ's own Spirit in our hearts.

The union that gives power to the use of the Name may be the union of love. When a bride whose life has been one of poverty becomes united to the bridegroom, she gives up her own name to be called by his, and has the full right to use it. She purchases in his name, and that name is not refused. This is done because the bridegroom has chosen her for himself, counting on her to care for his interests because they are now one.

The heavenly Bridegroom does nothing less. Having loved us and made us one with Himself, what can He do but give those who bear His Name the right to present it before the Father, or to come with it to Himself for all they need? No one really gives himself up to live in the Name of Jesus without receiving in ever-increasing measure the spiritual capacity to ask for and receive in that Name whatever he desires. My bearing of the name of another shows that I have given up my own name and, with it, my own independent life. But just as surely, it shows I have possession of everything belonging to the name I have taken instead of my own.

The common comparison to a messenger sent to ask in the name of another, or a guilty person using the name of a guardian in his appeal, is defective. We are not praying in the name of someone who is absent. Jesus Himself is with the Father. When we pray to the Father, it must be in Jesus' Name. The Name represents the person. To ask in His Name is to ask in full union of interest, life, and love with Himself, as one who lives in and for Him.

Let the Name of Jesus have undivided supremacy in my heart and life! My faith will grow to the assurance that what I ask for in that Name cannot be refused. The Name and the power of asking go together. When the Name of Jesus has become the power that rules my life, its power in prayer with God will be seen, too.

Everything depends on my own relationship to the Name. The power it has on my life is the power it will have in my prayers. There is more than one expression in Scripture which can make this clear. "Do all in the Name of the Lord Jesus" is the counterpart of "Ask all. " To do all and ask all in His Name go together. "We shall walk in the Name of our God" means the power of the Name must rule in the whole life. Only then will it have power in prayer. God looks not to our lips, but to our lives to see what the Name is to us. When Scripture speaks of "men who have given their lives for the Name of the Lord Jesus," or of one "ready to die for the Name of the Lord Jesus," we see what our relationship to the Name must be. When it is everything to me, it will obtain everything for me. If I let it have all I have, it will let me have all it has.

" Whatsoever ye shall ask in my Name, that will I do." Jesus means that promise literally. Christians have sought to limit it because it looked too free. It was hardly safe to trust man so unconditionally. They did not understand that the phrase "in my Name" is its own safeguard. It is a spiritual power which no one can use further than his living and acting in that Name allows.

As we bear the Name before men, we have the power to use it before God. Let us plead for God's Holy Spirit to show us what the Name means, and what the right use of it is. It is through the Spirit that the Name, which is above every name in heaven, will take the place of supremacy in our hearts and lives, too. Disciples of Jesus! Let the lessons of this day go deeply into your hearts. The Master says, "Only pray in my Name; whatsoever ye ask will be given. Heaven is opened to you! The treasures and power of the spiritual world are placed at your disposal to help those around you.

Learn to pray in the Name of Jesus. He says to us as He said to the disciples, "Hitherto ye have not asked in my Name: ask, and ye shall receive." Let each disciple of Jesus seek to avail himself of the rights of his royal priesthood, to use the power placed at his disposal for his work. Let Christian awake and hear this message: Your prayers can obtain what would otherwise be withheld! They can accomplish what would otherwise remain undone O awake, and use the Name of Jesus to open the treasures of heaven for this perishing world!

Lord, Teach Us to Pray!

Blessed Lord! It seems as if each lesson You give me has such depth of meaning that if I could just learn that one, I would be able to pray properly. Right now I feel as if I only need to pray for one thing: Lord, please teach me what it is to pray in Your Name. Teach me to live and act, to walk and speak, to do everything in the Name of Jesus, so that my prayer cannot be anything else but in that blessed Name, too.

Lord! Teach me to fully grasp the precious promise that whatever I ask in Your name You will do. and the Father will give. I realize that I haven't fully attained, and that I don't completely understand, the wondrous union You mean when You say, "In my Name." Let me hold on to the promise until it fills my heart with the undoubting assurance that I can ask for anything in the Name of Jesus.

O my Lord! Let the Holy Spirit teach me this! You did describe Him as "the Comforter, Whom the Father shall send in My Name. "He knows what it is to be sent from heaven in Your Name, to reveal and to honor the power of that Name in Your servants; and to use that Name alone to glorify You. Lord Jesus! Let Your Spirit dwell in me and fill me! I yield my whole being to His rule and leading. Your Name and Your Spirit are one. Through Him, Your Name will be the strength of my life and my prayer. Then I will be able to forsake everything for Your Name's sake, speaking to men and to God in Your Name, and proving that this, indeed, is the Name above every name.

Lord Jesus! Please teach me by Your Holy Spirit to pray in Your Name. Amen.

The Holy Spirit and Prayer

"And in that day ye shall ask me nothing. Verily, verily, I say unto you, Whatsoever ye shall ask the Farther in my name, he will give it you. Hitherto have ye asked nothing in my name: ask, and ye shall receive, that your joy may be full" (John 16:23-24).

"At that day ye shall ask in my name: and I say not unto you, that I will pray the Father for you: For the Father himself loveth you" (John 16:26-27).
"Praying in the Holy Ghost, keep yourselves in the love of God" (Jude 20-21).

The words of John (I John 2:12-14) to little children, young men, and fathers suggest the thought that often in the Christian life there are three great stages of experience. The first, that of the new-born child, is filled with the assurance and the joy of forgiveness. The second, the transition stage of struggle and growth in knowledge and strength, is comparable to young men growing strong. God's Word is doing its work in them and giving them victory over the evil one. The final stage of maturity and ripeness is that of the fathers, who have entered deeply into the knowledge and fellowship of the Eternal One.

In Christ's teaching on prayer, three similar stages in prayer-life are apparent. The Sermon on the Mount describes the initial stage. All of His teaching is comprised in one word: Father. Pray to your Father; your Father sees, hears, knows, and will reward. How much more than any earthly father He is! Simply be childlike and trustful.

Then comes something like a transition stage of conflict and conquest. Words like these refer to it: "This sort goeth not out but by prayer and fasting""Shall not God avenge His own elect who cry day and night unto Him?"

Finally, we have in the parting words a higher stage: The children have become men. They are now the Master's friends, from whom He has no secrets, and to whom He says, "All things that I heard from my Father I made known unto you." In the frequently repeated "whatsoever ye will," He hands them the keys of the Kingdom. Now the time has come for the power of prayer in His Name to be proved.

The contrast between this final stage and the previous preparatory ones is marked most distinctly in the words: "Hitherto ye have asked nothing in my Name"; "At that day ye shall ask in my Name." "At that day" means the day of the outpouring of the Holy Spirit. The great work Christ was to do on the cross—the mighty power and the complete victory to be manifested in His resurrection and ascension would allow the glory of God to come down from heaven as never before, to dwell in men. The Spirit of the glorified Jesus was to come and be the life of His disciples. And one of the signs of that wonderful, new flow of the Spirit was to be a power in prayer that was up to that time unknown. Prayer in the Name of Jesus—asking for and obtaining everything—is to be the evidence of the reality of the Spirit's indwelling.

The coming of the Holy Spirit indeed began a new epoch in the prayer world. To understand this, we must remember Who He is, what His work is, and why His not being given until Jesus was glorified is significant. It is in the Spirit that God exists, for He is Spirit. It is in the Spirit that the Son was begotten of the Father, because in the fellowship of the Spirit, the Father and the Son are one. The Father's prerogative is eternal, continuous giving to the Son. The Son's right and blessedness is to ask and receive eternally. Through the Spirit, this communion of life and love is maintained. This has been true from all eternity.

It is especially true now, when the Son as Mediator lives to pray. The great work which Jesus began on earth of reconciling God and man in His own body, He carries on in heaven. To accomplish this, He took the conflict between God's righteousness and our sin into His own person. On the cross, He ended the struggle once and for all in His own body. Then He ascended to heaven, where He carries out the deliverance He obtained and manifests His victory in each member of His Body. This is why He lives to pray. In His unceasing intercession, He places Himself in living fellowship with the unceasing prayer of His redeemed ones. Or rather, it is His unceasing intercession which shows itself in their prayers, giving them a power they never had before.

He does this through the Holy Spirit. This Spirit of the glorified Jesus was not manifested and could not be until Jesus had been glorified (John 7:39). This gift of the Father was something distinctively new, entirely different from what the Old Testament saints had known. The work that the blood effected in heaven when Christ entered within the veil was totally true and new. The redemption of human nature into fellowship with His resurrection power and

His glory was intensely real. The taking up of our humanity through Christ into the life of the triune God was an event of such inconceivable significance, that the Holy Spirit was indeed no longer only what He had been in the Old Testament.

That "the Holy Spirit was not yet, for Christ was not yet glorified" was literally true. The Holy Spirit had come from Christ's exalted humanity to testify in our hearts of what Christ had accomplished. Just as Jesus, after having come to earth as a man, returned to heaven with power He didn't have before, so the Holy Spirit came to us with a new life which He hadn't had before. He came to us with that new life—as the Spirit of the glorified Jesus. Under the Old Testament He was invoked as the Spirit of God. At Pentecost He descended as the Spirit of the glorified Jesus, bringing down and communicating to us the full fruit and power of the accomplished redemption.

Christ's continuing intercession maintains the effectiveness and application of His redemption. The Holy Spirit descending from Christ to us draws us up into the great stream of His ascending prayers. The Spirit prays for us without words in the depths of a heart where even thoughts are at times formless. He takes us up into the wonderful flow of the life of the triune God. Through the Spirit, Christ's prayers become ours, and ours are made His. We ask for what we desire, and it is given to us. We then understand from experience, "Hitherto ye have not asked in my Name. At that day ye shall ask in my Name."

Brother! What we need in order to pray in the Name of Christ to ask that we may receive that our joy may be full—is the baptism of this Holy Spirit. This is more than the Spirit of God under the Old Testament. This is more than the Spirit of conversion and regeneration the disciples had before Pentecost. This is more than the Spirit with a portion of Christ's influence and power. This is the Holy Spirit, the Spirit of the glorified Jesus in His exaltation and power, coming to us as the Spirit of the indwelling Jesus, revealing the Son and the Father within us (John 14:16-23). This Spirit cannot simply be the Spirit of our hours of prayer. It must be the Spirit of our whole life and walk, glorifying Jesus in us by revealing the completeness of His work and making us wholly one with Him and like Him. Then we can pray in His Name, because we are in very deed one with Him. Then we have that immediate access to the Father of which Jesus says, "I say not unto you, that I will pray the Father for you" (John 16:26).

Oh! We need to understand and believe that to be filled with the Spirit of the Glorified One is the one need of God's believing people. Then we will be able "with all prayer and supplication to be praying at all seasons in the Spirit," and "praying in the Holy Ghost, to keep ourselves in the love of God." "At that day ye shall ask in my Name."

Once again, we learn this lesson: What our prayer achieves depends on what we are and what our lives are. Living in the Name of Christ is the secret of praying in the Name of Christ; living in the Spirit is necessary for praying in the Spirit. Abiding in Christ gives the right and power to ask for what we desire. The extent of our abiding is equivalent to our power in prayer. The Spirit dwelling within us prays, not always in words and thoughts, but in a breathing and a being that is deeper than utterance. There is as much real prayer in us as there is of Christ's Spirit. Let our lives be full of Christ and full of His Spirit, so that the wonderfully unlimited promises to our prayers will no longer appear strange. "Hitherto ye have asked nothing in my Name. Ask, and ye shall receive, that your joy may be full. At that day ye shall ask in my Name. Verily, verily, I say unto you, Whatsoever ye shall ask the Father in my Name, He will give it you."

Lord, Teach Us to Pray.

O my God! In holy awe I bow before You, the Three in One. Again I see how the mystery of prayer is the mystery of the Holy Trinity. I adore the Father Who always hears. I adore the Son Who lives eternally to pray. And I love the Holy Spirit Who comes from the Father and the Son, lifting us up into the fellowship of that blessed, never-ceasing asking and receiving. I bow, my God, in adoring worship before the infinite power which, through the Holy Spirit, takes us and our prayers into Your Divine life and its fellowship of love.

O my blessed Lord Jesus! Teach me to understand this lesson: The indwelling Spirit streaming from You and uniting us to You is the Spirit of prayer. Teach me how, as an empty, wholly consecrated vessel, to yield myself to His being my life. Teach me to honor Him and to trust Him, as a living Person, to lead my life and my prayer. Teach me especially in prayer to wait in holy silence, giving Him time to breathe His unutterable intercession within me. And teach me that through Him it is possible to pray without ceasing and to pray without failing, because He makes me a partaker of the never-ceasing and never-failing intercession in which You appear before the Father.

O Lord! Fulfill in me Your promise, "At that day ye shall ask in my Name. Verily, verily, I say unto you, Whatsoever ye shall ask the Father in my Name, that will He give." Amen.

Author's Note

Prayer has often been compared to breathing. We have to carry out the comparison fully to see how wonderful the place is which the Holy Spirit occupies. With every breath, we expel impure air which would soon cause our death, and inhale fresh air to which we owe our life. In confession we release our sins, and in prayer we release the needs and desires of our hearts. And we inhale the fresh air of the promises, the love, and the life of God in Christ. We do this through the Holy Spirit, Who is the breath of our life.

He is also the breath of God. The Father breathes Him into us to unite Himself with our life. Just as every expiration is followed by the inhaling of the next breath, so God inhales His breath, and the Spirit returns to Him laden with the desires and needs of our hearts.

Thus the Holy Spirit is the breath of the life of God and the breath of the new life in us. As God breathes Him out, we receive Him in answer to prayer: as we breathe Him back again, He rises to God carrying our petitions. It is though the Holy Spirit that the Father and the Son are one, and that the intercession of the Son reaches the Father. He is our Spirit of prayer. True prayer is the living experience of the truth of the Holy Trinity. The Spirit's breathing, the Son's intercession, and the Father's will become one in us.

Christ the Intercessor

"But I have prayed for thee, that thy faith fail not" (Luke 22:32).

"I say not unto you, that I will pray the Father for you"(John 16:26).

"He ever liveth to make intercession for them" (Hebrews 7:25).

All growth in the spiritual life is connected with clearer insight into what Jesus is to us. The more I realize that Christ must be everything to me and in me, that everything in Christ is indeed for me, the more I learn to live the real life of faith. This life dies to self and lives wholly in Christ. The Christian life is no longer a vain struggle to live right, but a resting in Christ to find strength in Him as life. He helps us fight and gain the victory of faith!

This is especially true of the life of prayer. It, too, comes under the law of faith alone, and is seen in the light of the fullness and completeness there is in Jesus. The believer understands that prayer is no longer a matter of strain or anxious care, but an experience of what Christ will do for him and in him. It is a participation in the life of Christ, which is the same on earth as in heaven, always ascending to the Father as prayer. So he begins to pray. Such a believer not only trusts the merits of Jesus, or His intercession, by which our unworthy prayers are made acceptable: He also trusts in that near and close union through which He prays in us and we in Him. Having Him within us, we abide in Him and He in us through the Holy Spirit perfecting our union with Him, so that we ourselves can come directly to the Father in His Name.

The whole of salvation is Christ Himself: He has given Himself to us. He Himself lives in us. Because He prays, we pray, too. Just like the disciples, when they saw Jesus praying and asked Him to make them partakers of what He knew of prayer, we know that He makes us participate with Himself in the life of prayer. He is now our Intercessor on the throne.

This comes out quite clearly in the last night of His life. In His high-priestly prayer (John 17), He shows us how and what He has to pray to the Father, and what He will pray when He ascends to heaven. He had in His parting address repeatedly connected His going to the Father with their new life of prayer. The two would be ultimately connected. His entrance on the work of His eternal intercession would be the commencement and the power of their new prayer-life in His Name. It is the sight of Jesus in His intercession that gives us power to pray in His Name. All right and power of prayer is Christ's; He makes us share in His intercession.

To understand this, think first of His intercession. He lives to intercede. The work of Christ on earth as Priest was just a beginning. As Aaron, who offered the blood sacrifice, Jesus shed His blood. As Melchizedek, He now lives within the veil to continue His work for the power of the eternal life.

"It is Christ that died: yea rather, who is even at the right hand of God, who maketh intercession for us." That intercession is an intense reality—a work that is absolutely necessary—and without which the continued application of redemption cannot take place. Through the incarnation and resurrection of Jesus, the wondrous reconciliation took place, and man became partaker of the Divine life and blessedness.

But the real, personal use of this reconciliation cannot take place without the unceasing exercise of His Divine power by the Head in heaven. In all conversion and sanctification, in every victory over sin and the world, there is a real exercise of Christ's power. This exercise takes place only through His prayer: He asks of the Father and receives from the Father. "He is able to save them to the uttermost because He ever liveth to make intercession" (Hebrews 7:25). He receives every need of His people in intercession, extending to them what the Godhead has to give. His mediation on the throne is as real and indispensable as it was on the cross. Nothing takes place without Christ's intercession. It engages all His time and all His power. It is His unceasing occupation at the right hand of the Father.

We participate, not only in the benefits of HIS work, but in the work itself. This is because we are His Body. The Head and the members are one: "The head cannot say to the feet, I have no need of thee" (I Corinthians 12:21). We share with Jesus everything He is and has. "The glory which Thou gavest me, I have given them" (John 17:22). We are partakers of His life, His righteousness, and His work. We share His intercession, too. He cannot do it without us.

"Christ is our life"; "No longer I, but Christ liveth in me." The life in Him and in us is identical; it is one and the same. His life in heaven is a life of continuous prayer. When it descends and takes possession of us, it does not lose its character. It becomes a life of continuous prayer in us, too. It is a life that without ceasing asks and receives from God.

This is not as if there were two separate currents of prayer rising upwards—one from Him and one from His people. A substantial life-union is also a prayer-union. What He prays passes though us, and what we pray passes through Him. He is the angel with the golden censer. "Unto Him there was given much incense"—the secret of acceptable prayer —"that He should offer it with the prayers of all the saints upon the golden altar" (Revelation 8:3). We live and abide in Him, the Interceding One.

The Only-begotten is the only One Who has the right to pray. To Him alone it was said, "Ask, and it shall be given Thee." Just as the fullness for all things dwells in Him, a true fullness in prayer dwells in Him, too. He alone has the power of prayer. Growth of the spiritual life consists of a deeper belief that all treasures are in Him, and that we, too, are in Him. We receive each moment what we possess in Him. Prayer-life is the same. Our faith in the intercession of Jesus must not only be in His praying for us when we do not or cannot pray. As the Author of our life and our faith, He draws us to pray in unison with Himself. Our prayer must be a work of faith in the sense that as we know that Jesus communicates His whole life in us, He also breathes our praying into us.

To many a believer, it was a new epoch in his spiritual life when it was revealed to him how truly and entirely Christ was his life, standing responsible for his remaining faithful and obedient. It was then, that he really began to live a life of faith. No less blessed will be the discovery that Christ is responsible for our prayer-life, too. As the center and embodiment of all prayer, it is communicated by Him through the Holy Spirit to His people.

"He ever liveth to make intercession" as the Head of the Body. He is the Leader in that new and living way which He has opened up as the Author and the Perfecter of our faith. He provides everything for the life of His redeemed ones by giving His own life in them. He cares for their life of prayer by taking them up into His heavenly prayer-life, giving and maintaining His prayer-life within them. "I have prayed for thee," not to render thy faith needless, but "that thy faith fail not." Our faith and prayer of faith is rooted in His. If we pray with and in the eternal Intercessor, abiding in Him, "ask whatsoever ye will, and it shall be done unto you."

The thought of our fellowship in the intercession of Jesus reminds us of what He has taught us more than once before. All these wonderful prayer-promises have the glory of God, in the manifestation of His Kingdom and the salvation of sinners, as their aim. As long as we pray chiefly for ourselves, the promises of the last night must remain a sealed book to us. The promises are given to the fruit-bearing branches of the Vine, to disciples sent into the world to live for perishing men as the Father sent Him, to His faithful servants and intimate friends who take up the work He leaves behind. Like their Lord, they have become seed-corn, losing their lives to multiply them.

Let us each find out what our work is, and which souls are entrusted to our special prayers. Let us make our intercession for them our life of fellowship with God. We will not only discover the truth to the promises of power in prayer. We will begin to realize how our abiding in Christ and His abiding in us makes us share in His own joy of blessing and saving men.

O most wonderful intercession of our Blessed Lord Jesus! We not only owe everything to that intercession, but in it we are taken up as active partners and fellow-workers! Now we understand what it is to pray in the Name of Jesus, and why it has such power. To pray in His Name, in His Spirit, in Himself, and in perfect union with Him is the active and effective intercession of Christ Jesus. When will we ever be wholly taken up into it?

Lord, teach us to pray!

Blessed Lord! In lowly adoration I again bow before You. All of Your work of redemption has now passed into prayer. You are completely occupied with praying, to maintain and dispense what You purchased with Your blood. You live to pray. And because we abide in You, we have direct access to the Father. Our lives can be lives of unceasing prayer, and the answer to our prayer is certain.

Blessed Lord! You have invited Your people to be Your fellow-workers in a life of prayer. You have united Yourself with Your people. As Your Body, they share the ministry of intercession with You. Only through this ministry can the world be filled with the fruit of Your redemption and the glory of the Father. With more liberty than ever I come to You, my Lord, and plead with You to teach me to pray. Your life is prayer; Your life is mine. Lord! Teach me to pray in You and like You.

And, O my Lord! Let me know, just as You promised Your disciples, that You are in the Father, I am in You, and You are in me. Let the uniting power of the Holy Spirit make my whole life an abiding in You and in Your intercession. May my prayer be its echo, so that the Father hears me in You and You in me. Lord Jesus! In everything, let Your mind be in me! In everything, let my life be in You! In this way, I will be prepared to be the channel, Through which Your intercession pours its blessing on the world. Amen.

Christ the High Priest

"Father, I will that they also, whom thou hast given me, be with me where I am
'(John 17:24).

In His parting address, Jesus gives His disciples the full revelation of what
the new life was to be when the Kingdom of God had come in power. They
were to find their calling and their blessedness in the indwelling of the Holy
Spirit, in union with Jesus, the heavenly Vine, and in their witnessing and
suffering for Him. As He described their future life, the Lord had repeatedly
given the most unlimited promises as to the power their prayers might have.

Now in closing, He Himself proceeds to pray. To let His disciples have the
joy Of knowing what His intercession for them in heaven as their High Priest
will be, He gives them this precious legacy of His prayer to the Father. He
does this because, as priests, they are to share in His work of intercession, and
they must know how to perform this holy work.

In the teaching of our Lord on this last night (John, chapter 17), we
recognize that these astonishing prayer-promises have not been given for our
benefit, but in the interest of the Lord and His Kingdom. Only from the Lord
Himself can we learn what prayer in His Name is to be and what it can
obtain. To pray in His Name is to pray in perfect unity with Himself. The
High-Priestly prayer will teach everyone that prayer in the Name of Jesus may
ask for and expect everything. This prayer is ordinarily divided into three
parts. Our Lord first prays for Himself (verses 1-5), then for His disciples
(verses 6-19), and last for all the believing people of all ages (verses 20-26).
The follower of Jesus who gives himself to the work of intercession, and who
would like to know how much of a blessing he can pray down upon his circle
in the Name of Jesus, should in all humility let himself be led of the Spirit to
study this wonderful prayer as one of the most important lessons of the school
of prayer.

First of all, Jesus prays for Himself, for His being glorified, so that He may
glorify the Father. "Father! Glorify Thy Son. And now, Father, glorify Me."
He presents reasons for His praying this way. A holy covenant was concluded

between the Father and the Son in heaven. The Father promised Him power over all flesh as the reward for His work. Now Jesus had done the work, He had glorified the Father, and His one purpose was to further glorify Him. With the utmost boldness He asks the Father to glorify Him, so that He may now be and do for His people everything He has undertaken.

Disciple of Jesus! Here you have the first lesson in your work of priestly intercession, to be learned from the example of your great High Priest. To pray in the Name of Jesus is to pray in unity and in sympathy with Him. The Son began His prayer by clarifying His relationship to the Father, speaking of His work and obedience and His desire to see the Father glorified. You should pray like this. Draw near to the Father in Christ. Plead His finished work. Say that you are one with it, that you trust it, and live in it. Say that you, too, have given yourself to finish the work the Father has given you to do, and to live alone for His glory. Then ask confidently that the Son may be glorified in you.

This is praying in the Name, in the very words, and in the Spirit of Jesus, in union with Jesus Himself. Such prayer has power. If with Jesus you glorify the Father, the Father will glorify Jesus by doing what you ask in His Name. It is only when your own personal relationship, like Christ's, is clear with God—when you are glorifying Him and seeking everything for His glory—that, like Christ, you will have power to intercede for those around you.

Our Lord next prays for the circle of His disciples. He speaks of them as those whom the Father has given Him. Their distinguishing characteristic is that they have received Christ's Word. He says He is now sending them into the world in His place, just as the Father had sent Him. He asks two things for them: that the Father would keep them from the evil one, and that He would sanctify them through His Word.

Just like the Lord, each believing intercessor has his own immediate circle for whom he prays first. Parents have their children, teachers their pupils, pastors their flocks, and all believers have those whose care lies on their hearts. It is of great consequence that intercession should be personal, pointed, and definite. Our first prayer must always be that they receive the Word.

But this prayer will not work unless we say to the Lord, "I have given them Your Word." This gives us liberty and power in intercession for souls. Don't just pray for them, but speak to them. When they have received the Word, pray for their being kept from the evil one and for their being sanctified through that Word. Instead of being hopeless or judging, or giving up on those who fall, let us pray, "Father! Keep them in Your Name! Sanctify them through Your truth!" Prayer in the Name of Jesus accomplishes much: "What ye will shall be done unto you."

Next our Lord prays for a still wider circle. "I pray not only for these, but for them who through their word shall believe." His priestly heart enlarges itself to embrace all places and all time. He prays that everyone who belongs to Him may everywhere be one, as God's proof to the world of the divinity of His mission. He then prays that they may always be with Him in His glory. Until then, He asks "that the love wherewith Thou last loved me may be in them, and I in them."

The disciple of Jesus who has first proved the power of prayer in his own circle cannot confine himself within its limits. He then prays for the universal Church and its different branches. He prays especially for the unity of the Spirit and of love. He prays for its being one in Christ, as a witness to the world that Christ, Who has made love triumph over selfishness and separation, is indeed the Son of God sent from heaven. Every believer ought to pray that the unity of the Church, not in external organizations, but in spirit and in truth, is manifested.

Jesus says, "Father! I will (or I desire)." Based on His right as Son, the Father's promise to Him, and His finished work, He can do so. The Father had said to Him, "Ask of me, and I will give Thee." He simply availed Himself of the Father's promise. Jesus has given us a similar promise: "Whatsoever ye will shall be done unto you." He asks me in His Name to say what I will, what I desire. Abiding in Him, in a living union with Him in which man is nothing and Christ is everything, the believer has the liberty to take up that word of His High Priest. In answer to the question, "What wilt thou? "to say, "Father! I will all that You have promised."

This is nothing but true faith. It honors God that I have such confidence in saying what I desire is indeed acceptable to Him. At first sight, our hearts shrink from the expression. We feel neither the liberty nor the power to speak in such a manner. But grace will most assuredly be given to each one who loses his will in his Lord's. Whoever gives up his will entirely will find it again renewed and strengthened with a Divine strength.

"Father! I will. " This is the keynote of the everlasting, ever-active, all-powerful intercession of our Lord in heaven. It is only in union with Him that our prayer is effective and accomplishes much. If we abide in Him, living, walking, and doing all things in His Name; if we take each separate petition, tested and touched by His Word and Spirit, and cast it into the mighty stream of intercession that goes up from Him to be presented before the

Father; then we will have the full confidence that we receive what we ask for. The cry "Father! I will "will be breathed into us by the Spirit Himself. We will lose ourselves in Him and become nothing, finding that in our impotence we have power to succeed.

Disciples of Jesus! You are called to be like your Lord in His priestly intercession! When will we awaken to the glory of our destiny to pray to God for perishing men and be answered? When will we shake off the sloth that clothes itself in the pretense of humility and yield ourselves wholly to God's Spirit, that He might fill our wills with light and power to know, to take, and to possess everything that our God is waiting to give?

Lord, Teach Us to Pray.

O my Blessed High Priest! Who am I that You should invite me to share Your power of intercession? And why, O my Lord, am I so slow of heart to understand, believe, and exercise this wonderful privilege to which You have redeemed Your people? O Lord! Give me Your grace, that my life's work may become praying without ceasing, to draw down the blessing of heaven on all my surrroundings on earth.

Blessed Lord! I come now to accept my calling, for which I will give up everything and follow You. Into Your hands I will believingly yield my whole being. Form, train, and inspire me to be one of Your prayer force, those who watch and strive in prayer, who have power and victory. Take possession of my heart, and fill it with the desire to glorify God in the gathering, sanctification, and union of those whom the Father has given You. Take my mind and give me wisdom to know when prayer can bring a blessing. Take me wholly and prepare me as You would a priest, to stand always before God and to bless His Name.

Blessed Lord! Now and through all my spiritual life, let me want everything for You, and nothing for myself. Let it be my experience that the person who has and asks for nothing for himself, receives everything, including the wonderful grace of sharing Your everlasting ministry of intercession. Amen.

Christ the Sacrifice

"And he said, Abba, Father, all things are possible unto thee; take away this cup from me: nevertheless, not what I will, but what thou wilt" (Mark 14:36).

What a contrast within the space of a few hours! What a transition from the quiet elevation of that, "He lifted up His eyes to heaven, and said, Father! I will," to that falling on the ground and crying in agony, "My Father! not what I will." In the one we see the High Priest within the veil in His all powerful intercession; in the other, the sacrifice on the altar opening the way through the rent veil. The High-Priestly "Father! I will" precedes the sacrificial "Father! not what I will," but this was only to show what the intercession would be once the sacrifice was brought. The prayer before the throne, "Father! I will," had its origin and its power in the prayer at the altar, "Father! not what I will." From the entire surrender of His will in Gethsemane, the High Priest on the throne has the power to ask what He will, and the right to make His people share that power, asking what they will.

For everyone who wants to learn to pray in the school of Jesus, this Gethsemane lesson is one of the most sacred and precious. To a superficial scholar, it may appear to take away the courage to pray in faith. If even the earnest supplication of the Son was not heard, if even He had to say, "Not what I will!" how much more we must need to say it! Thus it appears impossible that the promises which the Lord had given only a few hours previously, "Whatsoever ye shall ask," "Whatsoever ye will," could have been meant literally.

A deeper insight into the meaning of Gethsemane would teach us the sure way to the assurance of an answer to our prayers. Gaze in reverent and adoring wonder on this great sight: God's Son praying through His tears, and not obtaining what He asks. He Himself is our Teacher and will open up to us the mystery of His holy sacrifice, as revealed in this wondrous prayer.

To understand the prayer, let us note the infinite difference between what our Lord prayed earlier as royal High Priest, and what He here prays in His weakness. There He prayed to glorify the Father and to glorify Himself and

His people as the fulfillment of distinct promises that had been given to Him. He asked what He knew would be according to the Word and the will of the Father. He could boldly say, "Father! I will."

Here He prays for something in regard to which the Father's will is not yet clear to Him. As far as He knows, it is the Father's will that He should drink the cup. He had told His disciples of the cup He must drink. A little later He would again say, "The cup which my Father hath given me, shall I not drink it?" It was for this He had come to this earth. But in the unutterable agony of soul that gripped Him as the power of darkness overcame Him, He began to taste the first drops of death—the wrath of God against sin. His human nature, as it shuddered in the presence of the awful reality of being made a curse, gave utterance in this cry of anguish. Its desire was that, if God's purpose could be accomplished without it, He might be spared the awful cup: "Let this cup pass from me." That desire was the evidence of the intense reality of His humanity.

The "Not as I will" kept that desire from being sinful. He pleadingly cries, "All things are possible with Thee," and returns again to still more earnest prayer that the cup may be removed. "Not what I will," repeated three times, constitutes the very essence and worth of His sacrifice. He had asked for something of which He could not say, "I know it is Thy will." He had pleaded God's power and love, and had then withdrawn his plea in His final, "Thy will be done." The prayer that the cup should pass away could not be answered. The prayer of submission that God's will be done was heard and gloriously answered in His victory first over the fear, and then over the power of death.

In this denial of His will, this complete surrender of His will to the will of the Father, Christ's obedience reached its highest perfection. From the sacrifice of the will in Gethsemane, the sacrifice of the life on Calvary derives its value. It is here, as Scripture says, that He learned obedience and became the Author of everlasting salvation to everyone who obeys Him. Because in that prayer He became obedient until death—the death of the cross—God exalted Him highly and gave Him the power to ask what He will. It was in that"Father! not what I will," that He obtained the power for the "Father! I will." By Christ's submittal in Gethsemane, He secured for His people the right to say to them, "Ask whatsoever ye will."

Let us look at the deep mysteries that Gethsemane offers. First, the Father offers His Well-beloved the cup of wrath. Second, the Son, Who is always so obedient, shrinks back and implores that He may not have to drink it. Third, the Father does not grant the Son His request, but still gives the cup. And last, the Son yields His will, is content that His will be not done, and goes out to Calvary to drink the cup. O Gethsemane! In you I see how my Lord could give me such unlimited assurance of an answer to my prayers. He won it for me by His consent to have His petition unanswered.

This is in harmony with the whole scheme of redemption. Our Lord always wins for us the opposite of what He suffered. He was bound so that we could go free. He was made sin so that we could become the righteousness of God. He died so that we could live. He bore God's curse so that God's blessing would be ours. He endured God's not answering His prayer, so that our prayers could find an answer. He said, "Not as I will, "so that He could say to us, "If ye abide in me, ask what ye will, and it shall be done unto you."

"If ye abide in me": Here in Gethsemane the word acquires new force and depth. Christ is our Head, Who stands in our place and bears what we would otherwise have had to bear forever. We deserved that God should turn a deaf ear to us and never listen to our cries. Christ came and suffered for us. He suffered what we had merited. For our sins, He suffered beneath the burden of that unanswered prayer. But now His suffering succeeds for me. What He has borne is taken away from me. His merit has won for me the answer to every prayer, if I abide in Him.

Yes, in Him, as He bows there in Gethsemane, I must abide. As my Head, He not only once suffered for me, but He always lives in me, breathing and working His own nature in me. The Spirit through which He offered Himself to God is the Spirit that dwells in me, too. He makes me a partaker of the very same obedience and the sacrifice of the will to God. That Spirit teaches me to yield my will entirely to the will of the Father, to give it up even unto death. He teaches me to distrust whatever is of my own mind, thought, and will, even though it may not be directly sinful. He opens my ear to wait in great gentleness and teachableness of soul for what the Father day by day has to speak and to teach. He shows me how union with God's will (and the love of it) is union with God Himself. Entire surrender to God's will is the Father's claim, the Son's example, and the true blessedness of the soul.

The Spirit leads my will into the fellowship of Christ's death and resurrection. My will dies in Him, and in Him is made alive again. He breathes into it a holy insight into God's perfect will, a holy joy in yielding itself to be an instrument of that will, and a holy liberty and power to lay hold of God's will to answer prayer. With my whole will, I learn to live for the interests of God and His Kingdom and to exercise the power of that will—crucified but risen again —in nature and in prayer, on earth and in heaven, with men and with God.

The more deeply I enter into the "Father! not what I will" of Gethsemane, and into Him Who said it, the fuller is my spiritual access to the power of His "Father! I will." The soul experiences that the will has become nothing in order that God's will may be everything. It is now inspired with a Divine strength to really will what God wills, and to claim what has been promised to it in the Name of Christ.

Listen to Christ in Gethsemane as He calls, "If ye abide in me, ye shall ask what ye will, and it shall be done unto you." Be of one mind and spirit with Him in His giving up everything to God's will; live like Him in obedience and surrender to the Father. This is abiding in Him—the secret of power in prayer.

Lord, teach us to pray

Blessed Lord Jesus! Gethsemane was the school where You learned to pray and to obey. It is still Your school, where You lead all Your disciples who wish to learn to obey and to pray just like You Lord! Teach me there to pray, in the faith that You have atoned for and conquered our self-will and can indeed give us grace to pray like you.

O Lamb of God! I want to follow You to Gethsemane! There I want to become one with You and abide in You, as You to the very death yield Your will to the Father. With You, through You, and in You, I yield my will in absolute and entire surrender to the will of the Father. Conscious of my own weakness and the secret power with which self-will would assert itself and again take its place on the throne, I claim in faith the power of Your victory. You have triumphed over it and delivered me from it. In Your death, I will daily live. In Your life, I will daily die. Abiding in You, may my will, through the power of Your eternal Spirit, become a finely tuned instrument which yields to every touch of the will of my God. With my whole soul, I say with You and in You. "Father! not as I will, but as Thou wilt."

Blessed Lord! Open my heart, and the hearts of all Your people, to fully take in the glory of the truth: That a will, given up to God, is a will God accepts for use in His service, to desire, determine, and will what is according to God's will. Let mine be a will which, by the power of the Holy Spirit, exercises its royal prerogative in prayer. Let it loose and bind in heaven and on earth, asking whatever it chooses, and saying it will be done.

O Lord Jesus! Teach me to pray. Amen.

Our Boldness in Prayer

"And this is the confidence that we have in him, that, if we ask any thing according to his will, he heareth us: And if we know that he hear us, whatsoever we ask, we know that we have the petitions that we desired of him" (1 John 5:14-15).

One of the greatest hindrances to believing prayer is undoubtedly this: Many don't know if what they ask is according to the will of God. As long as they are in doubt on this point, they cannot have the boldness to ask in the assurance that they will certainly receive. They soon begin to think that, once they have made known their requests and receive no answer, it is best to leave it to God to do according to His good pleasure. The words of John, "If we ask anything according to His will, He heareth us," as they understand them, make certainty as to an answer to prayer impossible, because they cannot be sure of what the will of God really may be. They think of God's will as His hidden counsel: How can man fathom the purpose of a God Who is wise in all things?

This is the very opposite of John's purpose writing this. He wanted to stir boldness and confidence in us, until we had the full assurance of faith in prayer. He says that we should have the boldness to the Father that we know we are asking according to His will, and we know that He hears us. With such boldness, He will hear us no matter what we ask for, as long as it is according to His will. In faith we should know that we have the answer. And even as we are praying, we should be able to receive what we have asked.

John supposes that when we pray, we first find if our prayers are according to the will of God. They may be according to God's will, and yet not answered at once, or without the persevering prayer of faith. It is to give us courage to persevere and to be strong in faith that He tells us we can have boldness or confidence in prayer, because if we ask anything according to His will, He hears us. It is evident that if we are uncertain whether our petitions are according to His will, we cannot have the comfort of His promise, "We know that we have the petitions which we have asked of Him."

But this is just the difficulty. More than one believer says, "I do not know if what I desire is according to the will of God. God's will is the purpose of His infinite wisdom. It is impossible for me to know whether He considers something else better for me than what I desire. He may have reasons for holding what I asked." Everyone should understand that with such thoughts the prayer of faith becomes an impossibility. There may still be a prayer of submission or of trust in God's wisdom. But there cannot be a prayer of faith.

The great mistake here is that God's children do not really believe that it is possible to know God's will. Or if they believe this, they do not take the time and trouble to find it out. What we need is to see clearly how the Father leads His waiting, teachable child to know that his petition is according to His will. Through God's holy Word—taken up and kept in the heart, the life, and the will—and through God's Holy Spirit accepted in His dwelling and leading we will learn to know that our petitions are according to His will.

First, let us consider the Word. There is a secret will of God, with which we often fear that our prayers may be at variance. But this is not the will of God that we should be concerned with in our prayers. His will as revealed in His Word should be our concern. Our notions of a secret will that makes decrees, rendering the answers to our prayers impossible, are erroneous. Childlike faith in what He is willing to do for His children simply accepts the Father's assurance that it is His will to hear prayer and to do what faith in His Word desires and accepts. In the Word, the Father has revealed in general promises the great principles of His will with His people. The child has to take the promise and apply it to the special circumstances in His life to which it has reference. Whatever he asks within the limits of that revealed will, he may confidently expect, knowing it to be according to the will of God.

In His Word, God has given us the revelation of His will. He shows us His plans for us, His people, and for the world. With the most precious promises of grace and power, He carries out these plans through His people. As faith becomes strong and bold enough to claim the fulfillment of the general promise in the special case, we may have the assurance that our prayers are heard, because they are according to God's will. Take the words of John the verse following our text as an illustration: "If any man sees his brother sinning a sin not unto death, he shall ask and God will give him life." This is the general promise. The believer who pleads on the grounds of this promise, prays according to the will of God, and John wants him to feel the boldness to know that he has the petition for which he asks.

God's will is something spiritual and must be spiritually discerned. It is not a matter of logic that we can argue about. Not every Christian has the same gift or calling. While the general will revealed in the promises is the same for everyone, each person has a specific, individual role to fulfill in God's purpose. The wisdom of the saints is in knowing the specific will of God according to the measure of grace given us, and to ask in prayer just what God has prepared and made possible for each. The Holy Spirit dwells in us to communicate this wisdom. The personal application of the general promises of the Word to our specific personal needs is given to us by the leading of the Holy Spirit.

It is this union of the teaching of the Word and the Spirit that many do not understand. This causes a twofold difficulty in knowing what God's will may be. Some seek the will of God in an inner feeling or conviction, and expect the Spirit to lead them without the Word. Others seek it in the Word, without the living leading of the Holy Spirit. The two must be united. Only in the Word and in the Spirit can we know the will of God and learn to pray according to it. In the heart, the Word and Spirit must meet. Only by indwelling can we experience their teaching. The Word must abide in us; our heart and life must be under its influence daily.

The quickening of the Word by the Spirit comes from within, not from without. Only he who yields himself entirely, in his whole life, to the supremacy of the Word and the will of God can expect to discern what that Word and will permit him to ask boldly in specific cases. The same is true of the Spirit. If I desire His leading in prayer to assure me what God's will is, my whole life must be yielded to that leading. Only in this way can mind and heart become spiritual and capable of knowing God's holy will. He who through Word and Spirit lives in the will of God by doing it; will know to pray according to that will in the confidence that He hears.

If only Christians could see what incalculable harm they do themselves by thinking that because their prayer is possibly not according to God's will, they must be content without an answer. God's Word tells us that the great reason for unanswered prayer is that we do not pray right: Ye ask and receive not, because ye ask amiss." In not granting an answer, the Father tells us that there is something wrong in our praying. He wants us to discover it and confess it, and so to teach us true believing and effective prayer. He can only attain this object when He brings us to the place where we see that we are to blame for the withholding of the answer. Our aims, our faith, or our lives are not what they should be. God is frustrated as long as we are content to say "Perhaps it is because my prayer is not according to His will that He does not hear me."

O let us no longer throw the blame for our unanswered prayers on the secret will of God, but on our own faulty praying! Let that word, "Ye receive not because ye ask amiss," be a lantern of the Lord, searching heart and life to prove that we are indeed those to whom Christ gave His promises of certain answers! Let us believe that we can know if our prayers are according to God's will! Let us yield our hearts to the indwelling of the Word of the Father to have Christ's Word abiding in us. We should live day by day with the anointing that teaches all things. If we yield ourselves unreservedly to the Holy Spirit as He teaches us to abide in Christ and to dwell in the Father's presence, we will soon understand how the Father's love longs for the child to know His will. In the confidence that that will includes every thing His power and love have promised to do, we should know, too, that He hears all of our prayers. "This is the boldness which we have, that if we ask anything according to His will, He heareth us."

Lord, Teach Us to Pray.

Blessed Master! With my whole heart I thank You for the blessed lesson that the path to a life full of answers to prayer is through the will of God. Lord! Teach me to know this blessed will by living it, loving it, and always doing it. In this way, I will learn to offer prayers according to that will. In their harmony with God's blessed will, I will find boldness in prayer and confidence in accepting the answer.

Father! It is Your will that Your child should enjoy Your presence and blessing. It is Your will that everything in Your child's life should be in accordance with Your will, and that the Holy Spirit should work this in him. It is Your will that Your child should live in the daily experience of distinct answers to prayer, in order to enjoy living and direct fellowship with Yourself. It is Your will that Your Name should be glorified in and through Your children, and that it will be in those who trust You. O my Father! Let this will of Yours be my confidence in everything I ask.

Blessed Savior! Teach me to believe in the glory of this will. That will is the eternal love that, with Divine power, works out its purpose in each human will that yields itself to it. Lord! Teach me this! You can make me see how every promise and every command of the Word is indeed the will of God, and that its fulfillment is given to me by God Himself. Let His will become the sure rock on which prayer and my assurance of an answer always rest Amen.

Author's Note

There is often great confusion as to the will of God. People think that what God wills must inevitably take place. This is by no means the case. God wills a great deal of blessing to His people which never comes to them. He wills it most earnestly, but they do not will it. Hence, it cannot come to them. This is the great mystery of man's creation with a free will and the renewal of his will in redemption. God has made the execution of His will dependent on the will of man. God's will as revealed in His promises will be fulfilled as much as our faith allow. Prayer is the power by which something comes to pass which otherwise would not have taken place. And faith the power which determines how much of God's will is done in us. Once God reveals to a soul what He is willing to do for it, the responsibility for the execution of that will rests with us.

Some are afraid that this is putting too much power into the hands of man. But all power is put into the hands of man through Christ Jesus (Luke 10:19). The key to prayer and all power is His. When we learn to understand that He is just as much one with us as with the Father, see how natural, right, and safe it is that such power is given. Christ the Son has the right to ask whatever I chooses. Through our abiding in Him and His abiding in us, His Spirit breathes in us what He wants to ask and obtain through us. We pray in His Name. The prayers are as much ours as they are His.

Others fear that to believe that prayer has such power limits the liberty and the love of God. O if we only knew how we are limiting His liberty and His love by not allowing Him to act in the only way in which He chooses to act, now that He has taken us up into fellowship with Himself! Our prayer is like pipes, though which water is carried from a large mountain stream to a town some distance away. Such water pipes don't make the water willing to flow down from the hills, nor do they give it its power of blessing and refreshment. This is its very nature. All they do is to determine its direction.

In the same way, the very nature of God is to love and to bless. His love longs to come down to us with its quickening and refreshing streams. But He has left it to prayer to say where the blessing is channeled. He has committed it to His believing people to bring the living water to the desert places. The will of God to bless is dependent on the will of man to say where the blessing goes.

The Ministry of Intercession

"A holy priesthood, to offer up spiritual sacrifices, acceptable to God by Jesus Christ" (I Peter 2:5)

"Ye shall be named the Priests of the Lord." (Isaiah 61:6).

"The Spirit of the Lord God is upon me: because the Lord hath anointed me." These are the words of Jesus in Isaiah, chapter sixty-one. As the fruit of His work, all redeemed ones are priests—fellow-partakers with Him of His anointing with the Spirit as High Priest. This anointing is "Like the precious ointment upon the beard of Aaron, that went down to the skirts of his garments" (Psalm 133:2). Like every son of Aaron, every member of Jesus' Body has a right to the priesthood. But not everyone exercises it. Many are still entirely ignorant of it. And yet it is the highest privilege of a child of God, the mark of greatest nearness and likeness to Him "Whoever liveth to pray." Do you doubt this? Think of what constitutes priesthood.

There is, first, the work of the priesthood. This has two sides: one Godward, the other manward. "Every priest is ordained for men in things pertaining to God" (Hebrews 5:1). Or, as it is said by Moses (Deuteronomy 10:8, 21:5, 33:10; Malachi 2:6): "The Lord separated the tribe of Levi, to stand before the Lord to minister unto Him, and to bless His Name. " On the one hand, the priest had the power to draw nigh to God, to dwell with Him in His house, and to present Him with the blood of the sacrifice or the burning incense. This work he did not do, however, on his own behalf, but for the sake of the people whose representative he was. This is the other side of his work. He received people's sacrifices, presented them to God, and then came out to bless in His Name, giving the assurance of His favor and teaching them His law.

A priest is thus a man who does not live for himself. He lives with God and for God. His work as God's servant is to care for His house, His honor, and His worship, making known to men His love and His will. He lives with men and for men (Hebrews 5:2). His work is to find out their sins and needs, bring these before God, offer sacrifice and incense in their names, obtain forgiveness and blessing for them, and then to come out and bless them in His Name.

This is the high calling of every believer. They have been redeemed with the one purpose of being God's priests in the midst of the perishing millions around them. In conformity to Jesus, the Great High Priest, they are to be the ministers and stewards of the grace of God.

Secondly, there is the walk of the priesthood, harmony with its work. As God is holy, so the priest was to be especially holy. This means not only separated from everything unclean, but holy unto God-being set apart and given up to God for His use. Separation from the world and being given to God were indicated in many ways.

It was seen in the clothing. The holy garment made according to God's own orders, marked the priests as His (Exodus 28). It was seen in the command as to their special purity and freedom from contact with death and defilement. Much that was allowed to an ordinary Israelite was forbidden them. Priests could have no bodily defects or blemishes. Bodily perfection was to be the model wholeness and holiness in God's service. The priestly tribes were to have no inheritance with the other tribes. God was to be their inheritance. Their life was to be one of faith—set apart unto God; they were to live on Him as well as for Him. All this symbolic of what the character of the New Testament priest is to be. Our priestly power with God depends on our personal life and walk. Jesus must be able to say of our walk on earth, "They have not defiled their garments."

In our separation from the world, we must prove that our desire to be holy to the Lord is whole-hearted and entire. The bodily perfection of the priest must have its counterpart in our also being "without spot or blemish." We must be "the man of God, perfect, thoroughly furnished unto all good works," "perfect and entire, wanting nothing" (Leviticus 21:17-21; Ephesians 5:27; 2 Timothy 3:17; James 1:4). Above all, we must consent to give up all inheritance on earth. We must forsake everything and like Christ have need only of God and keep everything for Him alone. This marks the true priest, the man who only lives for God and his fellow-men.

Thirdly, there is the way to the priesthood. God had chosen all of Aaron's sons to be priests. Each of them was a priest by birth. Yet he could not begin his work without a special act of ordinance—his consecration. Every child of God is a priest by right of his birth—his blood relationship to the Great High Priest. But he can exercise his power only as he accepts and realizes his consecration.

With Aaron and his sons it took place thus (Exodus 29): After being washed and clothed, they were anointed with the holy oil. Sacrifices were then offered, and the right ear, the right hand, and the right foot were touched with the blood. They and their garments were then sprinkled with the blood and the oil together. In the same way, as the blood and the Spirit work more fully in the child of God, the power of the Holy Priesthood will also work in him. The blood will take away all sense of unworthiness; the Spirit will take away all sense of unfitness.

Notice what was new in the application of the blood to the priest. If he had ever as a penitent sought forgiveness by bringing a sacrifice for his sin, the blood was sprinkled on the altar, but not on his person. But now, for priestly consecration, there was to be closer contact with the blood. The ear, hand and foot were by a special act brought under its power, and the whole being sanctified for God. When the believer is led to seek full priestly access God, he feels the need of a fuller and more enduring experience of the power of the blood. Where he had previously been content to have the blood sprinkled only on the mercy seat as what he needed for pardon, he now needs a more personal sprinkling a cleansing of his heart from an evil conscience. Through this, he has "no more conscience of sin" (Hebrews 10:2); he is cleansed from all sin. As he gets to enjoy this, his consciousness is awakened to his wonderful right of intimate access to God, and the full assurance that his intercessions are acceptable.

As the blood gives the right, the Spirit gives the power for believing intercession. He breathes into the priestly spirit a burning love for God's honor and the saving of souls. He makes us one with Jesus to the extent that prayer in His Name is reality. The more the Christian is truly filled with the Spirit of Christ, the more spontaneous will be his giving himself up to the life of priestly intercession.

Beloved fellow-Christians! God needs priests who can draw close to Him, live in His presence, and by their intercession draw down the blessings of His grace on others. And the world needs priests who will bear the burden of the perishing ones and intercede on their behalf.

Are you willing to offer yourself for this holy work? You know the surrender it demands—nothing less than the Christ-like giving up of everything, so that the salvation of God's love may be accomplished among men. Don't be one of those who are content with being saved, just doing enough work to keep themselves warm and lively! Let nothing keep you back from giving yourselves to be wholly and only priests of the Most High God!

The thought of unworthiness or of unfitness need not keep you back. In the blood, the objective power of the perfect redemption works in you. In the Spirit, the full, subjective, personal experience of a Divine life is secured. The blood provides an infinite worthiness to make your prayers acceptable. The Spirit provides a Divine fitness, teaching you to pray exactly according to the will of God.

Every priest knew that when he presented a sacrifice according to the law of the sanctuary, it was accepted. Under the covering of the blood and the Spirit, you have the assurance that all the wonderful promises of prayer in the Name of Jesus will be fulfilled in you. Abiding in union with the Great High Priest, "You shall ask what you will, and it shall be done unto you." You will have power to pray the effective prayer of the righteous man that accomplishes a great deal. You will not only join in the general prayer of the Church for the world, but be able in your own sphere to take up your own special work in prayer. As priests, you will work on a personal basis with God to receive and know the answer, and so to bless in His Name.

Come, brother, come! Be a priest, only a priest, and all priest! Walk before the Lord in the full consciousness that you have been set apart for the holy ministry of intercession. This is the true blessedness of conformity to the image of God's Son.

Lord, Teach Us to Pray.

O my blessed High Priest! Accept the consecration in which my soul responds to Your message! I believe in the holy priesthood of Your saints I believe that I am a priest, having the power to appear before the Father in prayer that will bring down many blessings on the perishing souls around me.

I believe in the power of Your precious blood to cleanse me from all sin. It gives me perfect confidence in God and brings me near to Him in the full assurance of faith that my intercession will be heard.

I believe in the anointing of the Spirit. It comes down to me daily from You, my Great High Priest, to sanctify me. It fills me with the consciousness my priestly calling and with the love of souls. It also teaches me what is according to God's will and how to pray the prayer of faith.

I believe that, just as You are in all things in life, You are in my prayer life, drawing me up in it the fellowship of Your wondrous work of intercession.

In this faith, I yield myself today to my God as one of His anointed priests. I stand before Him to intercede on behalf of sinners, and then return to bless them in His Name.

Holy Lord Jesus! Accept and seal my consecration. Lay Your hands on me and consecrate me Yourself to this holy work. Let me walk among men with the consciousness and the character of a priest or the Most High God.

And to Him Who loved us—Who washed us from our sins in His own blood, and Who made us kings and priests before God, His Father—to Him be glory and power forever! Amen.

A Life of Prayer

"Rejoice evermore. Pray without ceasing. In everything give thanks" (I Thessalonians 5:16-18).

Our Lord told the parable of the widow and the unjust judge to teach us that men ought to pray without ceasing. The widow persevered in seeking one definite thing. The parable appears to refer to persevering in prayer for some special blessing, when God delays or appears to refuse. The Epistles, which speak of continuing in prayer, watching for the answer, and praying always in the Spirit, appear to refer to something different—the whole life being one of prayer. As the soul longs for the manifestation of God's glory to us, in us, through us, and around us, the inmost life of the soul is continually rising upward in dependence, faith, longing desire, and trustful expectation.

What is needed to live such a life of prayer? The first thing is undoubtedly an entire sacrifice of one's life to God's Kingdom and glory. If you try to pray without ceasing because you want to be very pious and good, you will never succeed. Yielding ourselves to live for God and His honor enlarges the heart and teaches us to regard everything in the light of God and His will. We instinctively recognize in everything around us the need for God's help and blessing, and an opportunity for His being glorified.

Everything is weighed and tested by the one thing that fills the heart: the glory of God. The soul has learned that only what is of God can really glorify Him. Through the heart and soul, the whole life becomes a looking up, a crying from the inmost heart, for God to prove His power and love, and reveal His glory. The believer awakes to the consciousness that he is one of the watchmen on Zion's walls, whose call really does touch and move the King in heaven to do what would otherwise not be done. He understands how real Paul's exhortation was: "praying always with all prayer and supplication in the Spirit for all the saints and for me," and "continue in prayer, with all praying also for us." To forget oneself—to live for God and His Kingdom among men—is the way to learn to pray without ceasing.

This life devoted to God must be accompanied by the deep confidence that our prayer is effective. In His prayer lessons, our Blessed Lord insisted on faith in the Father as a God Who most certainly does what we ask. "Ask and ye shall receive." To count confidently on an answer is the beginning and the end of His teaching. (Compare Matthew 7:8 and John 16:24.)

As we gain the assurance that our prayers are effective and that God does what we ask, we dare not neglect the use of this wonderful power. Our souls should turn wholly to God, and our lives should become prayer. The Lord needs and takes time, because we and everyone around us are creatures of time, subject to the law of growth. But know that not one single prayer of faith can possibly be lost, and that sometimes there is a necessity for accumulating prayer. Know that persevering prayer pleases God. Prayer becomes the quiet, persistent living of our life of desire and faith in the presence of our God.

Don't limit such free and sure promises of the living God with your reasoning any longer! Don't rob them of their power, and ourselves of the wonderful confidence they are meant to inspire! The hindrance is not in God, not in His secret will, and not in the limitations of His promises. It is in us. We are not what we should be to obtain the promise. Open your whole heart to God's words of promise in all their simplicity and truth! They will search us and humble us. They will lift us up and make us glad and strong. To the faith that knows it gets what it asks for, prayer is not a work or a burden, but a joy and a triumph. It becomes a necessity and a second nature.

This union of strong desire and firm confidence is nothing but the life of the Holy Spirit within us. The Holy Spirit dwells in us, hides Himself in the depths of our being, and stirs our desire for the Unseen and the Divine-God Himself. It is always the Holy Spirit Who draws out the heart to thirst for God and to long for His being recognized and glorified. Sometimes He speaks through us in groanings that cannot be uttered, sometimes in clear and conscious assurance, sometimes in distinct petitions for the deeper revelation of Christ to ourselves, and sometimes in pleas for a soul, a work, the Church or the world. Where the child of God really lives and walks in the Spirit—where he is not content to remain carnal, but tries to be a fit, spiritual organ for the Divine Spirit to reveal the life of Christ and Christ Himself—there the never-ceasing life of intercession of the Blessed Son must reveal and repeat itself. Because it is the Spirit of Christ Who prays in us, our prayers must be heard. Because it is we who pray in the Spirit, there is need of time, patience, and continual renewing of the prayer until every obstacle is conquered, and the harmony between God's Spirit and ours is perfect.

The chief thing we need for a life of unceasing prayer is to know that Jesus teaches us to pray. We have begun to understand a little of what His teaching is. It isn't the communication of new thoughts or views, the discovery of failure or error, nor the arousal of desire and faith, however important all this may be. Jesus' teaching takes us up into the fellowship of His own prayer-life before the Father. This is how Jesus really teaches. It was the sight of Jesus praying that made the disciples ask to be taught to pray. The faith of Jesus' continuous prayer truly teaches us to pray.

We know why: He Who prays is our Head and our life. All He has is ours and is given to us when we give ourselves completely to Him. By His blood, He leads us into the immediate presence of God. The inner sanctuary is our home; we live there. Living so close to God and knowing we have been taken there to bless those who are far away, we cannot help but pray.

Christ makes us partakers with Himself of His prayer-power and prayer-life. Our true aim must not be to work a great deal and pray just enough to keep the work right. We should pray a great deal and then work enough for the power and blessing obtained in prayer to find its way through us to men. Christ lives to pray eternally; He saves and reigns. He communicates His prayer-life to us and maintains it in us if we trust Him. He is responsible for our praying without ceasing. Christ teaches us to pray by showing us how He does it, by doing it in us, and by leading us to do it in Him and like Him. Christ is everything—the life and the strength—for a never ceasing prayer-life. Seeing Christ's continuous praying as our life enables us to pray without ceasing. Because His priesthood is the power of an endless life—that resurrection life that never fades and never fails—and because His life is our life, praying without ceasing can become the joy of heaven here on earth. The Apostle says, "Rejoice evermore: pray without ceasing: in everything give thanks." Supported by never-ceasing joy and never-ceasing praise, never-ceasing prayer is the manifestation of the power of the eternal life where Jesus always prays.

The union between the Vine and the branch is indeed a prayer union. The highest conformity to Christ—the most blessed participation in the glory of His heavenly life—is that we take part in His work of intercession. He and we live forever to pray. In union with Him, praying without ceasing becomes a possibility—a reality, the holiest and most blessed part of our holy and blessed fellowship with God. We abide within the veil in the presence of the Father. What the Father says, we do. What the Son asks, the Father does. Praying without ceasing is the earthly manifestation of heaven, a foretaste of the life where they rest neither day nor night in their song of worship and adoration.

Lord, Teach Us to Pray.

O my Father! With my whole heart I praise You for this wondrous life of continuous prayer, continuous fellowship, continuous answers, and continuous oneness with Him Who lives to pray forever! O my God! Keep me abiding and walking in the presence of Your glory, so that prayer may be the spontaneous expression of my life with You.

Blessed Savior! With my whole heart I praise You for coming from heaven to share my needs and my pleas, so that I could share Your all— powerful intercession. Thank You for taking me into Your school of prayer, teaching me the blessedness and the power of a life that is totally comprised of prayer. And most of all, thank You for taking me up into the fellowship of Your life of intercession. Now through me, too, Your blessings can be dispensed to those around me.

Holy Spirit! With deep reverence I thank You for Your work in me. Through You I am lifted up into communication with the Son and the Father, entering the fellowship of the life and love of the Holy Trinity.

Spirit of God! Perfect Your work in me! Bring me into perfect union with Christ, My Intercessor! Let Your unceasing indwelling make my life one of unceasing intercession. And let my life unceasingly glorify the Father and bless those around me. Amen.

Abide in Christ

Table of Contents

JOHN 15:1-12: 1 I am the true vine, and my Father is the husbandman. 2 Every branch in me that beareth not fruit he taketh away; and every branch that beareth fruit, he purgeth it, that it may bring forth more fruit. 3 Now ye are clean through the word which I have spoken unto you. 4 Abide in me, and I in you. As the branch cannot bear fruit of itself, except it abide in the vine; no more can ye, except ye abide in me. 5 I am the vine, ye are the branches: he that abideth in me, and I in him, the same bringeth forth much fruit: for without me ye can do nothing. 6 If a man abide not in me, he is cast forth as a branch, and is withered; and men gather them, and cast them into the fire, and they are burned. 7 If ye abide in me, and my words abide in you, ye shall ask what ye will, and it shall be done unto you. 8 Herein is my Father glorified, that ye bear much fruit; so shall ye be my disciples. 9 As the Father hath loved me, so have I loved you: continue ye in my love. 10. If ye keep my commandments, ye shall abide in my love; even as I have kept my Father's commandments and abide in his love. 11 These things have I spoken unto you, that my joy might remain in you, and that your joy might be full. 12 This is my commandment, That ye love one another, as I have loved you.

Preface

During the life of Jesus on earth, the word He chiefly used when speaking of the relations of the disciples to Himself was: "Follow me." When about to leave for heaven, He gave them a new word, in which their more intimate and spiritual union with Himself in glory should be expressed. That chosen word was: "Abide in me."

It is to be feared that there are many earnest followers of Jesus from whom the meaning of this word, with the blessed experience it promises, is very much hidden. While trusting in their Savior for pardon and for help, and seeking to some extent to obey Him, they have hardly realized to what closeness of union, to what intimacy of fellowship, to what wondrous oneness of life and interest, He invited them when He said, "Abide in me." This is not only an unspeakable loss to themselves, but the Church and the world suffer in what they lose.

If we ask the reason why those who have indeed accepted the Savior, and been made partakers of the renewing of the Holy Ghost, thus come short of the full salvation prepared for them, I am sure the answer will in very many cases be, that ignorance is the cause of the unbelief that fails of the inheritance. If, in our orthodox Churches, the abiding in Christ, the living union with Him, the experience of His daily and hourly presence and keeping, were preached with the same distinctness and urgency as His atonement and pardon through His blood, I am confident that many would be found to accept with gladness the invitation to such a life, and that its influence would be manifest in their experience of the purity and the power, the love and the joy, the fruit-bearing, and all the blessedness which the Savior connected with the abiding in Him.

It is with the desire to help those who have not yet fully understood what the Savior meant with His command, or who have feared that it was a life beyond their reach, that these meditations are now published. It is only by frequent repetition that a child learns its lessons. It is only by continuously fixing the mind for a time on some one of the lessons of faith, that the believer is gradually helped to take and thoroughly assimilate them. I have the hope that to some, especially young believers, it will be a help to come and for a month day after day spell over the precious words, "Abide in me," with the lessons connected with them in the parable of the Vine. Step by step we shall get to see how truly this promise-precept is meant for us, how surely grace is provided to enable us to obey it, how indispensable the experience of its blessing is to a healthy Christian life, and how unspeakable the blessings are that flow from it. As we listen, and meditate, and pray—as we surrender ourselves, and accept in faith the whole Jesus as He offers Himself to us in it—the Holy Spirit will make the word to be spirit and life; this word of Jesus, too, will become to us the power of God unto salvation, and through it will come the faith that grasps the long desired blessing.

I pray earnestly that our gracious Lord may be pleased to bless this little book, to help those who seek to know Him fully, as He has already blessed it in its original issue in a different (the Dutch) language. I pray still more earnestly that He would, by whatever means, make the multitudes of His dear children who are still living divided lives, to see how He claims them wholly for Himself, and how the wholehearted surrender to abide in Him alone brings the joy unspeakable and full of glory. Oh, let each of us who has begun to taste the sweetness of this life, yield himself wholly to be a witness to the grace and power of our Lord to keep us united with Himself, and seek by word and walk to win others to follow Him fully. It is only in such fruit-bearing that our own abiding can be maintained.

In conclusion, I ask to be permitted to give one word of advice to my reader. It is this. It needs time to grow into Jesus the Vine: do not expect to abide in Him unless you will give Him that time. It is not enough to read God's Word, or meditations as here offered, and when we think we have hold of the thoughts, and have asked God for His blessing, to go out in the hope that the blessing will abide. No, it needs day by day time with Jesus and with God. We all know the need of time for our meals each day—every workman claims his hour for dinner; the hurried eating of so much food is not enough. If we are to live through Jesus, we must feed on Him (John 6:57); we must thoroughly take in and assimilate that heavenly food the Father has given us in His life. Therefore, my brother, who would learn to abide in Jesus, take time each day, ere you read, and while you read, and after you read, to put yourself into living contact with the living Jesus, to yield yourself distinctly and consciously to His blessed influence; so will you give Him the opportunity of taking hold of you, of drawing you up and keeping you safe in His almighty life.

And now, to all God's children whom He allows me the privilege of pointing to the Heavenly Vine, I offer my fraternal love and salutations, with the prayer that to each one of them may be given the rich and full experience of the blessedness of abiding in Christ. And may the grace of Jesus, and the love of God, and the fellowship of the Holy Spirit, be their daily portion. Amen.

All You Who Have Come to Him

"Come unto me."—MATT. 11:28

"Abide in me."—JOHN 15:4

Ii is to you who have heard and hearkened to the call, "Come unto me," that this new invitation comes, "Abide in me." The message comes from the same loving Savior. You doubtless have never repented having come at His call. You experienced that His word was truth; all His promises He fulfilled; He made you partakers of the blessings and the joy of His love. Was not His welcome most hearty, His pardon full and free, His love most sweet and precious? You more than once, at your first coming to Him, had reason to say, "The half was not told me."

And yet you have had to complain of disappointment: as time went on, your expectations were not realized. The blessings you once enjoyed were lost; the love and joy of your first meeting with your Savior, instead of deepening, have become faint and feeble. And often you have wondered what the reason could be, that with such a Savior, so mighty and so loving, your experience of salvation should not have been a fuller one.

The answer is very simple. You wandered from Him. The blessings He bestows are all connected with His "Come to ME," and are only to be enjoyed in close fellowship with Himself. You either did not fully understand, or did not rightly remember, that the call meant, "Come to me to stay with me." And yet this was in very deed His object and purpose when first He called you to Himself. It was not to refresh you for a few short hours after your conversion with the joy of His love and deliverance, and then to send you forth to wander in sadness and sin. He had destined you to something better than a short-lived blessedness, to be enjoyed only in times of special earnestness and prayer, and then to pass away, as you had to return to those duties in which far the greater part of life has to be spent. No, indeed; He had prepared for you an abiding dwelling with Himself, where your whole life and every moment of it might be spent, where the work of your daily life might be done, and where all the while you might be enjoying unbroken communion with Himself. It was even this He meant when to that first word, "Come to me," He added this, "Abide in me." As earnest and faithful, as loving and tender, as the compassion that breathed in that blessed "Come," was the grace that added this no less blessed "Abide." As mighty as the attraction with which that first word drew you, were the bonds with which this second, had you but listened to it, would have kept you. And as great as were the blessings with which that coming was rewarded, so large, yea, and much greater, were the treasures to which that abiding would have given you access.

And observe especially, it was not that He said, "Come to me and abide with me," but, "Abide in me." The intercourse was not only to be unbroken, but most intimate and complete. He opened His arms, to press you to His bosom; He opened His heart, to welcome you there; He opened up all His divine fulness of life and love, and offered to take you up into its fellowship, to make you wholly one with Himself. There was a depth of meaning you cannot yet realize in His words: "Abide *in Me.*"

And with no less earnestness than He had cried, "Come to me," did He plead, had you but noticed it, "Abide in me." By every motive that had induced you to come, did He beseech you to abide. Was it the fear of sin and its curse that first drew you? the pardon you received on first coming could, with all the blessings flowing from it, only be confirmed and fully enjoyed on abiding in Him. Was it the longing to know and enjoy the Infinite Love that was calling you? the first coming gave but single drops to taste—'tis only the abiding that can really satisfy the thirsty soul, and give to drink of the rivers of pleasure that are at His right hand. Was it the weary longing to be made free from the bondage of sin, to become pure and holy, and so to find rest, the rest of God for the soul? this too can only be realized as you abide in Him—only abiding in Jesus gives rest in Him. Or if it was the hope of an inheritance in glory, and an everlasting home in the presence of the Infinite One: the true preparation for this, as well as its blessed foretaste in this life, are granted only to those who abide in Him. In very truth, there is nothing that moved you to come, that does not plead with thousandfold greater force: "Abide in Him." You did well to come; you do better to abide. Who would, after seeking the King's palace, be content to stand in the door, when he is invited in to dwell in the King's presence, and share with Him in all the glory of His royal life? Oh, let us enter in and abide, and enjoy to the full all the rich supply His wondrous love hath prepared for us!

And yet I fear that there are many who have indeed come to Jesus, and who yet have mournfully to confess that they know but little of this blessed abiding in Him. With some the reason is, that they never fully understood that this was the meaning of the Savior's call. With others, that though they heard the word, they did not know that such a life of abiding fellowship was possible, and indeed within their reach. Others will say that, though they did believe that such a life was possible, and seek after it, they have never yet succeeded discovering the secret of its attainment. And others, again, alas! will confess that it is their own unfaithfulness that has kept them from the enjoyment of the blessing. When the Savior would have kept them, they were not found ready to stay; they were not prepared to give up everything, and always, only, wholly to abide in Jesus.

To all such I come now in the name of Jesus, their Redeemer and mine, with the blessed message: "Abide in me." In His name I invite them to come, and for a season meditate with me daily on its meaning, its lessons, its claims, and its promises. I know how many, and, to the young believer, how difficult, the questions are which suggest themselves in connection with it. There is especially the question, with its various aspects, to the possibility, in the midst of wearying work and continual distraction, of keeping up, or rather being kept in, the abiding communion. I do not undertake to remove all difficulties; this Jesus Christ Himself alone must do by His Holy Spirit. But what I would fain by the grace of God be permitted to do is, to repeat day by day the Master's blessed command, "Abide in me," until it enter the heart and find a place there, no more to be forgotten or neglected. I would fain that in the light of Holy Scripture we should Meditate on its meaning, until the understanding, that gate to the heart, opens to apprehend something of what it offers and expects. So we shall discover the means of its attainment, and learn to know what keeps us from it, and what can help us to it. So we shall feel its claims, and be compelled to acknowledge that there can be no true allegiance to our King without simply and heartily accepting this one, too, of His commands. So we shall gaze on its blessedness, until desire be inflamed, and the will with all its energies be roused to claim and possess the unspeakable blessing.

Come, my brethren, and let us day by day set ourselves at His feet, and meditate on this word of His, with an eye fixed on Him alone. Let us set ourselves in quiet trust before Him, waiting to hear His holy voice—the still small voice that is mightier than the storm that rends the rocks—breathing its quickening spirit within us, as He speaks: "Abide in me." The soul that truly hears Jesus Himself speak the word, receives with the word the power to accept and to hold the blessing He offers.

And it may please Thee, blessed Savior, indeed, to speak to us; let each of us hear Thy blessed voice. May the feeling of our deep need, and the faith of Thy wondrous love, combined with the sight of the wonderfully blessed life Thou art waiting to bestow upon us, constrain us to listen and to obey, as often as Thou speakest: "Abide in me." Let day by day the answer from our heart be clearer and fuller: "Blessed Savior, I do abide in Thee. "

And You Shall Find Rest to Your Souls

"Come unto me, and I will give you rest. Take my yoke upon you, and learn of me; and ye shall find rest to your souls —MATT.11:28-29

Rest for the soul: Such was the first promise with which the Savior sought to win the heavy-laden sinner. Simple though it appears, the promise is indeed as large and comprehensive as can be found. Rest for the soul—does it not imply deliverance from every fear, the supply of every want, the fulfilment of every desire? And now nothing less than this is the prize with which the Savior woos back the wandering one—who is mourning that the rest has not been so abiding or so full as it had hoped—to come back and abide in Him. Nothing but this was the reason that the rest has either not been found, or, if found, has been disturbed or lost again: you did not abide with, you did not abide in Him.

Have you ever noticed how, in the original invitation of the Savior to come to Him, the promise of rest was repeated twice, with such a variation in the conditions as might have suggested that abiding rest could only be found in abiding nearness. First the Savior says, "Come unto me, and I will give you rest"; the very moment you come, and believe, I will give you rest—the rest of pardon and acceptance—the rest in my love. But we know that all that God bestows needs time to become fully our own; it must be held fast, and appropriated, and assimilated into our inmost being; without this not even Christ's giving can make it our very own, in full experience and enjoyment. And so the Savior repeats His promise, in words which clearly speak not so much of the initial rest with which He welcomes the weary one who comes, but of the deeper and personally appropriated rest of the soul that abides with Him. He now not only says, "Come unto me," but "Take my yoke upon you and learn of me"; become my scholars, yield yourselves to my training, submit in all things to my will, let your whole life be one with mine—in other words, Abide in me. And then He adds, not only, "I will give," but "ye shall find rest to your souls." The rest He gave at coming will become something you have really found and made your very own—the deeper the abiding rest which comes from longer acquaintance and closer fellowship, from entire surrender and deeper sympathy. "Take my yoke, and learn of me," "Abide in me"—this is the path to abiding rest.

Do not these words of the Savior discover what you have perhaps often sought in vain to know, how it is that the rest you at times enjoy is so often lost. It must have been this: you had not understood how entire surrender to Jesus is the secret of perfect rest. Giving up one's whole life to Him, for Him alone to rule and order it; taking up His yoke, and submitting to be led and taught, to learn of Him; abiding in Him, to be and do only what He wills—these are the conditions of discipleship without which there can be no thought of maintaining the rest that was bestowed on first coming to Christ. The rest is in Christ, and not something He gives apart from Himself, and so it is only in having Him that the rest can really be kept and enjoyed.

It is because so many a young believer fails to lay hold of this truth that the rest so speedily passes away. With some it is that they really did not know; they were never taught how Jesus claims the undivided allegiance of the whole heart and life; how there is not a spot in the whole of life over which He does not wish to reign; how in the very least things His disciples must only seek to please Him. They did not know how entire the consecration was that Jesus claimed. With others, who had some idea of what a very holy life a Christian ought to lead, the mistake was a different one: they could not believe such a life to be a possible attainment. Taking, and bearing, and never for a moment laying aside the yoke of Jesus, appeared to them to require such a strain of effort, and such an amount of goodness, as to be altogether beyond their reach. The very idea of always, all the day, abiding in Jesus, was too high—something they might attain to after a life of holiness and growth, but certainly not what a feeble beginner was to start with. They did not know how, when Jesus said, "My yoke is easy," He spoke the truth; how just the yoke gives the rest, because the moment the soul yields itself to obey, the Lord Himself gives the strength and joy to do it. They did not notice how, when He said, "Learn of me," He added, "I am meek and lowly in heart," to assure them that His gentleness would meet their every need, and bear them as a mother bears her feeble child. Oh, they did not know that when He said, "Abide in me," He only asked the surrender to Himself, His almighty love would hold them fast, and keep and bless them. And so, as some had erred from the want of full consecration, so these failed because they did not fully trust. These two, consecration and faith, are the essential elements of the

Christian life—the giving up all to Jesus, the receiving all from Jesus. They are implied in each other; they are united in the one word—surrender. A full surrender is to obey as well as to trust, to trust as well as to obey.

With such misunderstanding at the outset, it is no wonder that the disciple life was not one of such joy or strength as had been hoped. In some things you were led into sin without knowing it, because you had not learned how wholly Jesus wanted to rule you, and how you could not keep right for a moment unless you had Him very near you. In other things you knew what sin was, but had not the power to conquer, because you did not know or believe how entirely Jesus would take charge of you to keep and to help you. Either way, it was not long before the bright joy of your first love was lost, and your path, instead of being like the path of the just, shining more and more unto the perfect day, became like Israel's wandering in the desert—ever on the way, never very far, and yet always coming short of the promised rest. Weary soul, since so many years driven to and fro like the panting hart, O come and learn this day the lesson that there is a spot where safety and victory, where peace and rest, are always sure, and that that spot is always open to thee—the heart of Jesus.

But, alas! I hear someone say, it is just this abiding in Jesus, always bearing His yoke, to learn of Him, that is so difficult, and the very effort to attain to this often disturbs the rest even more than sin or the world. What a mistake to speak thus, and yet how often the words are heard! Does it weary the traveler to rest in the house or on the bed where he seeks repose from his fatigue? Or is it a labor to a little child to rest in its mother's arms? Is it not the house that keeps the traveler within its shelter? do not the arms of the mother sustain and keep the little one? And so it is with Jesus. The soul has but to yield itself to Him, to be still and rest in the confidence that His love has undertaken, and that His faithfulness will perform, the work of keeping it safe in the shelter of His bosom. Oh, it is because the blessing is so great that our little hearts cannot rise to apprehend it; it is as if we cannot believe that Christ, the Almighty One, will in very deed teach and keep us all the day. And yet this is just what He has promised, for without this He cannot really give us rest. It is as our heart takes in this truth that, when He says, "Abide in me," "Learn of me," He really means it, and that it is His own work to keep us abiding when we yield ourselves to Him, that we shall venture to cast ourselves into the arms of His love, and abandon ourselves to His blessed keeping. It is not the yoke, but resistance to the yoke, that makes the difficulty; the whole-hearted surrender to Jesus, as at once our Master and our Keeper, finds and secures the rest.

Come, my brother, and let us this very day commence to accept the word of Jesus in all simplicity. It is a distinct command this: "Take my yoke, and learn of me, " "Abide in me. " A command has to be obeyed. The obedient scholar asks no questions about possibilities or results; he accepts every order in the confidence that his teacher has provided for all that is needed. The power and the perseverance to abide in the rest, and the blessing in abiding—it belongs to the Savior to see to this; 'tis mine to obey, 'tis His to provide. Let us this day in immediate obedience accept the command, and answer boldly, "Savior, I abide in Thee. At Thy bidding I take Thy yoke; I undertake the duty without delay; I abide in Thee." Let each consciousness of failure only give new urgency to the command, and teach us to listen more earnestly than ever till the Spirit again give us to hear the voice of Jesus saying, with a love and authority that inspire both hope and obedience, "Child, abide in me." That word, listened to as coming from Himself, will be an end of all doubting—a divine promise of what shall surely be granted. And with ever-increasing simplicity its meaning will be interpreted. Abiding in Jesus is nothing but the giving up of oneself to be ruled and taught and led, and so resting in the arms of Everlasting Love.

Blessed rest! the fruit and the foretaste and the fellowship of God's own rest! found of them who thus come to Jesus to abide in Him. It is the peace of God, the great calm of the eternal world, that passeth all understanding, and that keeps the heart and mind. With this grace secured, we have strength for every duty, courage for every struggle, a blessing in every cross, and the joy of life eternal in death itself.

O my Savior! if ever my heart should doubt or fear again, as if the blessing were too great to expect, or too high to attain, let me hear Thy voice to quicken my faith and obedience: "Abide in me"; "Take my yoke upon you, and learn of me; ye shall find rest to your souls."

Trusting Him to Keep You

"I follow after, if that I may apprehend that for which I also am apprehended of Christ Jesus."—PHIL.3:12

More than one admits that it is a sacred duty and a blessed privilege to abide in Christ, but shrinks back continually before the question: Is it possible, a life of unbroken fellowship with the Savior? Eminent Christians, to whom special opportunities of cultivating this grace have been granted, may attain to it; for the large majority of disciples, whose life, by a divine appointment, is so fully occupied with the affairs of this life, it can scarce be expected. The more they hear of this life, the deeper their sense of its glory and blessedness, and there is nothing they would not sacrifice to be made partakers of it. But they are too weak, too unfaithful—they never can attain to it.

Dear souls! how little they know that the abiding in Christ is just meant for the weak, and so beautifully suited to their feebleness. It is not the doing of some great thing, and does not demand that we first lead a very holy and devoted life. No, it is simply weakness entrusting itself to a Mighty One to be kept—the unfaithful one casting self on One who is altogether trustworthy and true. Abiding in Him is not a work that we have to do as the condition for enjoying His salvation, but a consenting to let Him do all for us, and in us, and through us. It is a work He does for us—the fruit and the power of His redeeming love. Our part is simply to yield, to trust, and to wait for what He has engaged to perform.

It is this quiet expectation and confidence, resting on the word of Christ that in Him there is an abiding place prepared, which is so sadly wanting among Christians. They scarce take the time or the trouble to realize that when He says "Abide *in Me*," He offers Himself, the Keeper of Israel that slumbers not nor sleeps, with all His power and love, as the living home of the soul, where the mighty influences of His grace will be stronger to keep than all their feebleness to lead astray. The idea they have of grace is this—that their conversion and pardon are God's work, but that now, in gratitude to

God, it is their work to live as Christians, and follow Jesus. There is always the thought of a work that has to be done, and even though they pray for help, still the work is theirs. They fail continually, and become hopeless; and the despondency only increases the helplessness. No, wandering one; as it was Jesus who drew you when He spake "Come," so it is Jesus who keeps you when He says "Abide." The grace to come and the grace to abide are alike from Him alone. That word Come, heard, meditated on, accepted, was the cord of love that drew you nigh; that word Abide is even so the band with which He holds you fast and binds you to Himself. Let the soul but take time to listen to the voice of Jesus. "In me," He says, "is thy place—in my almighty arms. It is I who love thee so, who speak Abide in me; surely thou canst trust me." The voice of Jesus entering and dwelling in the soul cannot but call for the response: "Yes, Savior, in Thee I can, I will abide."

Abide in me: These words are no law of Moses, demanding from the sinful what they cannot perform. They are the command of love, which is ever only a promise in a different shape. Think of this until all feeling of burden and fear and despair pass away, and the first thought that comes as you hear of abiding in Jesus be one of bright and joyous hope: it is for me, I know I shall enjoy it. You are not under the law, with its inexorable Do, but under grace, with its blessed Believe what Christ will do for you. And if the question be asked, "But surely there is something for us to do?" the answer is, "Our doing and working are but the fruit of Christ's work in us." It is when the soul becomes utterly passive, looking and resting on what Christ is to do, that its energies are stirred to their highest activity, and that we work most effectually because we know that He works in us. It is as we see in that word IN ME the mighty energies of love reaching out after us to have us and to hold us, that all the strength of our will is roused to abide in Him.

This connection between Christ's work and our work is beautifully expressed in the words of Paul: "I follow after, if that I may apprehend that whereunto I also am apprehended of Christ Jesus." It was because he knew that the mighty and the faithful One had grasped him with the glorious purpose of making him one with Himself, that he did his utmost to grasp the glorious prize. The faith, the experience, the full assurance, "Christ hath apprehended me," gave him the courage and the strength to press on and apprehend that whereunto he was apprehended. Each new insight of the great end for which Christ had apprehended and was holding him, roused him afresh to aim at nothing less.

Paul's expression, and its application to the Christian life, can be best understood if we think of a father helping his child to mount the side of some steep precipice. The father stands above, and has taken the son by the hand to help him on. He points him to the spot on which he will help him to plant his feet, as he leaps upward. The leap would be too high and dangerous for the child alone; but the father's hand is his trust, and he leaps to get hold of the point for which his father has taken hold of him. It is the father's strength that secures him and lifts him up, and so urges him to use his utmost strength.

Such is the relation between Christ and you, O weak and trembling believer! Fix first your eyes on the whereunto for which He has apprehended you. It is nothing less than a life of abiding, unbroken fellowship with Himself to which He is seeking to lift you up. All that you have already received—pardon and peace, the Spirit and His grace—are but preliminary to this. And all that you see promised to you in the future—holiness and fruitfulness and glory everlasting—are but its natural outcome. Union with Himself, and so with the Father, is His highest object. Fix your eye on this, and gaze until it stand out before you clear and unmistakable: Christ's aim is to have me abiding in Him.

And then let the second thought enter your heart: Unto this I am apprehended of Christ. His almighty power hath laid hold on me, and offers now to lift me up to where He would have me. Fix your eyes on Christ. Gaze on the love that beams in those eyes, and that asks whether you cannot trust Him, who sought and found and brought you nigh, now to keep you. Gaze on that arm of power, and say whether you have reason to be assured that He is indeed able to keep you abiding in Him.

And as you think of the spot whither He points—the blessed whereunto for which He apprehended you—and keep your gaze fixed on Himself, holding you and waiting to lift you up, O say, could you not this very day take the upward step, and rise to enter upon this blessed life of abiding in Christ? Yes, begin at once, and say, "O my Jesus, if Thou biddest me, and if Thou engagest to lift and keep me there, I will venture. Trembling, but trusting, I will say: Jesus, I do abide in Thee. "

My beloved fellow-believer, go, and take time alone with Jesus, and say this to Him. I dare not speak to you about abiding in Him for the mere sake of calling forth a pleasing religious sentiment. God's truth must at once be acted on. O yield yourself this very day to the blessed Savior in the surrender of the one thing He asks of you: give up yourself to abide in Him. He Himself will work it in you. You can trust Him to keep you trusting and abiding.

And if ever doubts again arise, or the bitter experience of failure tempt you to despair, just remember where Paul found His strength: "I am apprehended of Jesus Christ." In that assurance you have a fountain of strength. From that you can look up to the whereunto on which He has set His heart, and set yours there too. From that you gather confidence that the good work He hath begun He will also perform. And in that confidence you will gather courage, day by day, afresh to say, " `I follow on, that I may also apprehend that for which I am apprehended of Christ Jesus.' It is because Jesus has taken hold of me, and because Jesus keeps me, that I dare to say: Savior, I abide in Thee. "

As the Branch in the Vine

"I am the vine, ye are the branches."—JOHN 15:5

It was in connection with the parable of the Vine that our Lord first used the expression, "Abide in me." That parable, so simple, and yet so rich in its teaching, gives us the best and most complete illustration of the meaning of our Lord's command, and the union to which He invites us.

The parable teaches us the nature of that union. The connection between the vine and the branch is a living one. No external, temporary union will suffice; no work of man can effect it: the branch, whether an original or an engrafted one, is such only by the Creator's own work, in virtue of which the life, the sap, the fatness, and the fruitfulness of the vine communicate themselves to the branch. And just so it is with the believer too. His union with his Lord is no work of human wisdom or human will, but an act of God, by which the closest and most complete life-union is effected between the Son of God and the sinner. "God hath sent forth the Spirit of His Son into your hearts." The same Spirit which dwelt and still dwells in the Son, becomes the life of the believer; in the unity of that one Spirit, and the fellowship of the same life which is in Christ, he is one with Him. As between the vine and branch, it is a life-union that makes them one.

The parable teaches us the completeness of the union. So close is the union between the vine and the branch, that each is nothing without the other, that each is wholly and only for the other.

Without the vine the branch can do nothing. To the vine it owes its right of place in the vineyard, its life and its fruitfulness. And so the Lord says, "Without me ye can do nothing." The believer can each day be pleasing to God only in that which he does through the power of Christ dwelling in him. The daily inflowing of the life-sap of the Holy Spirit is his only power to bring forth fruit. He lives alone in Him and is for each moment dependent on Him alone.

Without the branch the vine can also do nothing. A vine without branches can bear no fruit. No less indispensable than the vine to the branch, is the branch to the vine. Such is the wonderful condescension of the grace of Jesus, that just as His people are dependent on Him, He has made Himself dependent on them. Without His disciples He cannot dispense His blessing to the world; He cannot offer sinners the grapes of the heavenly Canaan. Marvel not! It is His own appointment; and this is the high honor to which He has called His redeemed ones, that as indispensable as He is to them in heaven, that from Him their fruit may be found, so indispensable are they to Him on earth, that through them His fruit may be found. Believers, meditate on this, until your soul bows to worship in presence of the mystery of the perfect union between Christ and the believer.

There is more: as neither vine nor branch is anything without the other, so is neither anything except for the other.

All the vine possesses belongs to the branches. The vine does not gather from the soil its fatness and its sweetness for itself—all it has is at the disposal of the branches. As it is the parent, so it is the servant of the branches. And Jesus, to whom we owe our life, how completely does He give Himself for us and to us: "The glory Thou gavest me, I have given them"; "He that believeth in me, the works that I do shall he do also; and greater works shall he do." All His fullness and all His riches are for thee, O believer; for the vine does not live for itself, keeps nothing for itself, but exists only for the branches. All that Jesus is in heaven, He is for us: He has no interest there separate from ours; as our representative He stands before the Father.

And all the branch possesses belongs to the vine. The branch does not exist for itself, but to bear fruit that can proclaim the excellence of the vine: it has no reason of existence except to be of service to the vine. Glorious image of the calling of the believer, and the entireness of his consecration to the service of his Lord. As Jesus gives Himself so wholly over to him, he feels himself urged to be wholly his Lord's. Every power of his being, every moment of his life, every thought and feeling, belong to Jesus, that from Him and for Him he may bring forth fruit. As he realizes what the vine is to the branch, and what the branch is meant to be to the vine, he feels that he has but one thing to think of and to live for, and that is, the will, the glory, the work, the kingdom of his blessed Lord—the bringing forth of fruit to the glory of His name.

The parable teaches us the object of the union. The branches are for fruit and fruit alone. "Every branch that beareth not fruit He taketh away." The branch needs leaves for the maintenance of its own life, and the perfection of its fruit: the fruit itself it bears to give away to those around. As the believer enters into his calling as a branch, he sees that he has to forget himself, and to live entirely for his fellow-men. To love them, to seek for them, and to save them, Jesus came: for this every branch on the Vine has to live as much as the Vine itself. It is for fruit, much fruit, that the Father has made us one with Jesus.

Wondrous parable of the Vine—unveiling the mysteries of the Divine love, of the heavenly life, of the world of Spirit—how little have I understood thee! Jesus the living Vine in heaven, and I the living branch on earth! How little have I understood how great my need, but also how perfect my claim, to all His fullness! How little understood, how great His need, but also how perfect His claim, to my emptiness! Let me, in its beautiful light, study the wondrous union between Jesus and His people, until it becomes to me the guide into full communion with my beloved Lord. Let me listen and believe, until my whole being cries out, "Jesus is indeed to me the True Vine, bearing me, nourishing me, supplying me, using me, and filling me to the full to make me bring forth fruit abundantly." Then shall I not fear to say, "I am indeed a branch to Jesus, the True Vine, abiding in Him, resting on Him, waiting for Him, serving Him, and living only that through me, too, He may show forth the riches of His grace, and give His fruit to a perishing world."

It is when we try thus to understand the meaning of the parable, that the blessed command spoken in connection with it will come home to us in its true power. The thought of what the vine is to the branch, and Jesus to the believer, will give new force to the words, "Abide in me!" It will be as if He says, "Think, soul, how completely I belong to thee. I have joined myself inseparably to thee; all the fulness and fatness of the Vine are thine in very deed. Now thou once art in me, be assured that all I have is wholly thine. It is my interest and my honor to have thee a fruitful branch; only Abide in me. Thou art weak, but I am strong; thou art poor, but I am rich. Only abide in me; yield thyself wholly to my teaching and rule; simply trust my love, my grace, my promises. Only believe; I am wholly thine; I am the Vine, thou art the branch. Abide in me."

What sayest thou, 0 my soul? Shall I longer hesitate, or withhold consent? Or shall I not, instead of only thinking how hard and how difficult it is to live like a branch of the True Vine, because I thought of it as something I had to accomplish—shall I not now begin to look upon it as the most blessed and joyful thing under heaven? Shall I not believe that, now I once am in Him, He Himself will keep me and enable me to abide? On my part, abiding is nothing but the acceptance of my position, the consent to be kept there, the surrender of faith to the strong Vine still to hold the feeble branch. Yes, I will, I do abide in Thee, blessed Lord Jesus.

O Savior, how unspeakable is Thy love! "Such knowledge is too wonderful for me: it is high, I cannot attain unto it." I can only yield myself to Thy love with the prayer that, day by day, Thou wouldest unfold to me somewhat of its precious mysteries, and so encourage and strengthen Thy loving disciple to do what his heart longs to do indeed—ever, only, wholly to abide in Thee.

As You Came to Him, by Faith

"As ye have received Christ Jesus the Lord, so walk ye in Him: rooted and built up in Him, and stablished in the faith, abounding therein. "COL.2:6-7

In these words the apostle teaches us the weighty lesson, that it is not only by faith that we first come to Christ and are united to Him, but that it is by faith that we are to be rooted and established in our union with Christ. Not less essential than for the commencement, is faith for the progress of the spiritual life. Abiding in Jesus can only be by faith.

There are earnest Christians who do not understand this; or, if they admit it in theory, they fail to realize its application in practice. They are very zealous for a free gospel, with our first acceptance of Christ, and justification by faith alone. But after this they think everything depends on our diligence and faithfulness. While they firmly grasp the truth, "The sinner shall be justified by faith," they have hardly found a place in their scheme for the larger truth, "The just shall live by faith." They have never understood what a perfect Savior Jesus is, and how He will each day do for the sinner just as much as He did the first day when he came to Him. They know not that the life of grace is always and only a life of faith, and that in the relationship to Jesus the one daily and unceasing duty of the disciple is to believe, because believing is the one channel through which divine grace and strength flow out into the heart of man. The old nature of the believer remains evil and sinful to the last; it is only as he daily comes, all empty and helpless, to his Savior to receive of His life and strength, that he can bring forth the fruits of righteousness to the glory of God. Therefore it is: "As ye have received Christ Jesus the Lord, so walk ye in Him: rooted in Him, and stablished in the faith, abounding therein." As you came to Jesus, so abide in Him, by faith.

And if you would know how faith is to be exercised in thus abiding in Jesus, to be rooted more deeply and firmly in Him, you have only to look back to the time when first you received Him. You remember well what obstacles at that time there appeared to be in the way of your believing. There was first your vileness and guilt: it appeared impossible that the promise of pardon and love could be for such a sinner. Then there was the sense of weakness and death: you felt not the power for the surrender and the trust to which you were called. And then there was the future: you dared not undertake to be a disciple of Jesus while you felt so sure that you could not remain standing, but would speedily again be unfaithful and fall. These difficulties were like mountains in your way. And how were they removed? Simply by the word of God. That word, as it were, compelled you to believe that, notwithstanding guilt in the past, and weakness in the present, and unfaithfulness in the future, the promise was sure that Jesus would accept and save you. On that word you ventured to come, and were not deceived: you found that Jesus did indeed accept and save.

Apply this, your experience in coming to Jesus, to the abiding in Him. Now, as then, the temptations to keep you from believing are many. When you think of your sins since you became a disciple, your heart is cast down with shame, and it looks as if it were too much to expect that Jesus should indeed receive you into perfect intimacy and the full enjoyment of His holy love. When you think how utterly, in times past, you have failed in keeping the most sacred vows, the consciousness of present weakness makes you tremble at the very idea of answering the Savior's command with the promise, "Lord, from henceforth I will abide in Thee. " And when you set before yourself the life of love and joy, of holiness and fruitfulness, which in the future are to flow from abiding in Him, it is as if it only serves to make you still more hopeless: you, at least, can never attain to it. You know yourself too well. It is no use expecting it, only to be disappointed; a life fully and wholly abiding in Jesus is not for you.

Oh that you would learn a lesson from the time of your first coming to the Savior! Remember, dear soul, how you then were led, contrary to all that your experience, and your feelings, and even your sober judgment said, to take Jesus at His word, and how you were not disappointed. He did receive you, and pardon you; He did love you, and save you—you know it. And if He did this for you when you were an enemy and a stranger, what think you, now that you are His own, will He not much more fulfil His promise? Oh that you would come and begin simply to listen to His word, and to ask only the one question: Does He really mean that I should abide in Him? The answer His word gives is so simple and so sure: By His almighty grace you now are in Him; that same almighty grace will indeed enable you to abide in Him. By faith you became partakers of the initial grace; by that same faith you can enjoy the continuous grace of abiding in Him.

And if you ask what exactly it is that you now have to believe that you may abide in Him, the answer is not difficult. Believe first of all what He says: "I am the Vine." The safety and the fruitfulness of the branch depend upon the strength of the vine. Think not so much of yourself as a branch, nor of the abiding as your duty, until you have first had your soul filled with the faith of what Christ as the Vine is. He really will be to you all that a vine can be—holding you fast, nourishing you, and making Himself every moment responsible for your growth and your fruit. Take time to know, set yourself heartily to believe: My Vine, on whom I can depend for all I need, is Christ. A large, strong vine bears the feeble branch, and holds it more than the branch holds the vine. Ask the Father by the Holy Ghost to reveal to you what a glorious, loving, mighty Christ this is, in whom you have your place and your life; it is the faith in what Christ is, more than anything else, that will keep you abiding in Him. A soul filled with large thoughts of the Vine will be a strong branch, and will abide confidently in Him. Be much occupied with Jesus, and believe much in Him, as the True Vine.

And then, when Faith can well say, "He is my Vine," let it further say, "I am His branch, I am in Him." I speak to those who say they are Christ's disciples, and on them I cannot too earnestly press the importance of exercising their faith in saying, "I am in Him." It makes the abiding so simple. If I realize clearly as I meditate: Now I am in Him, I see at once that there is nothing wanting but just my consent to be what He has made me, to remain where He has placed me. I am in Christ: This simple thought, carefully, prayerfully, believingly uttered, removes all difficulty as if there were some great attainment to be reached. No, I am in Christ, my blessed Savior. His love has prepared a home for me with Himself, when He says, "Abide in my love"; and His power has undertaken to keep the door, and to keep me in, if I will but consent. I am in Christ: I have now but to say, "Savior, I bless Thee for this wondrous grace. I consent; I yield myself to Thy gracious keeping; I do abide in Thee."

It is astonishing how such a faith will work out all that is further implied in abiding in Christ. There is in the Christian life great need of watchfulness and of prayer, of self-denial and of striving, of obedience and of diligence. But "all things are possible to him that believeth." "This is the victory that overcometh, even our faith." It is the faith that continually closes its eyes to the weakness of the creature, and finds its joy in the sufficiency of an Almighty Savior, that makes the soul strong and glad. It gives itself up to be led by the Holy Spirit into an ever deeper appreciation of that wonderful Savior whom God hath given us—the Infinite Immanuel. It follows the leading of the Spirit from page to page of the blessed Word, with the one desire to take each revelation of what Jesus is and what He promises as its nourishment and its life. In accordance with the promise, "If that which ye have heard from the beginning abide in you, ye shall also abide in the Father and the Son," it lives by every word that proceedeth out of the mouth of God. And so it makes the soul strong with the strength of God, to be and to do all that is needed for abiding in Christ.

Believer, you would abide in Christ: only believe. Believe always; believe now. Bow even now before your Lord, and say to Him in childlike faith, that because He is your Vine, and you are His branch, you will this day abide in Him.

Note

" `I am the True Vine.' He who offers us the privilege of an actual union with Himself is the great *I Am*, the almighty God, who upholds all things by the word of His power. And this almighty God reveals Himself as our perfect Savior, even to the unimaginable extent of seeking to renew our fallen natures by grafting them into His own Divine nature.

"To realize the glorious Deity of Him whose call sounds forth to longing hearts with such exceeding sweetness, is no small step towards gaining the full privilege to which we are invited. But longing is by itself of no use; still less can there be any profit in reading of the blessed results to be gained from a close and personal union with our Lord, if we believe that union to be practically beyond our reach. His words are meant to be a living, an eternal, precious reality. And this they can never become unless we are sure that we may reasonably expect their accomplishment. But what could make the accomplishment of such an idea possible—what could make it reasonable to suppose that we poor, weak, selfish creatures, full of sin and full of failures, might be saved out of the corruption of our nature and made partakers of the holiness of our Lord—except the fact, the marvellous, unalterable fact, that He who proposes to us so great a transformation is Himself the everlasting God, as able as He is willing to fulfil His own word. In meditating, therefore, upon these utterances of Christ, containing as they do the very essence of His teaching, the very concentration of His love, let us, at the outset, put away all tendency to doubt. Let us not allow ourselves so much as to question whether such erring disciples as we are can be enabled to attain the holiness to which we are called through a close and intimate union with our Lord. If there be any impossibility, any falling short of the proposed blessedness, it will arise from the lack of earnest desire on our part. There is no lack in any respect on His part who puts forth the invitation; with *God* there can be no shortcoming in the fulfilment of His promise."—The Life of Fellowship; Meditations on John 15:1,11 by A. M. James.

It is perhaps necessary to say, for the sake of young or doubting Christians, that there is something more necessary than the effort to exercise faith in each separate promise that is brought under our notice. What is of even greater importance is the cultivation of a trustful disposition towards God, the habit of always thinking of Him, of His ways and His works, with bright confiding hopefulness. In such soil alone can the individual promises strike root and grow up. In a little work published by the Tract Society, Encouragements to Faith, by James Kimball, there will be found many most suggestive and helpful thoughts, all pleading for the right God has to claim that He shall be trusted. The Christian's Secret of a Happy Life is another little work that has been a great help to many. Its bright and buoyant tone, its loving and unceasing repetition of the keynote—we may indeed depend on Jesus to do all He has said, and more than we can think —has breathed hope and joy into many a heart that was almost ready to despair of ever getting on. In Frances Havergal's Kept for the Master's Use, there is the same healthful, hope-inspiring tone.

God Himself Has United You to Him

"Ye are in Christ Jesus." The believers at Corinth were still feeble and carnal, only babes in Christ. And yet Paul wants them, at the outset of his teaching, to know distinctly that they are in Christ Jesus. The whole Christian life depends on the clear consciousness of our position in Christ. Most essential to the abiding in Christ is the daily renewal of our faith's assurance, "I am in Christ Jesus." All fruitful preaching to believers must take this as its starting point: "Ye are in Christ Jesus."

But the apostle has an additional thought, of almost greater importance: "*of God* are ye in Christ Jesus." He would have us not only remember our union to Christ, but specially that it is not our own doing, but the work of God Himself. As the Holy Spirit teaches us to realize this, we shall see what a source of assurance and strength it must become to us. If it is of God alone that I am in Christ, then God Himself, the Infinite One, becomes my security for all I can need or wish in seeking to abide in Christ.

Let me try to understand what it means, this wonderful "*of God* in Christ." In becoming partakers of the union with Christ, there is a work God does and a work we have to do. God does His work by moving us to do our work. The work of God is hidden and silent; what we do is something distinct and tangible. Conversion and faith, prayer and obedience, are conscious acts of which we can give a clear account; while the spiritual quickening and strengthening that come from above are secret and beyond the reach of human sight. And so it comes that when the believer tries to say, "I am in Christ Jesus," he looks more to the work he did, than to that wondrous secret work of God by which he was united to Christ. Nor can it well be otherwise at the commencement of the Christian course. "I know that I have believed," is a valid testimony. But it is of great consequence that the mind should be led to see that at the back of our turning, and believing, and accepting of Christ, there was God's almighty power doing its work—inspiring our will, taking possession of us, and carrying out its own purpose of love in planting us into Christ Jesus. As the believer enters into this, the divine side of the work of salvation, he will learn to praise and to worship with new exultation, and to rejoice more than ever in the divineness of that salvation he has been made partaker of. At each step he reviews, the song will come, "This is the Lord's doing"—Divine Omnipotence working out what Eternal Love had devised. "*of God* I am in Christ Jesus."

The words will lead him even further and higher, even to the depths of eternity. "Whom He hath predestinated, them He also called." The calling in time is the manifestation of the purpose in eternity. Ere the world was, God had fixed the eye of His sovereign love on you in the election of grace, and chosen you in Christ. That you know yourself to be in Christ, is the stepping-stone by which you rise to understand in its full meaning the word, "*of God* I am in Christ Jesus." With the prophet, your language will be, "The Lord hath appeared of old unto me: yea, I have loved thee with an everlasting love, therefore with loving-kindness have I drawn thee." And you will recognize your own salvation as a part of that "mystery of His will, according to the good pleasure of His will which He purposed in Himself," and join with the whole body of believers in Christ as these say, "In whom we also have obtained an inheritance, being predestinated according to the purpose of Him who worketh all things after the counsel of His own will." Nothing will more exalt free grace, and make man bow very low before it, than this knowledge of the mystery "*of God* in Christ."

It is easy to see what a mighty influence it must exert on the believer who seeks to abide in Christ. What a sure standing-ground it gives him, as he rests his right to Christ and all His fulness on nothing less than the Father's own purpose and work! We have thought of Christ as the Vine, and the believer as the branch; let us not forget that other precious word, "My Father is the husbandman." The Savior said, "Every plant which my heavenly Father hath not planted, shall be rooted up"; but every branch grafted by Him in the True Vine, shall never be plucked out of His hand. As it was the Father to whom Christ owed all He was, and in whom He had all His strength and His life as the Vine, so to the Father the believer owes his place and his security in Christ. The same love and delight with which the Father watched over the beloved Son Himself, watch over every member of His body, every one who is in Christ Jesus.

What confident trust this faith inspires—not only as to the being kept in safety to the end, but specially as to the being able to fulfil in every point the object for which I have been united to Christ. The branch is as much in the charge and keeping of the husbandman as the vine; his honor as much concerned in the well-being and growth of the branch as of the vine. The God who chose Christ to be Vine fitted Him thoroughly for the work He had as Vine to perform. The God who has chosen me and planted me in Christ, has thereby engaged to secure, if I will but let Him, by yielding myself to Him, that I in every way be worthy of Jesus Christ. Oh that I did but fully realize this! What confidence and urgency it would give to my prayer to the God and Father of Jesus Christ! How it would quicken the sense of dependence, and make me see that praying without ceasing is indeed the one need of my life—an unceasing waiting, moment by moment, on the God who has united me to Christ, to perfect His own divine work, to work in me both to will and to do of His good pleasure.

And what a motive this would be for the highest activity in the maintenance of a fruitful branch-life! Motives are mighty powers; it is of infinite importance to have them high and clear. Here surely is the highest: "You are God's workmanship, created in Christ Jesus unto good works": grafted by Him into Christ, unto the bringing forth of much fruit. Whatever God creates is exquisitely suited to its end. He created the sun to give light: how perfectly it does its work! He created the eye to see: how beautifully it fulfils its object! He created the new man unto good works: how admirably it is fitted for its purpose.

of God I am in Christ: created anew, made a branch of the Vine, fitted for fruit-bearing. Would to God that believers would cease looking most at their old nature, and complaining of their weakness, as if God called them to what they were unfitted for! Would that they would believingly and joyfully accept the wondrous revelation of how God, in uniting them to Christ, has made Himself chargeable for their spiritual growth and fruitfulness! How all sickly hesitancy and sloth would disappear, and under the influence of this mighty motive—the faith in the faithfulness of Him of whom they are in Christ—their whole nature would rise to accept and fulfil their glorious destiny!

O my soul! yield yourself to the mighty influence of this word: "*of God* ye are in Christ Jesus." It is the same *God of whom* Christ is made all that He is for us, *of whom* we also are in Christ, and will most surely be made what we must be to Him. Take time to meditate and to worship, until the light that comes from the throne of God has shone into you, and you have seen your union to Christ as indeed the work of His almighty Father. Take time, day after day, and let, in your whole religious life, with all it has of claims and duties, of needs and wishes, God be everything. See Jesus, as He speaks to you, "Abide in me," pointing upward and saying, "My *Father is the husbandman*. Of Him you are in me, through Him you abide in me, and to Him and to His glory shall be the fruit you bear." And let your answer be, Amen, Lord! So be it. From eternity Christ and I were ordained for each other; inseparably we belong to each other: it is God's will; I shall abide in Christ. It is of God I am in Christ Jesus.

As Your Wisdom

"Of God are ye in Christ Jesus, who was made unto us wisdom from God, both righteousness and sanctification, and redemption."—I COR. 1:30 (R.V. marg.).

Jesus Christ is not only Priest to purchase, and King to secure, but also Prophet to reveal to us the salvation which God hath prepared for them that love Him. Just as at the creation the light was first called into existence, that in it all God's other works might have their life and beauty, so in our text wisdom is mentioned first as the treasury in which are to be found the three precious gifts that follow. The life is the light of man; it is in revealing to us, and making us behold the glory of God in His own face, that Christ makes us partakers of eternal life. It was by the tree of knowledge that sin came; it is through the knowledge that Christ gives that salvation comes. He is made of God unto us wisdom. In Him are hid all the treasures of wisdom and knowledge.

And of God you are in Him, and have but to abide in Him, to be made partaker of these treasures of wisdom. In Him you are, and in Him the wisdom is; dwelling in Him, you dwell in the very fountain of all light; abiding in Him, you have Christ the wisdom of God leading your whole spiritual life, and ready to communicate, in the form of knowledge, just as much as is needful for you to know. Christ is made unto us wisdom: you are in Christ.

It is this connection between what Christ has been made of God to us, and how we have it only as also being in Him, that we must learn to understand better. We shall thus see that the blessings prepared for us in Christ cannot be obtained as special gifts in answer to prayer apart from the abiding in Him. The answer to each prayer must come in the closer union and the deeper abiding in Him; in Him, the unspeakable gift, all other gifts are treasured up, the gift of wisdom and knowledge too.

How often have you longed for wisdom and spiritual understanding that you might know God better, whom to know is life eternal! Abide in Jesus: your life in Him will lead you to that fellowship with God in which the only true knowledge of God is to be had. His love, His power, His infinite glory will, as you abide in Jesus, be so revealed as it hath not entered into the heart of man to conceive. You may not be able to grasp it with the understanding, or to express it in words; but the knowledge which is deeper than thoughts or words will be given—the knowing of God which comes of being known of Him. "We preach Christ crucified unto them which are called, Christ the power of God, and the wisdom of God."

Or you would fain count all things but loss for the excellency of the knowledge of Jesus Christ your Lord. Abide in Jesus, and be found in Him. You shall know Him in the power of His resurrection and the fellowship of His sufferings. Following Him, you shall not walk in darkness, but have the light of life. It is only when God shines into the heart, and Christ Jesus dwells there, that the light of the knowledge of God in the face of Christ can be seen.

Or would you understand his blessed work, as He wrought it on earth, or works it from heaven by His Spirit? Would you know how Christ can become our righteousness, and our sanctification, and redemption? It is just as bringing, and revealing, and communicating these that He is made unto us wisdom from God. There are a thousand questions that at times come up, and the attempt to answer them becomes a weariness and a burden. It is because you have forgotten you are in Christ, whom God has made to be your wisdom. Let it be your first care to abide in Him in undivided fervent devotion of heart; when the heart and the life are right, rooted in Christ, knowledge will come in such measure as Christ's own wisdom sees meet. And without such abiding in Christ the knowledge does not really profit, but is often most hurtful. The soul satisfies itself with thoughts which are but the forms and images of truth, without receiving the truth itself in its power. God's way is ever first to give us, even though it be but as a seed, the thing itself, the life and the power, and then the knowledge. Man seeks the knowledge first, and often, alas! never gets beyond it. God gives us Christ, and in Him hid the treasures of wisdom and knowledge. O let us be content to possess Christ, to dwell in Him, to make Him our life, and only in a deeper searching into Him, to search and find the knowledge we desire. Such knowledge is life indeed.

Therefore, believer, abide in Jesus as your wisdom, and expect from Him most confidently whatever teaching you may need for a life to the glory of the Father. In all that concerns your spiritual life, abide in Jesus as your wisdom. The life you have in Christ is a thing of infinite sacredness, far too high and holy for you to know how to act it out. It is He alone who can guide you, as by a secret spiritual instinct, to know what is becoming your dignity as a child of God, what will help and what will hinder your inner life, and specially your abiding in Him. Do not think of it as a mystery or a difficulty you must solve. Whatever questions come up as to the possibility of abiding perfectly and uninterruptedly in Him, and of really obtaining all the blessing that comes from it, always remember: He knows, all is perfectly clear to Him, and He is my wisdom. Just as much as you need to know and are capable of apprehending, will be communicated, if you only trust Him. Never think of the riches of wisdom and knowledge hid in Jesus as treasures without a key, or of your way as a path without a light. Jesus your wisdom is guiding you in the right way, even when you do not see it.

In all your intercourse with the blessed Word, remember the same truth: abide in Jesus, your wisdom. Study much to know the written Word; but study more to know the living Word, in whom you are of God. Jesus, the wisdom of God, is only known by a life of implicit confidence and obedience. The words He speaks are spirit and life to those who live in Him. Therefore, each time you read, or hear, or meditate upon the Word, be careful to take up your true position. Realize first your oneness with Him who is the wisdom of God; know yourself to be under His direct and special training; go to the Word abiding in Him, the very fountain of divine light—in His light you shall see light.

In all your daily life, its ways and its work, abide in Jesus as your wisdom. Your body and your daily life share in the great salvation: in Christ, the wisdom of God, provision has been made for their guidance too. Your body is His temple, your daily life the sphere for glorifying Him: it is to Him a matter of deep interest that all your earthly concerns should be guided aright. Only trust His sympathy, believe His love, and wait for His guidance—it will be given. Abiding in Him, the mind will be calmed and freed from passion, the judgment cleared and strengthened, the light of heaven will shine on earthly things, and your prayer for wisdom, like Solomon's, will be fulfilled above what you ask or think.

And so, especially in any work you do for God, abide in Jesus as your wisdom. "We are created in Christ Jesus unto good works, which God hath before ordained that we should walk in them"; let all fear or doubt lest we should not know exactly what these works are, be put far away. In Christ we are created for them: He will show us what they are, and how to do them. Cultivate the habit of rejoicing in the assurance that the divine wisdom is guiding you, even where you do not yet see the way.

All that you can wish to know is perfectly clear to Him. As Man, as Mediator, He has access to the counsels of Deity, to the secrets of Providence, in your interest, and on your behalf. If you will but trust Him fully, and abide in Him entirely, you can be confident of having unerring guidance.

Yes, abide in Jesus as your wisdom. Seek to maintain the spirit of waiting and dependence, that always seeks to learn, and will not move but as the heavenly light leads on. Withdraw yourself from all needless distraction, close your ears to the voices of the world, and be as a docile learner, ever listening for the heavenly wisdom the Master has to teach. Surrender all your own wisdom; seek a deep conviction of the utter blindness of the natural understanding in the things of God; and both as to what you have to believe and have to do, wait for Jesus to teach and to guide. Remember that the teaching and guidance come not from without: it is by His life in us that the divine wisdom does His work. Retire frequently with Him into the inner chamber of the heart, where the gentle voice of the Spirit is only heard if all be still. Hold fast with unshaken confidence, even in the midst of darkness and apparent desertion, His own assurance that He is the light and the leader of His own. And live, above all, day by day in the blessed truth that, as He Himself, the living Christ Jesus, is your wisdom, your first and last care must ever be this alone—to abide in Him. Abiding in Him, His wisdom will come to you as the spontaneous outflowing of a life rooted in Him. I am, I abide in Christ, who was made unto us wisdom from God; wisdom will be given me.

As Your Righteousness

"Of God are ye in Christ Jesus, who was made unto us wisdom from God, both righteousness and sanctification, and redemption."—I Cor.1:30 (R.V. marg.).

The first of the great blessings which Christ our wisdom reveals to us as prepared in Himself, is —righteousness. It is not difficult to see why this must be first.

There can be no real prosperity or progress in a nation, a home, or a soul, unless there be peace. As not even a machine can do its work unless it be in rest, secured on a good foundation, quietness and assurance are indispensable to our moral and spiritual well-being. Sin had disturbed all our relations; we were out of harmony with ourselves, with men, and with God. The first requirement of a salvation that should really bring blessedness to us was peace. And peace can only come with right. Where everything is as God would have it, in God's order and in harmony with His will, there alone can peace reign. Jesus Christ came to restore peace on earth, and peace in the soul, by restoring righteousness. Because He is Melchizedek, King of righteousness, He reigns as King of Salem, King of peace (Heb.7:2). He so fulfils the promise the prophets held out: "A king shall reign in righteousness: and the work of righteousness shall be peace, and the effect of righteousness, quietness and assurance for ever" (Isa.32:1,17). Christ is made of God unto us righteousness; of God we are in Him as our righteousness; we are made the righteousness of God in Him. Let us try to understand what this means.

When first the sinner is led to trust in Christ for salvation, he, as a rule, looks more to His work than His person.

As he looks at the Cross, and Christ suffering there, the Righteous One for the unrighteous, he sees in that atoning death the only but sufficient foundation for his faith in God's pardoning mercy. The substitution, and the curse-bearing, and the atonement of Christ dying in the stead of sinners, are what give him peace. And as he understands how the righteousness which Christ brings becomes his very own, and how, in the strength of that, he is counted righteous before God, he feels that he has what he needs to restore him to God's favor: "Being justified by faith, we have peace with God." He seeks to wear this robe of righteousness in the ever renewed faith in the glorious gift of righteousness which has been bestowed upon him.

But as time goes on, and he seeks to grow in the Christian life, new needs arise. He wants to understand more fully how it is that God can thus justify the ungodly on the strength of the righteousness of another. He finds the answer in the wonderful teaching of Scripture as to the true union of the believer with Christ as the second Adam. He sees that it is because Christ had made Himself one with His people, and they were one with Him; that it was in perfect accordance with all law in the kingdom of nature and of heaven, that each member of the body should have the full benefit of the doing and the suffering as of the life of the head. And so he is led to feel that it can only be in fully realizing his personal union with Christ as the Head, that he can fully experience the power of His righteousness to bring the soul into the full favor and fellowship of the Holy One. The work of Christ does not become less precious, but the Person of Christ more so; the work leads up into the very heart, the love and the life of the God-man.

And this experience sheds its light again upon Scripture. It leads him to notice, what he had scarce remarked before, how distinctly the righteousness of God, as it becomes ours, is connected with the Person of the Redeemer. "This is His name whereby *He* shall be called, *Jehovah Our Righteousness*." In *Jehovah* have I righteousness and strength." "Of God is *He* made unto us righteousness." "That we might be made the righteousness of God *In Him*." "That I may be found *In Him*, having the righteousness of God." He sees how inseparable righteousness and life in Christ are from each other: "The righteousness of one comes upon all unto justification of life." "They which receive the gift of righteousness shall reign in life by one, Jesus Christ." And he understands what deep meaning there is in the key-word of the Epistle to the Romans: "The righteous shall live by faith." He is not now content with only thinking of the imputed righteousness as his robe; but, putting on Jesus Christ, and seeking to be wrapped up in, to be clothed upon with Himself and His life, he feels how completely the righteousness of God is his, because the Lord our righteousness is his. Before he understood this, he too often felt it difficult to wear his white robe all the day: it was as if he specially had to put it on when he came into God's presence to confess his sins, and seek new grace. But now the living Christ Himself is his righteousness—that Christ who watches over, and keeps and loves us as His own; it is no longer an impossibility to walk all the day enrobed in the loving presence with which He covers His people.

Such an experience leads still further. The life and the righteousness are inseparably linked, and the believer becomes more conscious than before of a righteous nature planted within him. The new man created in Christ Jesus, is "created in righteousness and true holiness." "He that doeth righteousness is righteous, even as He is righteous." The union to Jesus has effected a change not only in the relation to God, but in the personal state before God. And as the intimate fellowship to which the union has opened up the way is maintained, the growing renewal of the whole being makes righteousness to be his very nature.

To a Christian who begins to see the deep meaning of the truth, "*He* is made to us righteousness," it is hardly necessary to say, "Abide in Him." As long as he only thought of the righteousness of the substitute, and our being counted judicially righteous for His sake, the absolute necessity of abiding in Him was not apparent. But as the glory of "Jehovah our righteousness" unfolds to the view, he sees that abiding in Him personally is the only way to stand, at all times, complete and accepted before God, as it is the only way to realize how the new and righteous nature can be strengthened from Jesus our Head. To the penitent sinner the chief thought was the righteousness which comes through Jesus dying for sin; to the intelligent and advancing believer, Jesus, the Living One, through whom the righteousness comes, is everything, because having Him he has the righteousness too.

Believer, abide in Christ as your righteousness. You bear about with you a nature altogether corrupt and vile, ever seeking to rise up and darken your sense of acceptance, and of access to unbroken fellowship with the Father. Nothing can enable you to dwell and walk in the light of God, without even the shadow of a cloud between, but the habitual abiding in Christ as your righteousness. To this you are called. Seek to walk worthy of that calling. Yield yourself to the Holy Spirit to reveal to you the wonderful grace that permits you to draw nigh to God, clothed in a divine righteousness. Take time to realize that the King's own robe has indeed been put on, and that in it you need not fear entering His presence. It is the token that you are the man whom the King delights to honor. Take time to remember that as much as you need it in the palace, no less do you require it when He sends you forth into the world, where you are the King's messenger and representative. Live your daily life in the full consciousness of being righteous in God's sight, an object of delight and pleasure in Christ. Connect every view you have of Christ in His other graces with this first one: "Of God He is made to you righteousness." This will keep you in perfect peace. Thus shall you enter into, and dwell in, the rest of God. So shall your inmost being be transformed into being righteous and doing righteousness. In your heart and life it will become manifest where you dwell; abiding in Jesus Christ, the Righteous One, you will share His position, His character, and His blessedness: "Thou lovest righteousness, and hatest iniquity: therefore God, thy God, hath anointed thee with the oil of gladness above thy fellows." Joy and gladness above measure will be your portion.

As Your Sanctification

"Of God are ye in Christ Jesus, who has made unto us wisdom from God, both righteousness and sanctification, and redemption." I COR.1:30(R.V. marg.).

"Paul, unto the Church of God which is at Corinth to them that are sanctified in Christ Jesus, called to be saints";—thus the chapter opens in which we are taught that Christ is our sanctification. In the Old Testament, believers were called the righteous; in the New Testament they are called saints, the holy ones, sanctified in Christ Jesus. Holy is higher than righteous.[1] Holy in God has reference to His inmost being; righteous, to His dealings with His creatures. In man, righteousness is but a stepping-stone to holiness. It is in this he can approach most near to the perfection of God (comp. Matt.5:48; I Pet.1:16). In the Old Testament righteousness was found, while holiness was only typified; in Jesus Christ, the Holy One, and in His people, His saints or holy ones, it is first realized.

As in Scripture, and in our text, so in personal experience righteousness precedes holiness. When first the believer finds Christ as his righteousness, he has such joy in the new-made discovery that the study of holiness hardly has a place. But as he grows, the desire for holiness makes itself felt, and he seeks to know what provision his God has made for supplying that need. A superficial acquaintance with God's plan leads to the view that while justification is God's work, by faith in Christ, sanctification is our work, to be performed under the influence of the gratitude we feel for the deliverance we have experienced, and by the aid of the Holy Spirit. But the earnest Christian soon finds how little gratitude can supply the power. When he thinks that more prayer will bring it, he finds that, indispensable as prayer is, it is not enough. Often the believer struggles hopelessly for years, until he listens to the teaching of the Spirit, as He glorifies Christ again, and reveals Christ, our sanctification, to be appropriated by faith alone.

Christ is made of God unto us sanctification. Holiness is the very nature of God, and that alone is holy which God takes possession of and fills with Himself. God's answer to the question, How could sinful man become holy?

is, "Christ, the Holy One of God." In Him, whom the Father sanctified and sent into the world, God's holiness was revealed incarnate, and brought within reach of man. "I sanctify myself for them, that they also may be sanctified in truth." There is no other way of our becoming holy, but by becoming partakers of the holiness of Christ. [2] And there is no other way of this taking place than by our personal spiritual union with Him, so that through His Holy Spirit His holy life flows into us. "Of God are ye in Christ, who is made unto us sanctification." Abiding by faith in Christ our sanctification is the simple secret of a holy life. The measure of sanctification will depend on the measure of abiding in Him; as the soul learns wholly to abide in Christ, the promise is increasingly fulfilled: "The very God of peace sanctify you wholly."

To illustrate this relation between the measure of the abiding and the measure of sanctification experienced, let us think of the grafting a tree, that instructive symbol of our union to Jesus. The illustration is suggested by the Savior's words, "Make the tree good, and his fruit good." I can graft a tree so that only a single branch bears good fruit, while many of the natural branches remain, and bear their old fruit—a type of believer in whom a small part of the life is sanctified, but in whom, from ignorance or other reasons, the carnal life still in many respects has full dominion. I can graft a tree so that every branch is cut off, and the whole tree becomes renewed to bear good fruit; and yet, unless I watch over the tendency of the stems to give sprouts, they may again rise and grow strong, and, robbing the new graft of the strength it needs, make it weak. Such are Christians who, when apparently powerfully converted, forsake all to follow Christ, and yet after a time, through unwatchfulness, allow old habits to regain their power, and whose Christian life and fruit are but feeble. But if I want a tree wholly made good, I take it when young, and, cutting the stem clean off on the ground, I graft it just where it emerges from the soil. I watch over every bud which the old nature could possibly put forth, until the flow of sap from the old roots into the new stem is so complete, that the old life has, as it were, been entirely conquered and covered by the new. Here I have a tree entirely renewed—emblem of the Christian who has learnt in entire consecration to surrender everything for Christ, and in a whole-hearted faith wholly to abide in Him.

If, in this last case, the old tree were a reasonable being that could co-operate with the gardener, what would his language be to it? Would it not be this: "Yield now yourself entirely to this new nature with which I have invested you; repress every tendency of the old nature to give buds or sprouts; let all your sap and all your life-powers rise up into this graft from yonder beautiful tree, which I have put on you; so shall you bring forth sweet and much fruit." And the language of the tree to the gardener would be: "When you graft me, O spare not a single branch; let everything of the old self, even the smallest bud, be destroyed, that I may no longer live in my own, but in that other life that was cut off and brought and put upon me, that I might be wholly new and good." And, once again, could you afterwards ask the renewed tree, as it was bearing abundant fruit, what it could say of itself, its answer would be this: "In me, that is, in my roots, there dwells no good thing. I am ever inclined to evil; the sap I collect from the soil is in its nature corrupt, and ready to show itself in bearing evil fruit. But just when the sap rises into the sunshine to ripen into fruit, the wise gardener has clothed me with a new life, through which my sap is purified, and all my powers are renewed to the bringing forth of good fruit. I have only to abide in that which I have received. He cares for the immediate repression and removal of every bud which the old nature still would put forth."

Christian, fear not to claim God's promises to make you holy. Listen not to the suggestion that the corruption of your old nature would render holiness an impossibility. In your flesh dwells no good thing, and that flesh, though crucified with Christ, is not yet dead, but will continually seek to rise and lead you to evil. But the Father is the Husbandman. He has grafted the life of Christ on your life. That holy life is mightier than your evil life; under the watchful care of the Husbandman, that new life can keep down the workings of the evil life within you. The evil nature is there, with its unchanged tendency to rise up and show itself. But the new nature is there too—the living Christ, your sanctification, is there—and through Him all your powers can be sanctified as they rise into life, and be made to bear fruit to the glory of the Father.

And now, if you would live a holy life, abide in Christ your sanctification. Look upon Him as the Holy One of God, made man that He might communicate to us the holiness of God. Listen when Scripture teaches that there is within you a new nature, a new man, created in Christ Jesus in righteousness and true holiness. Remember that this holy nature which is in you is singularly fitted for living a holy life, and performing all holy duties, as much so as the old nature is for doing evil. Understand that this holy nature within you has its root and life in Christ in heaven, and can only grow and become strong as the intercourse between it and its source is uninterrupted. And above all, believe most confidently that Jesus Christ Himself delights in maintaining that new nature within you, and imparting to it His own strength and wisdom for its work. Let that faith lead you daily to the surrender of all self-confidence, and the confession of the utter corruption of all there is in you by nature. Let it fill you with a quiet and assured confidence that you are indeed able to do what the Father expects of you as His child, under the covenant of His grace, because you have Christ strengthening you. Let it teach you to lay yourself and your services on the altar as spiritual sacrifices, holy and acceptable in His sight, a sweet-smelling savor. Look not upon a life of holiness as a strain and an effort, but as the natural outgrowth of the life of Christ within you. And let ever again a quiet, hopeful, gladsome faith hold itself assured that all you need for a holy life will most assuredly be given you out of the holiness of Jesus. Thus will you understand and prove what it is to abide in Christ our sanctification.

Note

The thought that in the personal holiness of our Lord a new holy nature was formed to be communicated to us, and that we make use of it by faith, is the central idea of Marshall's invaluable work, The Gospel Mystery of Sanctcation:

"One great mystery is, that the holy frame and disposition whereby our souls are furnished and enabled for immediate practice of the law, must be obtained by receiving it out of Christ's fulness, as a thing already prepared and brought to an existence for us in Christ, and treasured up in Him; and that, as we are justified by a righteousness wrought out in Christ, and imputed to us, so we are sanctified by such an holy frame and qualification as are first wrought out and completed in Christ for us, and then imparted to us. As our natural corruption was produced originally in the first Adam, and propagated from him to us, so our new nature and holiness is first produced in Christ, and derived from Him to us, or, as it were, propagated. So that we are not at all to work together with Christ in making or producing that holy frame in us, but only to take it to ourselves, and use it in our holy practice, as made ready to our hands. Thus we have fellowship with Christ, in receiving that holy frame of spirit that was originally in Him; for fellowship is where several persons have the same things in common. This mystery is so great, that notwithstanding all the light of the Gospel, we commonly think that we must get an holy frame by producing it anew in ourselves, and by pursuing it and working it out of our own heart" (see chap. 3). [3]

Footnotes:

1. "Holiness may be called spiritual perception, as righteousness is legal completeness." —Horatius Bonar in God's Way of Holiness.

2. See note at end of chapter.

3. I have felt so strongly that the teaching of Marshall is just what the Church needs to bring out clearly what the Scripture path of holiness is, that I have prepared an abridgment (all in the author's own words) of his work. By leaving out what was not essential to his argument, and shortening when he appeared diffuse, I hoped to bring his book within reach of many who might never read the larger work. It is published by Nisbet & Co. under the title, The Highway of Holiness. I cannot too earnestly urge every student of theology, and of Scripture, and of the art of holy living, to make himself master of the teaching of Marshall's third, fourth, and twelfth chapters.

Publisher's Note: The original complete work, The Gospel Mystery of Sanctification, was reissued by Oliphants Ltd. in 1955.

As Your Redemption

"Of God are ye in Christ Jesus, who was made unto us wisdom from God, both righteousness and sanctification, and redemption."—I COR.1:30(R.V. marg.).

Here we have the top of the ladder, reaching into heaven—the blessed end to which Christ and life in Him is to lead. The word redemption, though sometimes applied to our deliverance from the guilt of sin, here refers to our complete and final deliverance from all its consequences, when the Redeemer's work shall become fully manifest, even to the redemption of the body itself (comp. Rom.8:21-23; Eph.1.14; 4:30). The expression points us to the highest glory to be hoped for in the future, and therefore also to the highest blessing to be enjoyed in the present in Christ. We have seen how, as a Prophet, Christ is our wisdom, revealing to us God and His love, with the nature and conditions of the salvation that love has prepared. As a Priest, He is our righteousness, restoring us to right relations to God, and securing us His favor and friendship. As a King, He is our sanctification, forming and guiding us into the obedience to the Father's holy will. As these three offices work out God's one purpose, the grand consummation will be reached, the complete deliverance from sin and all its effects be accomplished, and ransomed humanity regain all that it had ever lost.

Christ is made of God unto us redemption. The word invites us to look upon Jesus, not only as He lived on earth, teaching us by word and example, as He died, to reconcile us with God, as He lives again, a victorious King, rising to receive His crown, but as, sitting at the right hand of God, He takes again the glory which He had with the Father, before the world began, and holds it there for us. It consists in this, that there His human nature, yea, His human body, freed from all the consequences of sin to which He once had been exposed, is now admitted to share the divine glory. As Son of Man, He dwells on the throne and in the bosom of the Father: the deliverance from what He had to suffer from sin is complete and eternal. The complete redemption is found embodied in His own Person: what He as man is and has in heaven is the complete redemption. *He* is made of God to us redemption.

We are in Him as such. And the more intelligently and believingly we abide in Him as our redemption, the more shall we experience, even here, of "the powers of the world to come." As our communion with Him becomes more intimate and intense, and we let the Holy Spirit reveal Him to us in His heavenly glory, the more we realize how the life in us is the life of One who sits upon the throne of heaven. We feel the power of an endless life working in us. We taste the eternal life. We have the foretaste of the eternal glory.

The blessings flowing from abiding in Christ as our redemption are great. The soul is delivered from all fear of death. There was a time when even the Savior feared death. But now no longer. He has triumphed over death; even His body has entered into the glory. The believer who abides in Christ as his full redemption, realizes even now his spiritual victory over death. It becomes to him the servant that removes the last rags of the old carnal vesture, ere he be clothed upon with the new body of glory. It carries the body to the grave, to lie there as the seed whence the new body will arise the worthy companion of the glorified spirit. The resurrection of the body is no longer a barren doctrine, but a living expectation, and even an incipient experience, because the Spirit of Him that raised Jesus from the dead, dwells in the body as the pledge that even our mortal bodies shall be quickened (Rom.8:11-23). This faith exercises its sanctifying influence in the willing surrender of the sinful members of the body to be mortified and completely subjected to the dominion of the Spirit, as preparation for the time when the frail body shall be changed and fashioned like to His glorious body.

This full redemption of Christ as extending to the body, has a depth of meaning not easily expressed. It was of man as a whole, soul and body that it is said that he was made in the image and likeness of God. In the angels, God had created spirits without material bodies; in the creation of the world, there was matter without spirit. Man was to be the highest specimen of divine art: the combination in one being, of matter and spirit in perfect harmony, as type of the most perfect union between God and His own creation. Sin entered in, and appeared to thwart the divine plan: the material obtained a fearful supremacy over the spiritual. The Word was made flesh, the divine fulness received an embodiment in the humanity of Christ, that the redemption might be a complete and perfect one; that the whole creation, which now groaneth and travaileth in pain together, might be delivered from the bondage of corruption into the liberty of the glory of the children of God. God's purpose will not be accomplished, and Christ's glory will not be manifested fully, until the body, with that whole of nature of which it is part and head, has been transfigured by the power of the spiritual life, and made the transparent vesture for showing forth the glory of the Infinite Spirit. Then only shall we understand: "Christ Jesus is made unto us (complete) redemption."

Meantime we are taught to believe: "Of God are ye in Christ, as your redemption." This is not meant as a revelation, to be left to the future; for the full development of the Christian life, our present abiding in Christ must seek to enter into and appropriate it. We do this as we learn to triumph over death. We do it as we learn to look upon Christ as the Lord of our body, claiming its entire consecration, securing even here, if faith will claim it (Mark 16:17-18), victory over the terrible dominion sin hath had in the body. We do this as we learn to look on all nature as part of the Kingdom of Christ, destined, even though it be through a baptism of fire, to partake in His redemption. We do it as we allow the powers of the coming world to possess us, and to lift us up into a life in the heavenly places, to enlarge our hearts and our views, to anticipate, even here, the things which have never entered into the heart of man to conceive.

Believer, abide in Christ as your redemption. Let this be the crown of your Christian life. Seek it not first or only, apart from the knowledge of Christ in His other relations. But seek it truly as that to which they are meant to lead you up. Abide in Christ as your redemption. Nothing will fit you for this but faithfulness in the previous steps of the Christian life. Abide in Him as your wisdom, the perfect revelation of all that God is and has for you. Follow, in the daily ordering of the inner and the outer life, with meek docility His teaching, and you shall be counted worthy to have secrets revealed to you which to most disciples are a sealed book. The wisdom will lead you into the mysteries of complete redemption. Abide in Him as your righteousness, and dwell clothed upon with Him in that inner sanctuary of the Father's favor and presence to which His righteousness gives you access. As you rejoice in your reconciliation, you shall understand how it includes all things, and how they too wait the full redemption; "for it pleased the Father by Him to reconcile all things unto Himself; by Him, I say, whether they be things on earth or things in heaven." And abide in Him as your sanctification; the experience of His power to make you holy, spirit and soul and body, will quicken your faith in a holiness that shall not cease its work until the bells of the horses and every pot in Jerusalem shall be holiness to the Lord. Abide in Him as your redemption, and live, even here, as the heir of the future glory. And as you seek to experience in yourself to the full, the power of His saving grace, your heart shall be enlarged to realize the position man has been destined to occupy in the universe, as having all things made subject to him, and you shall for your part be fitted to live worthy of that high and heavenly calling.

The Crucified One

"I am crucified with Christ: nevertheless I live; yet not I, but Christ liveth in me."—GAL.2:20.

"We have been planted together in the likeness of his death. "—Rom.6:5

"I am crucified with Christ." Thus the apostle expresses his assurance of his fellowship with Christ in His sufferings and death, and his full participation in all the power and the blessing of that death. And so really did he mean what he said, and know that he was now indeed dead, that he adds: "It is no longer I that live, but Christ that liveth in me."How blessed must be the experience of such a union with the Lord Jesus! To be able to look upon His death as mine, just as really as it was His—upon His perfect obedience to God, His victory over sin, and complete deliverance from its power, as mine; and to realize that the power of that death does by faith work daily with a divine energy in mortifying the flesh, and renewing the whole life into the perfect conformity to the resurrection life of Jesus! Abiding in Jesus, the Crucified One, is the secret of the growth of that new life which is ever begotten of the death of nature.

Let us try to understand this. The suggestive expression, "Planted into the likeness of His death," will teach us what the abiding in the Crucified One means. When a graft is united with the stock on which it is to grow, we know that it must be kept fixed, it must abide in the place where the stock has been cut, been wounded, to make an opening to receive the graft. No graft without wounding—the laying bare and opening up of the inner life of the tree to receive the stranger branch. It is only through such wounding that access can be obtained to the fellowship of the sap and the growth and the life of the stronger stem. Even so with Jesus and the sinner. Only when we are planted into the likeness of His death shall we also be in the likeness of His resurrection, partakers of the life and the power there are in Him. In the death of the Cross Christ was wounded, and in His opened wounds a place prepared where we might be grafted in. And just as one might say to a graft, and does practically say as it is fixed in its place, "Abide here in the wound of the stem, that is now to bear you"; so to the believing soul the message comes, "Abide in the wounds of Jesus; there is the place of union, and life, and growth. There you shall see how His heart was opened to receive you; how His flesh was rent that the way might be opened for your being made one with Him, and having access to all the blessings flowing from His divine nature."

You have also noticed how the graft has to be torn away from the tree where it by nature grew, and to be cut into conformity to the place prepared for it in the wounded stem. Even so the believer has to be made conformable to Christ's death—to be crucified and to die with Him. The wounded stem and the wounded graft are cut to fit into each other, into each other's likeness. There is a fellowship between Christ's sufferings and your sufferings. His experiences must become yours. The disposition He manifested in choosing and bearing the cross must be yours. Like Him, you will have to give full assent to the righteous judgment and curse of a holy God against sin. Like Him, you have to consent to yield your life, as laden with sin and curse, to death, and through it to pass to the new life. Like Him, you shall experience that it is only through the self-sacrifice of Gethsemane and Calvary that the path is to be found to the joy and the fruit-bearing of the resurrection life. The more clear the resemblance between the wounded stem and the wounded graft, the more exactly their wounds fit into each other, the surer and the easier, and the more complete will be the union and the growth.

It is in Jesus, the Crucified One, I must abide. I must learn to look upon the Cross as not only an atonement to God, but also a victory over the devil—not only a deliverance from the guilt, but also from the power of sin. I must gaze on Him on the Cross as wholly mine, offering Himself to receive me into the closest union and fellowship, and to make me partaker of the full power of His death to sin, and the new life of victory to which it is but the gateway. I must yield myself to Him in an undivided surrender, with much prayer and strong desire, imploring to be admitted into the ever closer fellowship and conformity of His death, of the Spirit in which He died that death.

Let me try and understand why the Cross is thus the place of union. On the Cross the Son of God enters into the fullest union with man—enters into the fullest experience of what it says to have become a son of man, a member of a race under the curse. It is in death that the Prince of life conquers the power of death; it is in death alone that He can make me partaker of that victory. The life He imparts is a life from the dead; each new experience of the power of that life depends upon the fellowship of the death. The death and the life are inseparable. All the grace which Jesus the Saving One gives is given only in the path of fellowship with Jesus the Crucified One. Christ came and took my place; I must put myself in His place, and abide there. And there is but one place which is both His and mine—that place is the Cross. His in virtue of His free choice; mine by reason of the curse of sin. He came there to seek me; there alone I can find Him. When He found me there, it was the place of cursing; this He experienced, for "cursed is every one that hangeth on a tree." He made it a place of blessing; this I experienced, for Christ has delivered us from the curse, being made a curse for us. When Christ comes in my place, He remains what He was, the beloved of the Father; but in the fellowship with me He shares my curse and dies my death. When I stand in His place, which is still always mine, I am still what I was by nature, the accursed one, who deserves to die; but as united to Him, I share His blessing, and receive His life. When He came to be one with me He could not avoid the Cross, for the curse always points to the Cross as its end and fruit. And when I seek to be one with Him, I cannot avoid the Cross either, for nowhere but on the Cross are life and deliverance to be found. As inevitably as my curse pointed Him to the Cross as the only place where He could be fully united to me, His blessing points me to the Cross too as the only place where I can be united to Him. He took my cross for His own; I must take His Cross as my own; I must be crucified with Him. It is as I abide daily, deeply in Jesus the Crucified One, that I shall taste the sweetness of His love, the power of His life, the completeness of His salvation.

Beloved believer! it is a deep mystery, this of the Cross of Christ. I fear there are many Christians who are content to look upon the Cross, with Christ on it dying for their sins, who have little heart for fellowship with the Crucified One. They hardly know that He invites them to it. Or they are content to consider the ordinary afflictions of life, which the children of the world often have as much as they, as their share of Christ's Cross. They have no conception of what it is to be crucified with Christ, that bearing the cross means likeness to Christ in the principles which animated Him in His path of obedience. The entire surrender of all self-will, the complete denial to the flesh of its every desire and pleasure, the perfect separation from the world in all its ways of thinking and acting, the losing and hating of one's life, the giving up of self and its interests for the sake of others—this is the disposition which marks him who has taken up Christ's Cross, who seeks to say, "I am crucified with Christ; I abide in Christ, the Crucified One."

Would you in very deed please your Lord, and live in as close fellowship with Him as His grace could maintain you in? O pray that His Spirit lead you into this blessed truth: this secret of the Lord for them that fear Him. We know how Peter knew and confessed Christ as the Son of the living God while the Cross was still an offence (Matt.16:16,17,21,23). The faith that believes in the blood that pardons, and the life that renews, can only reach its perfect growth as it abides beneath the Cross, and in living fellowship with Him seeks for perfect conformity with Jesus the Crucified.

O Jesus, our crucified Redeemer, teach us not only to believe on Thee, but to abide in Thee, to take Thy Cross not only as the ground of our pardon, but also as the law of our life. O teach us to love it not only because on it Thou didst bear our curse, but because on it we enter into the closest fellowship with Thyself, and are crucified with Thee. And teach us, that as we yield ourselves wholly to be possessed of the Spirit in which Thou didst bear the Cross, we shall be made partakers of the power and the blessing to which the Cross alone gives access.

God Himself Will Establish You in Him

"He which Establish us with you in Christ, is God."—2 COR.1:21

These words of Paul teach us a much needed and most blessed truth—that just as our first being united with Christ was the work of divine omnipotence, so we may look to the Father, too, for being kept and being fixed more firmly in Him. "The Lord will perfect that which concerneth me"—this expression of confidence should ever accompany the prayer, "Forsake not the work of Thine own hands." In all his longings and prayers to attain to a deeper and more perfect abiding in Christ, the believer must hold fast his confidence: "He which hath begun a good work in you, will perform it until the day of Jesus Christ." There is nothing that will so help to root and ground him in Christ as this faith: "He which Establish us in Christ is God."

How many there are who can witness that this faith is just what they need! They continually mourn over the variableness of their spiritual life. Sometimes there are hours and days of deep earnestness, and even of blessed experience of the grace of God. But how little is needed to mar their peace, to bring a cloud over the soul! And then, how their faith is shaken! All efforts to regain their standing appear utterly fruitless; and neither solemn vows, nor watching and prayer, avail to restore to them the peace they for a while had tasted. Could they but understand how just their own efforts are the cause of their failure, because it is God alone who can establish us in Christ Jesus. They would see that just as in justification they had to cease from their own working, and to accept in faith the promise that God would give them life in Christ, so now, in the matter of their sanctification, their first need is to cease from striving themselves to establish the connection with Christ more firmly, and to allow God to do it. "God is faithful, by whom ye were called unto the fellowship of His Son Jesus Christ." What they need is the simple faith that the establishing in Christ, day by day, is God's work—a work that He delights to do, in spite of all our weakness and unfaithfulness, if we will but trust Him for it.

To the blessedness of such a faith, and the experience it brings, many can testify. What peace and rest, to know that there is a Husbandman who cares for the branch, to see that it grows stronger, and that its union with the Vine becomes more perfect, who watches over every hindrance and danger, who supplies every needed aid! What peace and rest, fully and finally to give up our abiding into the care of God, and never have a wish or thought, never to offer a prayer or engage in an exercise connected with it, without first having the glad remembrance that what we do is only the manifestation of what God is doing in us! The eestablishing in Christ is His work: He accomplishes it by stirring us to watch, and wait, and work. But this He can do with power only as we cease interrupting Him by our self-working—as we accept in faith the dependent posture which honours Him and opens the heart to let Him work. How such a faith frees the soul from care and responsibility! In the midst of the rush and bustle of the world's stirring life, amid the subtle and ceaseless temptations of sin, amid all the daily cares and trials that so easily distract and lead to failure, how blessed it would be to be an established Christian—always abiding in Christ! How blessed even to have the faith that one can surely become it—that the attainment is within our reach!

Dear believer, the blessing is indeed within your reach. He that Establish you with us in Christ is God. What I want you to take in is this—that believing this promise will not only give you comfort, but will be the means of your obtaining your desire. You know how Scripture teaches us that in all God's leads of His people faith has everywhere been the one condition of the manifestation of His power. Faith is the ceasing from all nature's efforts, and all other dependence; faith is confessed helplessness casting itself upon God's promise, and claiming its fulfilment; faith is the putting ourselves quietly into God's hands for Him to do His work. What you and I need now is to take time, until this truth stands out before us in all its spiritual brightness: It is God Almighty, God the Faithful and Gracious One, who has undertaken to stablish me in Christ Jesus.

Listen to what the Word teaches you:—"The Lord shall establish thee an holy people unto Himself"; "O Lord God, stablish their heart unto Thee"; "Thy God loved Israel, to establish them for ever"; "Thou wilt establish the heart of the humble"; "Now to Him that is of power to establish you, be glory for ever"; "To the end He may establish your hearts unblameable in holiness" ; "*The Lord Is Faithful*, who shall stablish you and keep you from all evil"; "The God of all grace, who hath called us in Christ Jesus, make you perfect, stablish, strengthen, settle you." Can you take these words to mean anything less than that you too—however fitful your spiritual life has hitherto been, however unfavorable your natural character or your circumstances may appear—can be established in Christ Jesus—can become an established Christian? Let us but take time to listen, in simple childlike teachableness, to these words as the truth of God, and the confidence will come: As surely—as I am in Christ, I shall also, day by day, be established in Him.

The lesson appears so simple; and yet the most of us take so long to learn it. The chief reason is, that the grace the promise offers is so large, so God-like, so beyond all our thoughts, that we do not take it really to mean what it says. The believer who has once come to see and accept what it brings, can bear witness to the wonderful change there comes over the spiritual life. Hitherto he had taken charge of his own welfare; now he has a God to take charge of it. He now knows himself to be in the school of God, a Teacher who plans the whole course of study for each of His pupils with infinite wisdom, and delights to have them come daily for the lessons He has to give. All he asks is to feel himself constantly in God's hands, and to follow His guidance, neither lagging behind nor going before. Remembering that it is God who worketh both to will and to do, he sees his only safety to be in yielding himself to God's working. He lays aside all anxiety about his inner life and its growth, because the Father is the Husbandman under whose wise and watchful care each plant is well secured. He knows that there is the prospect of a most blessed life of strength and fruitfulness to every one who will take God alone and wholly as his hope.

Believer, you cannot but admit that such a life of trust must be a most blessed one. You say, perhaps, that there are times when you do, with your whole heart, consent to this way of living, and do wholly abandon the care of your inner life to your Father. But somehow it does not last. You forget again; and instead of beginning each morning with the joyous transference of all the needs and cares of your spiritual life to the Father's charge, you again feel anxious, and burdened, and helpless. Is it not, perhaps, my brother, because you have not committed to the Father's care this matter of daily remembering to renew your entire surrender? Memory is one of the highest powers in our nature. By it day is linked to day, the unity of life through all our years is kept up, and we know that we are still ourselves. In the spiritual life, recollection is of infinite value. For the sanctifying of our memory, in the service of our spiritual life, God has provided most beautifully. The Holy Spirit is the remembrancer, the Spirit of recollection. Jesus said, "He shall bring all things to your remembrance." "He which Establish us with you in Christ is God, who hath also sealed us, and given the earnest of the Spirit in our hearts." It is just for the establishing that the Holy Remembrancer has been given. God's blessed promises, and your unceasing acts of faith and surrender accepting of them—He will enable you to remember these each day. The Holy Spirit is—blessed be God—the memory of the new man.

Apply this to the promise of the text: "He that Establish us in Christ is God." As you now, at this moment, abandon all anxiety about your growth and progress to the God who has undertaken to stablish you in the Vine, and feel what a joy it is to know that God alone has charge, ask and trust Him by the Holy Spirit ever to remind you of this your blessed relation to Him. He will do it; and with each new morning your faith may grow stronger and brighter: I have a God to see that each day I become more firmly united to Christ.

And now, beloved fellow-believer, "the God of all grace, who hath called us in Christ Jesus, make you perfect, stablish, strengthen, settle you." What more can you desire? Expect it confidently, ask it fervently. Count on God to do His work. And learn in faith to sing the song, the notes of which each new experience will make deeper and sweeter: "Now to Him, that is of power to establish you, be glory for ever. Amen." Yes, glory to God, who has undertaken to establish us in Christ!

Every Moment

"In that day sing ye unto her, A vineyard of red wine. I the Lord do keep it; I will water it every moment: lest any hurt it, I will keep it night and day."—ISA.27:2,3.

The vineyard was the symbol of the people of Israel, in whose midst the True Vine was to stand. The branch is the symbol of the individual believer, who stands in the Vine. The song of the vineyard is also the song of the Vine and its every branch. The command still goes forth to the watchers of the vineyard—would that they obeyed it, and sang till every feeble-hearted believer had learned and joined the joyful strain—"Sing ye unto her: I, *Jehovah*, Do *keep it*; I will water it every moment: lest any hurt it, *I will keep* it night and day."

What an answer from the mouth of God Himself to the question so often asked: Is it possible for the believer always to abide in Jesus? Is a life of unbroken fellowship with the Son of God indeed attainable here in this earthly life? Truly not, if the abiding is our work, to be done in our strength. But the things that are impossible with men are possible with God. If the Lord Himself will keep the soul night and day, yea, will watch and water it every moment, then surely the uninterrupted communion with Jesus becomes a blessed possibility to those who can trust God to mean and to do what He says. Then surely the abiding of the branch of the vine day and night, summer and winter, in a never-ceasing life-fellowship, is nothing less than the simple but certain promise of your abiding in your Lord.

In one sense, it is true, there is no believer who does not always abide in Jesus; without this there could not be true life. "If a man abide not in me, he is cast forth." But when the Savior gives the command, "Abide in me," with the promise, "He that abideth in me bringeth forth much fruit," He speaks of that willing, intelligent, and whole-hearted surrender by which we accept His offer, and consent to the abiding in Him as the only life we choose or seek. The objections raised against our right to expect that we shall always be able thus voluntarily and consciously to abide in Jesus are chiefly two.

The one is derived from the nature of man. It is said that our limited powers prevent our being occupied with two things at the same moment. God's providence places many Christians in business, where for hours at a time the closest attention is required to the work they have to do. How can such a man, it is asked, with his whole mind in the work he has to do, be at the same time occupied with Christ, and keeping up fellowship with Him? The consciousness of abiding in Jesus is regarded as requiring such a strain, and such a direct occupation of the mind with heavenly thoughts, that to enjoy the blessing would imply a withdrawing of oneself from all the ordinary avocations of life. This is the same error as drove the first monks into the wilderness.

Blessed be God, there is no necessity for such a going out of the world. Abiding in Jesus is not a work that needs each moment the mind to be engaged, or the affections to be directly and actively occupied with it. It is an entrusting of oneself to the keeping of the Eternal Love, in the faith that it will abide near us, and with its holy presence watch over us and ward off the evil, even when we have to be most intently occupied with other things. And so the heart has rest and peace and joy in the consciousness of being kept when it cannot keep itself.

In ordinary life, we have abundant illustration of the influence of a supreme affection reigning in and guarding the soul, while the mind concentrates itself on work that requires its whole attention. Think of the father of a family, separated for a time from his home, that he may secure for his loved ones what they need. He loves his wife and children, and longs much to return to them. There may be hours of intense occupation when he has not a moment to think of them, and yet his love is as deep and real as when he can call up their images; all the while his love and the hope of making them happy urge him on, and fill him with a secret joy in his work. Think of a king: in the midst of work, and pleasure, and trial, he all the while acts under the secret influence of the consciousness of royalty, even while he does not think of it. A loving wife and mother never for one moment loses the sense of her relation to the husband and children: the consciousness and the love are there, amid all her engagements. And shall it be thought impossible for the Everlasting Love so to take and keep possession of our spirits, that we too shall never for a moment lose the secret consciousness: We are in Christ, kept in Him by His almighty power. Oh, it is possible; we can be sure it is. Our abiding in Jesus is even more than a fellowship of love—it is a fellowship of life. In work or in rest, the consciousness of life never leaves us. And even so can the mighty power of the Eternal Life maintain within us the consciousness of its presence. Or rather, Christ, who is our life, Himself dwells within us, and by His presence maintains our consciousness that we are in Him.

The second objection has reference to our sinfulness. Christians are so accustomed to look upon sinning daily as something absolutely inevitable, that they regard it as a matter of course that no one can keep up abiding fellowship with the Savior: we must sometimes be unfaithful and fail. As if it was not just because we have a nature which is naught but a very fountain of sin, that the abiding in Christ has been ordained for us as our only but our sufficient deliverance! As if it were not the Heavenly Vine, the living, loving Christ, in whom we have to abide, and whose almighty power to hold us fast is to be the measure of our expectations! As if He would give us the command, "Abide in me," without securing the grace and the power to enable us to perform it! As if, above all, we had not the Father as the Husbandman to keep us from falling, and that not in a large and general sense, but according to His own precious promise: "Night and day, every moment!" Oh, if we will but look to our God as the Keeper of Israel, of whom it is said, "Jehovah shall keep thee from all evil; He shall keep thy soul," we shall learn to believe that conscious abiding in Christ every moment, night and day, is indeed what God has prepared for them that love Him.

My beloved fellow-Christians, let nothing less than this be your aim. I know well that you may not find it easy of attainment; that there may come more than one hour of weary struggle and bitter failure. Were the Church of Christ what it should be—were older believers to younger converts what they should be, witnesses to God's faithfulness, like Caleb and Joshua, encouraging their brethren to go up and possess the land with their, "We are well able to overcome; if the Lord delight in us, then *He will bring* us into this land"—were the atmosphere which the young believer breathes as he enters the fellowship of the saints that of a healthy, trustful, joyful consecration, abiding in Christ would come as the natural outgrowth of being in Him. But in the sickly state in which such a great part of the body is, souls that are pressing after this blessing are sorely hindered by the depressing influence of the thought and the life around them. It is not to discourage that I say this, but to warn, and to urge to a more entire casting of ourselves upon the word of God Himself. There may come more than our hour in which you are ready to yield to despair; but be of good courage. Only believe. He who has put the blessing within your reach will assuredly lead to its possession.

The way in which souls enter into the possession may differ. To some it may come as the gift of a moment. In times of revival, in the fellowship with other believers in whom the Spirit is working effectually, under the leading of some servant of God who can guide, and sometimes in solitude too, it is as if all at once a new revelation comes upon the soul. It sees, as in the light of heaven, the strong Vine holding and bearing the feeble branches so securely, that doubt becomes impossible. It can only wonder how it ever could have understood the words to mean aught else than this: To abide unceasingly in Christ is the portion of every believer. It sees it; and to believe, and rejoice, and love, come as of itself.

To others it comes by a slower and more difficult path. Day by day, amid discouragement and difficulty, the soul has to press forward. Be of good cheer; this way too leads to the rest. Seek but to keep your heart set upon the promise: "*I the Lord Do Keep it*, night and day." Take from His own lips the watchword: "Every moment." In that you have the law of His love, and the law of your hope. Be content with nothing less. Think no longer that the duties and the cares, that the sorrows and the sins of this life must succeed in hindering the abiding life of fellowship. Take rather for the rule of your daily experience the language of faith: I am persuaded that neither death with its fears, nor life with its cares, nor things present with their pressing claims, nor things to come with their dark shadows, nor height of joy, nor depth of sorrow, nor any other creature, shall be able, for one single moment, to separate us from the love of God which is in Christ Jesus our Lord, and in which He is teaching me to abide. If things look dark and faith would fail, sing again the song of the vineyard: "I the Lord do keep it; I will water it every moment: lest any hurt it, I will keep it night and day." And be assured that, if Jehovah keep the branch night and day, and water it every moment, a life of continuous and unbroken fellowship with Christ is indeed our privilege.

Day by Day

"And the people shall go out and gather the portion of a day in his day."—Ex.16:4(marg.).

The day's portion in its day: Such was the rule for God's giving and man's working in the ingathering of the manna. It is still the law in all the dealings of God's grace with His children. A clear insight into the beauty and application of this arrangement is a wonderful help in understanding how one, who feels himself utterly weak, can have the confidence and the perseverance to hold on brightly through all the years of his earthly course. A doctor was once asked by a patient who had met with a serious accident: "Doctor, how long shall I have to lie here?" The answer, "Only a day at a time," taught the patient a precious lesson. It was the same lesson God had recorded for His people of all ages long before: The day's portion in its day.

It was, without doubt, with a view to this and to meet man's weakness, that God graciously appointed the change of day and night. If time had been given to man in the form of one long unbroken day, it would have exhausted and overwhelmed him; the change of day and night continually recruits and recreates his powers. As a child, who easily makes himself master of a book, when each day only the lesson for the day is given him, would be utterly hopeless if the whole book were given him at once; so it would be with man, if there were no divisions in time. Broken small and divided into fragments, he can bear them; only the care and the work of each day have to be undertaken—the day's portion in its day. The rest of the night fits him for making a fresh start with each new morning; the mistakes of the past can be avoided, its lessons improved. And he has only each day to be faithful for the one short day, and long years and a long life take care of themselves, without the sense of their length or their weight ever being a burden.

Most sweet is the encouragement to be derived from this truth in the life of grace. Many a soul is disquieted with the thought as to how it will be able to gather and to keep the manna needed for all its years of travel through such a barren wilderness. It has never learnt what unspeakable comfort there is in the word: The day's portion for its day. That word takes away all care for the morrow most completely. Only to-day is yours; to-morrow is the Father's. The question: What security have you that during all the years in which you have to contend with the coldness, or temptations, or trials of the world, you will always abide in Jesus? is one you need, yea, you may not ask. Manna, as your food and strength, is given only by the day; faithfully to fill the present is your only security for the future. Accept, and enjoy, and fulfil with your whole heart the part you have this day to perform. His presence and grace enjoyed to-day will remove all doubt whether you can entrust the morrow to Him too.

How great the value which this truth teaches us to attach to each single day! We are so easily led to look at life as a great whole, and to neglect the little to-day, to forget that the single days do indeed make up the whole, and that the value of each single day depends on its influence on the whole. One day lost is a link broken in the chain, which it often takes more than another day to mend. One day lost influences the next, and makes its keeping more difficult. Yea, one day lost may be the loss of what months or years of careful labor had secured. The experience of many a believer could confirm this.

Believer! would you abide in Jesus, let it be day by day. You have already heard the message: Moment by moment; the lesson of day by day has something more to teach. Of the moments there are many where there is no direct exercise of the mind on your part; the abiding is in the deeper recesses of the heart, kept by the Father, to whom you entrusted yourself. But just this is the work that with each new day has to be renewed for the day—the distinct renewal of surrender and trust for the life of moment by moment. God has gathered up the moments and bound them up into a bundle, for the very purpose that we might take measure of them. As we look forward in the morning, or look back in the evening, and weigh the moments, we learn how to value and how to use them rightly. And even as the Father, with each new morning, meets you with the promise of just sufficient manna for the day for yourself and those who have to partake with you, meet Him with the bright and loving renewal of your acceptance of the position He has given you in His beloved Son. Accustom yourself to look upon this as one of the reasons for the appointment of day and night. God thought of our weakness, and sought to provide for it. Let each day have its value from your calling to abide in Christ. As its light opens on your waking eyes, accept it on these terms: A day, just one day only, but still a day, given to abide and grow up in Jesus Christ. Whether it be a day of health or sickness, joy or sorrow, rest or work, of struggle or victory, let the chief thought with which you receive it in the morning thanksgiving be this: "A day that the Father gave; in it I may, I must become more closely united to Jesus." As the Father asks, "Can you trust me just for this one day to keep you abiding in Jesus, and Jesus to keep you fruitful?" you cannot but give the joyful response: "I will trust and not be afraid."

The day's portion for its day was given to Israel in the morning very early. The portion was for use and nourishment during the whole day, but the giving and the getting of it was the morning's work. This suggests how greatly the power to spend a day aright, to abide all the day in Jesus, depends on the morning hour. If the first-fruits be holy, the lump is holy. During the day there come hours of intense occupation in the rush of business or the throng of men, when only the Father's keeping can maintain the connection with Jesus unbroken. The morning manna fed all the day; it is only when the believer in the morning secures his quiet time in secret to renew distinctly and effectually loving fellowship with his Savior, that the abiding can be kept up all the day. But what cause for thanksgiving that it may be done! In the morning, with its freshness and quiet, the believer can look out upon the day. He can consider its duties and its temptations, and pass them through beforehand, as it were, with his Savior, throwing all upon Him who has undertaken to be everything to him. Christ is his manna, his nourishment, his strength, his life: he can take the day's portion for the day, Christ as his for all the needs the day may bring, and go on in the assurance that the day will be one of blessing and of growth.

And then, as the lesson of the value and the work of the single day is being taken to heart, the learner is all unconsciously being led on to get the secret of "day by day continually" (Ex.29:38). The blessed abiding grasped by faith for each day apart is an unceasing and ever-increasing growth. Each day of faithfulness brings a blessing for the next; makes both the trust and the surrender easier and more blessed. And so the Christian life grows: as we give our whole heart to the work of each day, it becomes all the day, and from that every day. And so each day separately, all the day continually, day by day successively, we abide in Jesus. And the days make up the life: what once appeared too high and too great to attain, is given to the soul that was content to take and use "every day his portion" (Ezra 3:4), "as the duty of every day required." Even here on earth the voice is heard: "Well done, good and faithful servant, thou hast been faithful over few, I will make thee ruler over many: enter thou into the joy of thy Lord." Our daily life becomes a wonderful interchange of God's daily grace and our daily praise: "Daily He loadeth us with His benefits"; "that I may daily perform my vows." We learn to understand God's reason for daily giving, as He most certainly gives, only enough, but also fully enough, for each day. And we get into His way, the way of daily asking and expecting only enough, but most certainly fully enough, for the day. We begin to number our days not from the sun's rising over the world, or by the work we do or the food we eat, but the daily renewal of the miracle of the manna—the blessedness of daily fellowship with Him who is the Life and the Light of the world. The heavenly life is as unbroken and continuous as the earthly; the abiding in Christ each day has for that day brought its blessing; we abide in Him every day, and all the day. Lord, make this the portion of each one of us.

At this Moment

"Behold, now is the accepted time; behold, now is the day of salvation." 2 Cor 6:2

The thought of living moment by moment is of such central importance—looking at the abiding in Christ from our side—that we want once more to speak of it. And to all who desire to learn the blessed art of living only a moment at a time, we want to say: The way to learn it is to exercise yourself in living in the present moment. Each time your attention is free to occupy itself with the thought of Jesus—whether it be with time to think and pray, or only for a few passing seconds—let your first thought be to say: Now, at this moment, I do abide in Jesus. Use such time, not in vain regrets that you have not been abiding fully, or still more hurtful fears that you will not be able to abide, but just at once take the position the Father has given you: "I am in Christ; this is the place God has given me. I accept it; here I rest; I do now abide in Jesus." This is the way to learn to abide continually. You may be yet so feeble as to fear to say of each day, "I am abiding in Jesus"; but the feeblest can, each single moment, say, as he consents to occupy his place as a branch in the vine, "Yes, I do abide in Christ." It is not a matter of feeling—it is not a question of growth or strength in the Christian life—it is the simple question whether the will at the present moment desires and consents to recognize the place you have in your Lord, and to accept it. If you are a believer, you are in Christ. If you are in Christ, and wish to stay there, it is your duty to say, though it be but for a moment, "Blessed Savior, I abide in Thee now; Thou keepest me now."

It has been well said that in that little word now lies one of the deepest secrets of the life of faith. At the close of a conference on the spiritual life, a minister of experience rose and spoke. He did not know that he had learnt any truth he did not know before, but he had learnt how to use aright what he had known. He had learnt that it was his privilege at each moment, whatever surrounding circumstances might be, to say, "Jesus saves me now." This is indeed the secret of rest and victory. If I can say, "Jesus is to me at this moment all that God gave Him to be—life, and strength, and peace"—I have but as I say it to hold still, and rest, and realize it, and for that moment I have what I need. As my faith sees how of God I am in Christ, and takes the place in Him my Father has provided, my soul can peacefully settle down: Now I abide in Christ.

Believer! when striving to find the way to abide in Christ from moment to moment, remember that the gateway is: Abide in Him at this present moment. Instead of wasting effort in trying to get into a state that will last, just remember that it is Christ Himself, the living, loving Lord, who alone can keep you, and is waiting to do so. Begin at once and act faith in Him for the present moment: this is the only way to be kept the next. To attain the life of permanent and perfect abiding is not ordinarily given at once as a possession for the future: it comes mostly step by step. Avail yourself, therefore, of every opportunity of exercising the trust of the present moment. Each time you bow in prayer, let there first be an act of simple devotion: "Father, I am in Christ; I now abide in Him." Each time you have, amidst the bustle of duty, the opportunity of self-recollection, let its first involuntary act be: "I am still in Christ, abiding in Him now." Even when overtaken by sin, and the heart within is all disturbed and excited, O let your first look upwards be with the words: "Father, I have sinned; and yet I come—though I blush to say it—as one who is in Christ. Father! here I am; I can take no other place; of God I am in Christ; I now abide in Christ." Yes, Christian, in every possible circumstance, every moment of the day, the voice is calling: Abide in me, do it now. And even now, as you are reading this, O come at once and enter upon the blessed life of always abiding, by doing it at once: do it now.

In the life of David there is a beautiful passage which may help to make this thought clearer (2 Sam.3:17,18). David had been anointed king in Judah. The other tribes still followed Ish-bosheth, Saul's son. Abner, Saul's chief captain, resolves to lead the tribes of Israel to submit to David, the God-appointed king of the whole nation. He speaks to the elders of Israel: "Ye sought for David in times past to be king over you; now, then, do it, for Jehovah hath spoken of David, saying, By the hand of my servant David will I save my people Israel out of the hand of the Philistines, and out of the hand of all their enemies." And they did it, and anointed David a second time to be king, now over all Israel, as at first only over Judah (2 Sam.5:3)—a most instructive type of the way in which a soul is led to the life of entire surrender and undivided allegiance, to the full abiding.

First you have the divided kingdom: Judah faithful to the king of God's appointment; Israel still clinging to the king of its own choosing. As a consequence, the nation divided against itself, and no power to conquer the enemies. Picture of the divided heart. Jesus accepted as King in Judah, the place of the holy mount, in the inner chamber of the soul; but the surrounding territory, the every-day life, not yet brought to subjection; more than half the life still ruled by self-will and its hosts. And so no real peace within and no power over the enemies.

Then there is the longing desire for a better state: "Ye sought for David in times past to be king over you." There was a time, when David had conquered the Philistines, that Israel believed in him; but they had been led astray. Abner appeals to their own knowledge of God's will, that David must rule over all. So the believer, when first brought to Jesus, did indeed want Him to be Lord over all, had hoped that He alone would be King. But, alas! unbelief and self-will had come in, and Jesus could not assert His power over the whole life. And yet the Christian is not content. How he longs—sometimes without daring to hope that it can be—for a better time.

Then follows God's promise. Abner says: "The Lord hath spoken, By the hand of David I will save my people from the hand of all their enemies." He appeals to God's promise: as David had conquered the Philistines, the nearest enemy in time past, so he alone could conquer those farther off. He should save Israel from the hand of all their enemies. Beautiful type of the promise by which the soul is now invited to trust Jesus for the victory over every enemy, and a life of undisturbed fellowship. "The Lord hath spoken"—this is our only hope. On that word rests the sure expectation (Luke 1:70-75): "As He spake, That we should be saved from the hand of all that hate us, to perform the oath which He sware, that He would grant unto us that we, being delivered from the hand of our enemies, should serve Him without fear, in holiness and righteousness before Him, all the days of our life." David reigning over every corner of the land, and leading a united and obedient people on from victory to victory: this is the promise of what Jesus can do for us, as soon as in faith in God's promise all is surrendered to Him, and the whole life given up to be kept abiding in Him.

"Ye sought for David in times past to be king over you," spake Abner, and added, "Then do it now." Do it now is the message that this story brings to each one of us who longs to give Jesus unreserved supremacy. Whatever the present moment be, however unprepared the message finds you, however sad the divided and hopeless state of the life may be, still I come and urge Christ's claim to an immediate surrender—this very moment. I know well that it will take time for the blessed Lord to assert His power, and order all within you according to His will—to conquer the enemies and train all your powers for

His service. This is not the work of a moment. But there are things which are the work of a moment—of this moment. The one is—your surrender of all to Jesus; your surrender of yourself entirely to live only in Him. As time goes on, and exercise has made faith stronger and brighter, that surrender may become clearer and more intelligent. But for this no one may wait. The only way ever to attain to it is to begin at once. Do it now. Surrender yourself this very moment to abide wholly, only, always in Jesus. It is the work of a moment. And just so, Christ's renewed acceptance of you is the work of a moment. Be assured that He has you and holds you as His own, and that each new "Jesus, I do abide in Thee," meets with an immediate and most hearty response from the Unseen One. No act of faith can be in vain. He does indeed anew take hold on us and draw us close to Himself. Therefore, as often as the message comes, or the thought of it comes, Jesus says: Abide in me, do it at once. Each moment there is the whisper: Do it now.

Let any Christian begin, then, and he will speedily experience how the blessing of the present moment is passed on to the next. It is the unchanging Jesus to whom he links himself; it is the power of a divine life, in its unbroken continuity, that takes possession of him. The do it now of the present moment—a little thing though it seems—is nothing less than the beginning of the ever-present now, which is the mystery and the glory of eternity. Therefore, Christian, abide in Christ: do it now.

Forsaking All for Him

"I have suffered the loss of all things, and do count them but dung, that I may win Christ, and be found in him.—PHIL.3:8-9.

Wherever there is life, there is a continual interchange of taking in and giving out, receiving and restoring. The nourishment I take is given out again in the work I do; the impressions I receive, in the thoughts and feelings I express. The one depends on the other—the giving out ever increases the power of taking in. In the healthy exercise of giving and taking is all the enjoyment of life.

It is so in the spiritual life too. There are Christians who look on its blessedness as consisting all in the privilege of ever receiving; they know not how the capacity for receiving is only kept up and enlarged by continual giving up and giving out—how it is only in the emptiness that comes from the parting with what we have, that the divine fulness can flow in. It was a truth our Savior continually insisted on. When He spoke of selling all to secure the treasure, of losing our life to find it, of the hundred-fold to those who forsake all, He was expounding the need of self-sacrifice as the law of the Kingdom for Himself as well as for His disciples. If we are really to abide in Christ, and to be found in Him—to have our life always and wholly in Him—we must each in our measure say with Paul, "I count all things but loss for the excellency of the knowledge of Christ Jesus my Lord, that I may win Christ, and be *found in* Him."

Let us try and see what there is to be forsaken and given up. First of all, there is sin. There can be no true conversion without the giving up of sin. And yet, owing to the ignorance of the young convert of what really is sin, of what the claims of God's holiness are, and what the extent to which the power of Jesus can enable us to conquer sin, the giving up of sin is but partial and superficial. With the growth of the Christian life there comes the want of a deeper and more entire purging out of everything that is unholy. And it is specially when the desire to abide in Christ uninterruptedly, to be always found in Him, becomes strong, that the soul is led to see the need of a new act of surrender, in which it afresh accepts and ratifies its death to sin in Christ, and parts indeed with everything that is sin. Availing himself, in the strength of God's Spirit, of that wonderful power of our nature by which the whole of one's future life can be gathered up and disposed of in one act of the will, the believer yields himself to sin no more—to be only and wholly a servant of righteousness. He does it in the joyful assurance that every sin surrendered is gain indeed—room for the inflowing of the presence and the love of Christ.

Next to the parting with unrighteousness, is the giving up of self-righteousness. Though contending most earnestly against our own works or merits, it is often long before we come really to understand what it is to refuse self the least place or right in the service of God. Unconsciously we allow the actings of our own mind and heart and will free scope in God's presence. In prayer and worship, in Bible reading and working for God, instead of absolute dependence on the Holy Spirit's leading, self is expected to do a work it never can do. We are slow to learn the lesson, "In me, that is, in my flesh, dwelleth no good thing." As it is learnt, and we see how corruption extends to everything that is of nature, we see that there can be no entire abiding in Christ without the giving up of all that is of self in religion—without giving it up to the death, and waiting for the breathings of the Holy Spirit as alone able to work in us what is acceptable in God's sight.

Then, again, there is our whole natural life, with all the powers and endowments bestowed upon us by the Creator, with all the occupations and interests with which Providence has surrounded us. It is not enough that, when once you are truly converted, you have the earnest desire to have all these devoted to the service of the Lord. The desire is good, but can neither teach the way nor give the strength to do it acceptably. Incalculable harm has been done to the deeper spirituality of the Church, by the idea that when once we are God's children the using of our gifts in His service follows as a matter of course. No; for this there is indeed needed very special grace. And the way in which the grace comes is again that of sacrifice and surrender. I must see how all my gifts and powers are, even though I be a child of God, still defiled by sin, and under the power of the flesh. I must feel that I cannot at once proceed to use them for God's glory. I must first lay them at Christ's feet, to be accepted and cleansed by Him. I must feel myself utterly powerless to use them aright. I must see that they are most dangerous to me, because through them the flesh, the old nature, self, will so easily exert its power. In this conviction I must part with them, giving them entirely up to the Lord. When He has accepted them, and set His stamp upon them, I receive them back, to hold them as His property, to wait on Him for the grace to use them aright day by day, and to have them act only under His influence. And so experience proves it true here too, that the path of entire consecration is the path of full salvation. Not only is what is thus given up received back again to become doubly our own, but the forsaking all is followed by the receiving all. We abide in Christ more fully as we forsake all and follow Him. As I count all things loss for His sake, I am found *in* Him.

The same principle holds good of all the lawful occupations and possessions with which we are entrusted of God. Such were the fish-nets on the Sea of Galilee, and the household duties of Martha of Bethany—the home and the friends of many a one among Jesus' disciples. Jesus taught them in very deed to forsake all for Him. It was no arbitrary command, but the simple application of a law in nature to the Kingdom of His grace—that the more perfectly the old occupant is cast out, the more complete can be the possession of the new, and the more entire the renewal of all within.

This principle has a still deeper application. The truly spiritual gifts which are the working of God's own Holy Spirit within us—these surely need not be thus given up and surrendered? They do indeed; the interchange of giving up and taking in is a life process, and may not cease for a moment. No sooner does the believer begin to rejoice in the possession of what he has, than the inflow of new grace is retarded, and stagnation threatens. It is only into the thirst of an empty soul that the streams of living waters flow. Ever thirsting is the secret of never thirsting. Each blessed experience we receive as a gift of God, must at once be returned back to Him from whom it came, in praise and love, in self-sacrifice and service; so only can it be restored to us again, fresh and beautiful with the bloom of heaven. Is not this the wonderful lesson Isaac on Moriah teaches us? Was he not the son of promise, the God-given life, the wonder-gift of the omnipotence of Him who quickeneth the dead? (Rom.4:17). And yet even he had to be given up, and sacrificed. that he might be received back again a thousandfold more precious than before—a type of the Only-begotten of the Father, whose pure and holy life had to be given up ere He could receive it again in resurrection power, and could make His people partakers of it. A type, too, of what takes place in the life of each believer, as, instead of resting content with past experiences or present grace, he presses on, forgetting and giving up all that is behind, and reaches out to the fullest possible apprehension of Christ His life.

And such surrender of all for Christ, is it a single step, the act and experience of a moment, or is it a course of daily renewed and progressive attainment? It is both. There may be a moment in the life of a believer when he gets a first sight, or a deeper insight, of this most blessed truth, and when, made willing in the day of God's power, he does indeed, in an act of the will, gather up the whole of life yet before him into the decision of a moment, and lay himself on the altar a living and an acceptable sacrifice. Such moments have often been the blessed transition from a life of wandering and failure to a life of abiding and power divine. But even then his daily life becomes, what the life must be of each one who has no such experience, the unceasing prayer for more light on the meaning of entire surrender, the ever-renewed offering up of all he has to God.

Believer, would you abide in Christ, see here the blessed path. Nature shrinks back from such self-denial and crucifixion in its rigid application to our life in its whole extent. But what nature does not love and cannot perform, grace will accomplish, and make to you a life of joy and glory. Do you but yield up yourself to Christ your Lord; the conquering power of His incoming presence will make it joy to cast out all that before was most precious. "A hundredfold in this life": this word of the Master comes true to all who, with whole-hearted faithfulness, accept His commands to forsake all. The blessed receiving soon makes the giving up most blessed too. And the secret of a life of close abiding will be seen to be simply this: As I give myself wholly to Christ, I find the power to take Him wholly for myself; and as I lose myself and all I have for Him, He takes me wholly for Himself, and gives Himself wholly to me.

Through the Holy Spirit

"The anointing which ye have received of him, abideth in you; and even as it hath taught you, ye shall abide in him."—I JOHN 2:27.

How beautiful the thought of a life always abiding in Christ! The longer we think of it, the more attractive it becomes. And yet how often it is that the precious words, "Abide in me," are heard by the young disciple with a sigh! It is as if he understands so little what they really mean, and can realize so little how this full enjoyment can be attained. He longs for some one who could make it perfectly clear, and continually again remind him that the abiding is in very deed within his reach. If such an one would but listen to the word we have from John this day, what hope and joy it would bring! It gives us the divine assurance that we have the anointing of the Holy Spirit to teach us all things, also to teach us how to abide in Christ.

Alas! someone answers, this word does not give me comfort, it only depresses me more. For it tells of another privilege I so little know to enjoy: I do not understand how the teaching of the Spirit is given—where or how I can discern His voice. If the Teacher is so unknown, no wonder that the promise of His teaching about the abiding does not help me much.

Thoughts like these come from an error which is very common among believers. They imagine that the Spirit, in teaching them, must reveal the mysteries of the spiritual life first to their intellect, and afterwards in their experience. And God's way is just the contrary of this. What holds true of all spiritual truth is specially true of the abiding in Christ: We must live and experience truth in order to know it. Life-fellowship with Jesus is the only school for the science of heavenly things. "What I do, thou knowest not now, but thou shalt know hereafter," is a law of the Kingdom, specially true of the daily cleansing of which it first was spoken, and the daily keeping. Receive what you do not comprehend, submit to what you cannot understand, accept and expect what to reason appears a mystery, believe what looks impossible, walk in a way which you know not—such are the first lessons in the school of God. "If ye abide in my word, ye shall understand the truth": in these and other words of God we are taught that there is a habit of mind and life which precedes the understanding of the truth. True discipleship consists in first following, and then knowing the Lord. The believing surrender to Christ, and the submission to His word to expect what appears most improbable, is the only way to the full blessedness of knowing Him.

These principles hold specially good in regard to the teaching of the Spirit. That teaching consists in His guiding the spiritual life within us to that which God has prepared for us, without our always knowing how. On the strength of God's promise, and trusting in His faithfulness, the believer yields himself to the leading of the Holy Spirit, without claiming to have it first made clear to the intellect what He is to do, but consenting to let Him do His work in the soul, and afterwards to know what He has wrought there. Faith trusts the working of the Spirit unseen in the deep recesses of the inner life. And so the word of Christ and the gift of the Spirit are to the believer sufficient guarantee that He will be taught of the Spirit to abide in Christ. By faith he rejoices in what he does not see or feel: he knows, and is confident that the blessed Spirit within is doing His work silently but surely, guiding him into the life of full abiding and unbroken communion. The Holy Spirit is the Spirit of life in Christ Jesus; it is His work, not only to breathe, but ever to foster and strengthen, and so to perfect the new life within. And just in proportion as the believer yields himself in simple trust to the unseen, but most certain law of the Spirit of life working within him, his faith will pass into knowledge. It will be rewarded by the Spirit's light revealing in the Word what has already been wrought by the Spirit's power in the life.

Apply this now to the promise of the Spirit's teaching us to abide in Christ. The Holy Spirit is indeed the mighty power of God. And He comes to us from the heart of Christ, the bearer of Christ's life, the revealer and communicator of Christ Himself within us. In the expression, "the fellowship of the Spirit," we are taught what His highest work is. He is the bond of fellowship between the Father and the Son: by Him they are one. He is the bond of fellowship between all believers: by Him they are one. Above all, He is the bond of fellowship between Christ and believers ; He is the life-sap through which Vine and branch grow into real and living oneness: by Him we are one. And we can be assured of it, that if we do but believe in His presence and working, if we do but watch not to grieve Him, because we know that He is in us, if we wait and pray to be filled with Him, He will teach us how to abide. First guiding our will to a whole-hearted cleaving to Christ, then quickening our faith into ever larger confidence and expectation, then breathing into our hearts a peace and joy that pass understanding, He teaches us to abide, we scarce know how. Then coming through the heart and life into the understanding, He makes us know the truth—not as mere thought-truth, but as the truth which is in Christ Jesus, the reflection into the mind of the light of what He has already made a reality in the life. "The life was the light of men."

In view of such teaching, it is clear how, if we would have the Spirit to guide us into the abiding life, our first need is—quiet restful faith. Amid all the questions and difficulties that may come up in connection with our striving to abide in Christ—amid all the longing we may sometimes feel to have a Christian of experience to aid us—amid the frequent painful consciousness of failure, of ignorance, of helplessness—do let us hold fast the blessed confidence: We have the unction of the Holy One to teach us to abide in Him. "*The anointing* which ye have received of Him, *abideth in* you; and even as it hath taught you, *ye shall abide in* Him." Make this teaching of His in connection with the abiding a matter of special exercise of faith. Believe that as surely as you have part in Christ, you have His Spirit too. Believe that He will do His work with power, if only you do not hinder Him. Believe that He is working,even when you cannot discern it. Believe that He will work mightily if you ask this from the Father. It is impossible to live the life of full abiding without being full of the Holy Spirit; believe that the fulness of the Spirit is indeed your daily portion. Be sure and take time in prayer to dwell at the footstool of the throne of God and the Lamb, whence flows the river of the water of life. It is there, and only there, that you can be filled with the Spirit. Cultivate carefully the habit of daily, yea, continually honoring Him by the quiet, restful confidence that He is doing His work within. Let faith in His indwelling make you jealous of whatever could grieve Him—the spirit of the world or the actings of self and the flesh. Let that faith seek its nourishment in the Word and all it says of the Spirit, His power, His comfort, and His work. Above all, let that faith in the Spirit's indwelling lead you specially, to look away to Jesus; as we have received the anointing of Him, it comes in ever stronger flow from Him as we are occupied with Him alone. Christ is the Anointed One. As we look up to Him, the holy anointing comes, "the precious ointment upon the head of Aaron, that went down to the skirts of his garments." It is faith in Jesus that brings the anointing; the anointing leads to Jesus, and to the abiding in Him alone.

Believer, abide in Christ, in the power of the Spirit. What think you, ought the abiding longer to be a fear or a burden? Surely not. Oh, if we did but know the graciousness of our Holy Comforter, and the blessedness of wholly yielding ourselves to His leading, we should indeed experience the divine comfort of having such a teacher to secure our biding in Christ. The Holy Spirit was given for this one purpose—that the glorious redemption and life in Christ might with divine power be conveyed and communicated to us. We have the Holy Spirit to make the living Christ, in all His saving power, and in the completeness of His victory over sin, ever present within us. It is this that constitutes Him the Comforter: with Him we need never mourn an absent Christ. Let us therefore, as often as we read, or meditate, or pray in connection with this abiding in Christ, reckon upon it as a settled thing that we have the Spirit of God Himself within us, teaching, and guiding, and working. Let us rejoice in the confidence that we must succeed in our desires, because the Holy Spirit is working all the while with secret but divine power in the soul that does not hinder Him by its unbelief.

In Stillness of Soul

"In returning and rest shall ye be saved; in quietness and confidence shall be your strength."—Isaih 30:15

"Be silent to the Lord, and wait patiently for him."—Ps.37:7 (marg.)

"Truly my soul is silent unto God."—Ps.62:1 (marg.)

There is a view of the Christian life that regards it as a sort of partnership, in which God and man have each to do their part. It admits that it is but little that man can do, and that little defiled with sin; still he must do his utmost—then only can he expect God to do His part. To those who think thus, it is extremely difficult to understand what Scripture means when it speaks of our being still and doing nothing, of our resting and waiting to see the salvation of God. It appears to them a perfect contradiction, when we speak of this quietness and ceasing from all effort as the secret of the highest activity of man and all his powers. And yet this is just what Scripture does teach. The explanation of the apparent mystery is to be found in this, that when God and man are spoken of as working together, there is nothing of the idea of a partnership between two partners who each contribute their share to a work. The relation is a very different one. The true idea is that of cooperation founded on subordination. As Jesus was entirely dependent on the Father for all His words and all His works, so the believer can do nothing of himself. What he can do of himself is altogether sinful. He must therefore cease entirely from his own doing, and wait for the working of God in him. As he ceases from self-effort, faith assures him that God does what He has undertaken, and works in him. And what God does is to renew, to sanctify, and waken all his energies to their highest power. So that just in proportion as he yields himself a truly passive instrument in the hand of God, will he be wielded of God as the active instrument of His almighty power. The soul in which the wondrous combination of perfect passivity with the highest activity is most completely realized, has the deepest experience of what the Christian life is.

Among the lessons to be learnt of those who are studying the blessed art of abiding in Christ, there is none more needful and more profitable than this one of stillness of soul. In it alone can we cultivate that teachableness of spirit, to which the Lord will reveal His secrets—that meekness to which He shows His ways. It is the spirit exhibited so beautifully in all the three Marys: In her whose only answer to the most wonderful revelation ever made to human being was, "Behold the handmaid of the Lord; be it unto me according to Thy word"; and of whom, as mysteries multiplied around her, it is written: "Mary kept all these things and pondered them in her heart." And in her who "sat at Jesus' feet, and heard His word," and who showed, in the anointing Him for His burial, how she had entered more deeply into the mystery of His death than even the beloved disciple. And in her, too, who sought her Lord in the house of the Pharisee, with tears that spake more than words. It is a soul silent unto God that is the best preparation for knowing Jesus, and for holding fast the blessings He bestows. It is when the soul is hushed in silent awe and worship before the Holy Presence that reveals itself within, that the still small voice of the blessed Spirit will be heard.

Therefore, beloved Christian, as often as you seek to understand better the blessed mystery of abiding in Christ, let this be your first thought (Ps.62:5, marg.): "My soul, only be silent unto God; for my expectation is from Him." Do you in very deed hope to realize the wondrous union with the Heavenly Vine? Know that flesh and blood cannot reveal it unto you, but only the Father in heaven. "Cease from thine own wisdom." You have but to bow in the confession of your own ignorance and impotence; the Father will delight to give you the teaching of the Holy Spirit. If but your ear be open, and your thoughts brought into subjection, and your heart prepared in silence to wait upon God, and to hear what He speaks, He will reveal to you His secrets. And one of the first secrets will be the deeper insight into the truth, that as you sink low before Him in nothingness and helplessness, in a silence and a stillness of soul that seeks to catch the faintest whisper of His love, teachings will come to you which you had never heard before for the rush and noise of your own thoughts and efforts. You shall learn how your great work is to listen, and hear, and believe what He promises; to watch and wait and see what He does; and then, in faith, and worship, and obedience, to yield yourself to His working who works in you mightily.

One would think that no message could be more beautiful or welcome than this, that we may rest and be quiet, and that our God will work for us and in us. And yet how far this is from being the case! And how slow many are to learn that quietness is blessedness, that quietness is strength, that quietness is the source of the highest activity—the secret of all true abiding in Christ! Let us try to learn it, and to watch against whatever interferes with it. The dangers that threaten the soul's rest are not a few.

There is the dissipation of soul which comes from entering needlessly and too deeply into the interests of this world. Every one of us has his divine calling; and within the circle pointed out by God Himself, interest in our work and its surroundings is a duty. But even here the Christian needs to exercise watchfulness and sobriety. And still more do we need a holy temperance in regard to things not absolutely imposed upon us by God. If abiding in Christ really be our first aim, let us beware of all needless excitement. Let us watch even in lawful and necessary things against the wondrous power these have to keep the soul so occupied, that there remains but little power or zest for fellowship with God. Then there is the restlessness and worry that come of care and anxiety about earthly things; these eat away the life of trust, and keep the soul like a troubled sea. There the gentle whispers of the Holy Comforter cannot be heard.

No less hurtful is the spirit of fear and distrust in spiritual things; with its apprehensions and its efforts, it never comes really to hear what God has to say. Above all, there is the unrest that comes of seeking in our own way and in our own strength the spiritual blessing which comes alone from above. The heart occupied with its own plans and efforts for doing God's will, and securing the blessing of abiding in Jesus, must fail continually. God's work is hindered by our interference. He can do His work perfectly only when the soul ceases from its work. He will do His work mightily in the soul that honours Him by expecting Him to work both to will and to do.

And, last of all, even when the soul seeks truly to enter the way of faith, there is the impatience of the flesh, which forms its judgment of the life and progress of the soul not after the divine but the human standard.

In dealing with all this, and so much more, blessed the man who learns the lesson of stillness, and fully accepts God's word: "In quietness and confidence shall be your strength." Each time he listens to the word of the Father, or asks the Father to listen to his words, he dares not begin his Bible reading or prayer without first pausing and waiting, until the soul be hushed in the presence of the Eternal Majesty. Under a sense of the divine nearness, the soul, feeling how self is always ready to assert itself, and intrude even into the holiest of all with its thoughts and efforts, yields itself in a quiet act of self-surrender to the teaching and working of the divine Spirit. It is still and waits in holy silence, until all is calm and ready to receive the revelation of the divine will and presence. Its reading and prayer then indeed become a waiting on God with ear and heart opened and purged to receive fully only what He says.

"Abide in Christ!" Let no one think that he can do this if he has not daily his quiet time, his seasons of meditation and waiting on God. In these a habit of soul must be cultivated, in which the believer goes out into the world and its distractions, the peace of God, that passeth all understanding, keeping the heart and mind. It is in such a calm and restful soul that the life of faith can strike deep root, that the Holy Spirit can give His blessed teaching, that the Holy Father can accomplish His glorious work. May each one of us learn every day to say, "Truly my soul is silent unto God." And may every feeling of the difficulty of attaining this only lead us simply to look and trust to Him whose presence makes even the storm a calm. Cultivate the quietness as a means to the abiding in Christ; expect the ever deepening quietness and calm of heaven in the soul as the fruit of abiding in Him.

In Affliction and Trial

"Every branch that bearest fruit, he purgeth it, that it may bring forth more fruit."—JOHN 15:2.

In the whole plant world there is not a tree to be found so specially suited to the image of man in his relation to God, as the vine. There is none of which the fruit and its juice are so full of spirit, so quickening and stimulating. But there is also none of which the natural tendency is so entirely evil—none where the growth is so ready to run into wood that is utterly worthless except for the fire. Of all plants, not one needs the pruning knife so unsparingly and so unceasingly. None is so dependent on cultivation and training, but with this none yields a richer reward to the husbandman. In His wonderful parable, the Savior, with a single word, refers to this need of pruning in the vine, and the blessing it brings. But from that single word what streams of light pour in upon this dark world, so full of suffering and of sorrow to believers! What treasures of teaching and comfort to the bleeding branch in its hour of trial: "Every branch that beareth fruit, He purgeth it, that it may bring forth more fruit." And so He has prepared His people, who are so ready when trial comes to be shaken in their confidence, and to be moved from their abiding in Christ, to hear in each affliction the voice of a messenger that comes to call them to abide still more closely. Yes, believer, most specially in times of trial, abide in Christ.

Abide in Christ! This is indeed the Father's object in sending the trial. In the storm the tree strikes deeper roots in the soil; in the hurricane the inhabitants of the house abide within, and rejoice in its shelter. So by suffering the Father would lead us to enter more deeply into the love of Christ. Our hearts are continually prone to wander from Him; prosperity and enjoyment all too easily satisfy us, dull our spiritual perception, and unfit us for full communion with Himself. It is an unspeakable mercy that the Father comes with His chastisement, makes the world round us all dark and unattractive, leads us to feel more deeply our sinfulness, and for a time lose our joy in what was becoming so dangerous. He does it in the hope that, when we have found our rest in Christ in time of trouble, we shall learn to choose abiding in Him as our only portion; and when the affliction is removed, have so grown more firmly into Him, that in prosperity He still shall be our only joy. So much has He set His heart on this, that though He has indeed no pleasure in afflicting us, He will not keep back even the most painful chastisement if He can but thereby guide His beloved child to come home and abide in the beloved Son. Christian! pray for grace to see in every trouble, small or great, the Father's finger pointing to Jesus, and saying, Abide in Him.

Abide in Christ: so will you become partaker of all the rich blessings God designed for you in the affliction. The purposes of God's wisdom will become clear to you, your assurance of the unchangeable love become stronger, and the power of His Spirit fulfil you the promise: "He chasteneth us for our profit, that we might be partakers of His holiness." Abide in Christ: and your cross becomes the means of fellowship with His cross, and access into its mysteries—the mystery of the curse which He bore for you, of the death to sin in which you partake with Him, of the love in which, as sympathizing High Priest, He descended into all your sorrows. Abide in Christ: growing in conformity to your blessed Lord in His sufferings, deeper experience of the reality and the tenderness of His love will be yours. Abide in Christ: in the fiery oven, one like the Son of Man will be seen as never before; the purging away of the dross and the refining of the gold will be accomplished, and Christ's own likeness reflected in you. O abide in Christ: the power of the flesh will be mortified, the impatience and self-will of the old nature be humbled, to make place for the meekness and gentleness of Christ. A believer may pass through much affliction, and yet secure but little blessing from it all. Abiding in Christ is the secret of securing all that the Father meant the chastisement to bring us.

Abide in Christ: in Him you shall find sure and abundant consolation. With the afflicted comfort is often first, and the profit of the affliction second. The Father loves us so, that with Him our real and abiding profit is His first object, but He does not forget to comfort too. When He comforts it is that He may turn the bleeding heart to Himself to receive the blessing in fellowship with Him; when He refuses comfort, His object is still the same. It is in making us partakers of His holiness that true comfort comes. The Holy Spirit is the Comforter, not only because He can suggest comforting thoughts of God's love, but far more, because He makes us holy, and brings us into close union with Christ and with God. He teaches us to abide in Christ; and because God is found there, the truest comfort will come there too. In Christ the heart of the Father is revealed, and higher comfort there cannot be than to rest in the Father's bosom. In Him the fulness of the divine love is revealed, combined with the tenderness of a mother's compassion—and what can comfort like this? In Him you see a thousand times more given you than you have lost; see how God only took from you that you might have room to take from Him what is so much better. In Him suffering is consecrated, and becomes the foretaste of eternal glory; in suffering it is that the Spirit of God and of glory rests on us. Believer! would you have comfort in affliction?—Abide in Christ.

Abide in Christ: so will you bear much fruit. Not a vine is planted but the owner thinks of the fruit, and the fruit only. Other trees may be planted for ornament, for the shade, for the wood—the vine only for the fruit. And of each vine the husbandman is continually asking how it can bring forth more fruit, much fruit. Believer! abide in Christ in times of affliction, and you shall bring forth more fruit. The deeper experience of Christ's tenderness and the Father's love will urge you to live to His glory. The surrender of self and self-will in suffering will prepare you to sympathize with the misery of others, while the softening that comes of chastisement will fit you for becoming, as Jesus was, the servant of all. The thought of the Father's desire for fruit in the pruning will lead you to yield yourself afresh, and more than ever, to Him, and to say that now you have but one object in life—making known and conveying His wonderful love to fellow-men. You shall learn the blessed art of forgetting self, and, even in affliction, availing yourself of your separation from ordinary life to plead for the welfare of others. Dear Christian, in affliction abide in Christ. When you see it coming, meet it in Christ; when it is come, feel that you are more in Christ than in it, for He is nearer you than affliction ever can be; when it is passing, still abide in Him. And let the one thought of the Savior, as He speaks of the pruning, and the one desire of the Father, as He does the pruning, be yours too: "Every branch that beareth fruit, He purgeth, that it may bring forth more fruit."

So shall your times of affliction become your times of choicest blessing—preparation for richest fruitfulness. Led into closer fellowship with the Son of God, and deeper experience of His love and grace—established in the blessed confidence that He and you entirely belong to each other—more completely satisfied with Him and more wholly given up to Him than ever before—with your own will crucified afresh, and the heart brought into deeper harmony with God's will—you shall be a vessel cleansed, meet for the Master's use, prepared for every good work. True believer! O try and learn the blessed truth, that in affliction your first, your only, your blessed calling is to abide in Christ. Be much with Him alone. Beware of the comfort and the distractions that friends so often bring. Let Jesus Christ Himself be your chief companion and comforter. Delight yourself in the assurance that closer union with Him, and more abundant fruit through Him, are sure to be the results of trial, because it is the Husbandman Himself who is pruning, and will ensure the fulfilment of the desire of the soul that yields itself lovingly to His work.

That You May Bear Much Fruit

"He that abideth in me, and I in him, the same bringeth forth much fruit Herein is my Father glorified, that ye bear much fruit."—JOHN 15:5,8.

We all know what fruit is. The produce of the branch, by which men are refreshed and nourished. The fruit is not for the branch, but for those who come to carry it away. As soon as the fruit is ripe, the branch gives it off, to commence afresh its work of beneficence, and anew prepare its fruit for another season. A fruit-bearing tree lives not for itself, but wholly for those to whom its fruit brings refreshment and life. And so the branch exists only and entirely for the sake of the fruit. To make glad the heart of the husbandman is its object, its safety, and its glory.

Beautiful image of the believer, abiding in Christ! He not only grows in strength, the union with the Vine becoming ever surer and firmer, he also bears fruit, yea, much fruit. He has the power to offer that to others of which they can eat and live. Amid all who surround him he becomes like a tree of life, of which they can taste and be refreshed. He is in his circle a center of life and of blessing, and that simply because he abides in Christ, and receives from Him the Spirit and the life of which he can impart to others. Learn thus, if you would bless others, to abide in Christ, and that if you do abide, you shall surely bless. As surely as the branch abiding in a fruitful vine bears fruit, so surely, yea, much more surely, will a soul abiding in Christ with His fulness of blessing be made a blessing.

The reason of this is easily understood. If Christ, the heavenly Vine, has taken the believer as a branch, then He has pledged Himself, in the very nature of things, to supply the sap and spirit and nourishment to make it bring forth fruit. "From ME is thy fruit found": these words derive new meaning from our parable. The soul need but have one care—to abide closely, fully, wholly. He will give the fruit. He works all that is needed to make the believer a blessing.

Abiding in Him, you receive of Him His Spirit of love and compassion towards sinners, making you desirous to seek their good. By nature the heart is full of selfishness. Even in the believer, his own salvation and happiness are often too much his only object. But abiding in Jesus, you come into contact with His infinite love; its fire begins to burn within your heart; you see the beauty of love; you learn to look upon loving and serving and saving your fellow-men as the highest privilege a disciple of Jesus can have. Abiding in Christ, your heart learns to feel the wretchedness of the sinner still in darkness, and the fearfulness of the dishonor done to your God. With Christ you begin to bear the burden of souls, the burden of sins not your own. As you are more closely united to Him, somewhat of that passion for souls which urged Him to Calvary begins to breathe within you, and you are ready to follow His footsteps, to forsake the heaven of your own happiness, and devote your life to win the souls Christ has taught you to love. The very spirit of the Vine is love; the spirit of love streams into the branch that abides in Him.

The desire to be a blessing is but the beginning. As you undertake to work, you speedily become conscious of your own weakness and the difficulties in your way. Souls are not saved at your bidding. You are ready to be discouraged, and to relax your effort. But abiding in Christ, you receive new courage and strength for the work. Believing what Christ teaches, that it is *He* who through you will give His blessing to the world, you understand that you are but the feeble instrument through which the hidden power of Christ does its work, that His strength may be perfected and made glorious in your weakness. It is a great step when the believer fully consents to his own weakness, and the abiding consciousness of it, and so works faithfully on, fully assured that his Lord is working through him. He rejoices that the excellence of the power is of God, and not of us. Realizing his oneness with his Lord, he considers no longer his own weakness, but counts on the power of Him of whose hidden working within he is assured. It is this secret assurance that gives a brightness to his look, and a gentle firmness to his tone, and a perseverance to all his efforts, which of themselves are great means of influencing those he is seeking to win. He goes forth in the spirit of one to whom victory is assured; for this is the victory that overcometh, even our faith. He no longer counts it humility to say that God cannot bless his unworthy efforts. He claims and expects a blessing, because it is not he, but Christ in him, that worketh. The great secret of abiding in Christ is the deep conviction that we are nothing, and He is everything. As this is learnt, it no longer seems strange to believe that our weakness need be no hindrance to His saving power. The believer who yields himself wholly up to Christ for service in the spirit of a simple, childlike trust, will assuredly bring forth much fruit. He will not fear even to claim his share in the wonderful promise: "He that believeth on me, the works that I do shall he do also; and greater works than these shall he do, because I go to the Father." He no longer thinks that He cannot have a blessing, and must be kept unfruitful, that he may be kept humble. He sees that the most heavily laden branches bow the lowest down. Abiding in Christ, he has yielded assent to the blessed agreement between the Vine and the branches, that of the fruit all the glory shall be to the Husbandman, the blessed Father.

Let us learn two lessons. If we are abiding in Jesus, let us begin to work. Let us first seek to influence those around us in daily life. Let us accept distinctly and joyfully our holy calling, that we are even now to live as the servants of the love of Jesus to our fellow-men. Our daily life must have for its object the making of an impression favorable to Jesus. When you look at the branch, you see at once the likeness to the Vine. We must live so that somewhat of the holiness and the gentleness of Jesus may shine out in us. We must live to represent Him. As was the case with Him when on earth, the life must prepare the way for the teaching. What the Church and the world both need is this: men and women full of the Holy Ghost and of love, who, as the living embodiments of the grace and power of Christ, witness for Him, and for His power on behalf of those who believe in Him. Living so, with our hearts longing to have Jesus glorified in the souls He is seeking after, let us offer ourselves to Him for direct work. There is work in our own home. There is work among the sick, the poor, and the outcast. There is work in a hundred different paths which the Spirit of Christ opens up through those who allow themselves to be led by Him. There is work perhaps for us in ways that have not yet been opened up by others. Abiding in Christ, let us work. Let us work, not like those who are content if they now follow the fashion, and take some share in religious work. No; let us work as those who are growing more like Christ, because they are abiding in Him, and who, like Him, count the work of winning souls to the Father the very joy and glory of heaven begun on earth.

And the second lesson is: If you work, abide in Christ. This is one of the blessings of work if done in the right spirit—it will deepen your union with your blessed Lord. It will discover your weakness, and throw you back on His strength. It will stir you to much prayer; and in prayer for others is the time when the soul, forgetful of itself, unconsciously grows deeper into Christ. It will make clearer to you the true nature of branch-life; its absolute dependence, and at the same time its glorious sufficiency—independent of all else, because dependent on Jesus. If you work, abide in Christ. There are temptations and dangers. Work for Christ has sometimes drawn away from

Christ, and taken the place of fellowship with Him. Work can sometimes give a form of godliness without the power. As you work, abide in Christ. Let a living faith in Christ working in you be the secret spring of all your work; this will inspire at once humility and courage. Let the Holy Spirit of Jesus dwell in you as the Spirit of His tender compassion and His divine power. Abide in Christ, and offer every faculty of your nature freely and unreservedly to Him, to sanctify it for Himself. If Jesus Christ is really to work through us, it needs an entire consecration of ourselves to Him, daily renewed. But we understand now, just this is abiding in Christ; just this it is that constitutes our highest privilege and happiness. To be a branch bearing much fruit—nothing less, nothing more—be this our only joy.

So Will You Have Power in Prayer

"If ye abide in me, and my words abide in you, ye shall ask what ye will, and it shall be done unto you. "— JOHN 15:7.

Prayer is both one of the means and one of the fruits of union to Christ. As a means it is of unspeakable importance. All the things of faith, all the pleadings of desire, all the yearnings after a fuller surrender, all the confessions of shortcoming and of sin, all the exercises in which the soul gives up self and clings to Christ, find their utterance in prayer. In each meditation on abiding in Christ, as some new feature of what Scripture teaches concerning this blessed life is apprehended, the first impulse of the believer is at once to look up to the Father and pour out the heart into His, and ask from Him the full understanding and the full possession of what he has been shown in the Word. And it is the believer, who is not content with this spontaneous expression of his hope, but who takes time in secret prayer to wait until he has received and laid hold of what he has seen, who will really grow strong in Christ. However feeble the soul's first abiding, its prayer will be heard, and it will find prayer one of the great means of abiding more abundantly.

But it is not so much as a means, but as a fruit of the abiding, that the Savior mentions it in the parable of the Vine. He does not think so much of prayer—as we, alas! too exclusively do—as a means of getting blessing for ourselves, but as one of the chief channels of influence by which, through us as fellow-workers with God, the blessings of Christ's redemption are to be dispensed to the world. He sets before Himself and us the glory of the Father, in the extension of His Kingdom, as the object for which we have been made branches; and He assures us that if we but abide in Him, we shall be Israels, having power with God and man. Ours shall be the effectual, fervent prayer of the righteous man, availing much, like Elijah's for ungodly Israel. Such prayer will be the fruit of our abiding in Him, and the means of bringing forth much fruit.

To the Christian who is not abiding wholly in Jesus, the difficulties connected with prayer are often so great as to rob him of the comfort and the strength it could bring. Under the guise of humility, he asks how one so unworthy could expect to have influence with the Holy One. He thinks of God's sovereignty, His perfect wisdom and love, and cannot see how his prayer can really have any distinct effect. He prays, but it is more because he cannot rest without prayer, than from a loving faith that the prayer will be heard. But what a blessed release from such questions and perplexities is given to the soul who is truly abiding in Christ! He realizes increasingly how it is in the real spiritual unity with Christ that we are accepted and heard. The union with the Son of God is a life union: we are in very deed one with Him—our prayer ascends as His prayer. It is because we abide in Him that we can ask what we will, and it is given to us.

There are many reasons why this must be so. One is, that abiding in Christ, and having His words abiding in us, teach us to pray in accordance with the will of God. With the abiding in Christ our self-will is kept down, the thoughts and wishes of nature are brought into captivity to the thoughts and wishes of Christ; like-mindedness to Christ grows upon us—all our working and willing become transformed into harmony with His. There is deep and oft-renewed heart-searching to see whether the surrender has indeed been entire; fervent prayer to the heart-searching Spirit that nothing may be kept back. Everything is yielded to the power of His life in us, that it may exercise its sanctifying influence even on ordinary wishes and desires. His Holy Spirit breathes through our whole being; and without our being conscious how, our desires, as the breathings of the divine life, are in conformity with the divine will, and are fulfilled. Abiding in Christ renews and sanctifies the will: we ask what we will, and it is given to us.

In close connection with this is the thought, that the abiding in Christ teaches the believer in prayer only to seek the glory of God. In promising to answer prayer, Christ's one thought (see John 14:13) is this, "that the Father may be glorified in the Son." In His intercession on earth (John 17), this was His one desire and plea; in His intercession in heaven, it is still His great object. As the believer abides in Christ, the Savior breathes this desire into him. The thought, *Only the Glory of God*, becomes more and more the keynote of the life hid in Christ. At first this subdues, and quiets, and makes the soul almost afraid to dare entertain a wish, lest it should not be to the Father's glory. But when once its supremacy has been accepted, and everything yielded to it, it comes with mighty power to elevate and enlarge the heart, and open it to the vast field open to the glory of God. Abiding in

Christ, the soul learns not only to desire, but spiritually to discern what will be for God's glory; and one of the first conditions of acceptable prayer is fulfilled in it when, as the fruit of its union with Christ, the whole mind is brought into harmony with that of the Son as He said: "Father, glorify Thy name."

Once more: Abiding in Christ, we can fully avail ourselves of the name of Christ. Asking in the name of another means that that other authorized me and sent me to ask, and wants to be considered as asking himself: he wants the favor done to him. Believers often try to think of the name of Jesus and His merits, and to argue themselves into the faith that they will be heard, while they painfully feel how little they have of the faith of His name. They are not living wholly in Jesus' name; it is only when they begin to pray that they want to take up that name and use it. This cannot be. The promise "Whatsoever ye ask in my name," may not be severed from the command, "Whatsoever ye do, do all in the name of the Lord Jesus." If the name of Christ is to be wholly at my disposal, so that I may have the full command of it for all I will, it must be because I first put myself wholly at His disposal, so that He has free and full command of me. It is the abiding in Christ that gives the right and power to use His name with confidence. To Christ the Father refuses nothing. Abiding in Christ, I come to the Father as one with Him. His righteousness is in me, His Spirit is in me; the Father sees the Son in me, and gives me my petition. It is not—as so many think—by a sort of imputation that the Father looks upon us as if we were in Christ, though we are not in Him. No; the Father wants to see us living in Him: thus shall our prayer really have power to prevail. Abiding in Christ not only renews the will to pray aright, but secures the full power of His merits to us.

Again: Abiding in Christ also works in us the faith that alone can obtain an answer. "According to your faith be it unto you": this is one of the laws of the kingdom. "Believe that ye receive, and ye shall have." This faith rests upon, and is rooted in the Word, but is something infinitely higher than the mere logical conclusion: God has promised, I shall obtain. No; faith, as a spiritual act, depends upon the words abiding in us as living powers, and so upon the state of the whole inner life. Without fasting and prayer (Mark 9:29), without humility and a spiritual mind (John 5:44), without a wholehearted obedience (1 John 3:22), there cannot be this living faith. But as the soul abides in Christ, and grows into the consciousness of its union with Him, and sees how entirely it is He who makes it and its petition acceptable, it dares to claim an answer because it knows itself one with Him. It was by faith it learnt to abide in Him; as the fruit of that faith, it rises to a larger faith in all that God has promised to be and to do. It learns to breathe its prayers in the deep, quiet, confident assurance: We know we have the petition we ask of Him.

Abiding in Christ, further, keeps us in the place where the answer can be bestowed. Some believers pray earnestly for blessing; but when God comes and looks for them to bless them, they are not to be found. They never thought that the blessing must not only be asked, but waited for, and received in prayer. Abiding in Christ is the place for receiving answers. Out of Him the answer would be dangerous—we should consume it on our lusts (Jas. 4:3). Many of the richest answers—say for spiritual grace, or for power to work and to bless—can only come in the shape of a larger experience of what God makes Christ to us. The fulness is *in* Him; abiding in Him is the condition of power in prayer, because the answer is treasured up and bestowed in Him.

Believer, abide in Christ, for there is the school of prayer—mighty, effectual, answer-bringing prayer. Abide in Him, and you shall learn what to so many is a mystery: That the secret of the prayer of faith is the life of faith—the life that abides in Christ alone.

And in His Love

"As the Father hath loved me, so have I loved you: abide ye in my love.' —John 15:9.[1]

Blessed Lord, enlighten our eyes to see aright the glory of this wondrous word. Open to our meditation the secret chamber of *thy love*, that our souls may enter in, and find there their everlasting dwelling-place. How else shall we know aught of a love that passeth knowledge?

Before the Savior speaks the word that invites us to abide in His love, He first tells us what that love is. What He says of it must give force to His invitation, and make the thought of not accepting it an impossibility: "As the Father hath loved me, so I have loved you!"

"As the Father hath loved me." How shall we be able to form right conceptions of this love? Lord, teach us. God is love. Love is His very being. Love is not an attribute, but the very essence of His nature, the center round which all His glorious attributes gather. It was because He was love that He was the Father, and that there was a Son. Love needs an object to whom it can give itself away, in whom it can lose itself, with whom it can make itself one. Because God is love, there must be a Father and a Son. The love of the Father to the Son is that divine passion with which He delights in the Son, and speaks, "My beloved Son, in whom I am well pleased." The divine love is as a burning fire; in all its intensity and infinity it has but one object and but one joy, and that is the only-begotten Son. When we gather together all the attributes of God—His infinity, His perfection, His immensity, His majesty, His omnipotence—and consider them but as the rays of the glory of His love, we still fail in forming any conception of what that love must be. It is a love that passeth knowledge.

And yet this love of God to His Son must serve, O my soul, as the glass in which you are to learn how Jesus loves you. As one of His redeemed ones, you are His delight, and all His desire is to you, with the longing of a love which is stronger than death, and which many waters cannot quench. His heart yearns after you, seeking your fellowship and your love. Were it needed,

He could die again to possess you. As the Father loved the Son, and could not live without Him, could not be God the blessed without Him—so Jesus loves you. His life is bound up in yours; you are to Him inexpressibly more indispensable and precious than you ever can know. You are one with Himself. "As the Father hath loved me, so have I loved you." What a love!

It is an eternal love. From before the foundation of the world-God's Word teaches us this—the purpose had been formed that Christ should be the Head of His Church, that He should have a body in which His glory could be set forth. In that eternity He loved and longed for those who had been given Him by the Father; and when He came and told His disciples that He loved them, it was indeed not with a love of earth and of time, but with the love of eternity. And it is with that same infinite love that His eye still rests upon each of us here seeking to abide in Him, and in each breathing of that love there is indeed the power of eternity. "I have loved thee with an everlasting love."

It is a perfect love. It gives all, and holds nothing back. "The Father loveth the Son, and hath given all things into His hand." And just so Jesus loves His own: all He has is theirs. When it was needed, He sacrificed His throne and crown for you: He did not count His own life and blood too dear to give for you. His righteousness, His Spirit, His glory, even His throne, all are yours. This love holds nothing, nothing back, but, in a manner which no human mind can fathom, makes you one with itself. O wondrous love! to love us even as the Father loved Him, and to offer us this love as our everyday dwelling.

It is a gentle and most tender love. As we think of the love of the Father to the Son, we see in the Son everything so infinitely worthy of that love. When we think of Christ's love to us, there is nothing but sin and unworthiness to meet the eye. And the question comes: How can that love within the bosom of the divine life and its perfections be compared to the love that rests on sinners? Can it indeed be the same love? Blessed be God, we know it is so. The nature of love is always one, however different the objects. Christ knows of no other law of love but that with which His Father loved Him. Our wretchedness only serves to call out more distinctly the beauty of love, such as could not be seen even in heaven. With the tenderest compassion He bows to our weakness, with patience inconceivable He bears with our slowness, with the gentlest loving-kindness He meets our fears and our follies. It is the love of the Father to the Son, beautified, glorified, in its condescension, in its exquisite adaptation to our needs.

And it is an unchangeable love. "Having loved His own which were in the world, He loved them to the end." "The mountains shall depart, and the hills be removed, but my kindness shall not depart from thee." The promise with which it begins its work in the soul is this: "I shall not leave thee, until I have done that which I have spoken to thee of." And just as our wretchedness was what first drew it to us, so the sin, with which it is so often grieved, and which may well cause us to fear and doubt, is but a new motive for it to hold to us all the more. And why? We can give no reason but this: "As the Father hath loved me, so I have loved you."

And now, does not this love suggest the motive, the measure, and the means of that surrender by which we yield ourselves wholly to abide in Him?

This love surely supplies a motive. Only look and see how this love stands and pleads and prays. Gaze, O gaze on the divine form, the eternal glory, the heavenly beauty, the tenderly pleading gentleness of the crucified love, as it stretches out its pierced hands and says, "Oh, wilt thou not abide with me? wilt thou not come and abide in me?" It points you up to the eternity of love whence it came to seek you. It points you to the Cross, and all it has borne to prove the reality of its affection, and to win you for itself. It reminds you of all it has promised to do for you, if you will but throw yourself unreservedly into its arms. It asks you whether, so far as you have come to dwell with it and taste its blessedness, it has not done well by you. And with a divine authority, mingled with such an inexpressible tenderness that one might almost think he heard the tone of reproach in it, it says, "Soul, as the Father hath loved me, so I have loved you: abide in my love." Surely there can be but one answer to such pleading: Lord Jesus Christ! here I am. Henceforth Thy love shall be the only home of my soul: in Thy love alone will I abide.

That love is not only the motive, but also the measure, of our surrender to abide in it. Love gives all, but asks all. It does so, not because it grudges us aught, but because without this it cannot get possession of us to fill us with itself. In the love of the Father and the Son, it was so. In the love of Jesus to us, it was so. In our entering into His love to abide there, it must be so too; our surrender to it must have no other measure than its surrender to us. O that we understood how the love that calls us has infinite riches and fulness of joy for us, and that what we give up for its sake will be rewarded a hundredfold in this life! Or rather, would that we understood that it is a *love* with a height and a depth and a length and a breadth that passes knowledge! How all thought of sacrifice or surrender would pass away, and our souls be filled with wonder at the unspeakable privilege of being loved with such a love, of being allowed to come and abide in it for ever.

And if doubt again suggest the question: But is it possible, can I always abide in His love? listen how that love itself supplies the only means for the abiding in Him: It is faith in that love which will enable us to abide in it. If this love be indeed so divine, such an intense and burning passion, then surely I can depend on it to keep me and to hold me fast. Then surely all my unworthiness and feebleness can be no hindrance. If this love be indeed so divine, with infinite power at its command, I surely have a right to trust that it is stronger than my weakness; and that with its almighty arm it will clasp me to its bosom, and suffer me to go out no more. I see how this is the one thing my God requires of me. Treating me as a reasonable being endowed with the wondrous power of willing and choosing, He cannot force all this blessedness on me, but waits till I give the willing consent of the heart. And the token of this consent He has in His great kindness ordered faith to be—that faith by which utter sinfulness casts itself into the arms of love to be saved, and utter weakness to be kept and made strong. O Infinite Love! Love with which the Father loved the Son! Love with which the Son loves us! I can trust thee, I do trust thee. O keep me abiding in Thyself.

[1] It is difficult to understand why in our English Bible one Greek word should in the first sixteen verses of John 15 have had three different translations: abide in ver. 4, continue in ver. 9, and remain in vers. 11 and 16. The Revised Version has of course kept the one word, abide.

As Christ in the Father

"As the Father hath loved me, so I have loved you. Abide in my love, even as I abide in my Father's love."—JOHN 15:9,10.

Christ had taught His disciples that to abide in Him was to abide in His love. The hour of His suffering is nigh, and He cannot speak much more to them. They doubtless have many questions to ask as to what that abiding in Him and His love is. He anticipates and meets their wishes, and gives them *his own life* as the best exposition of His command. As example and rule for their abiding in His love, they have to look to His abiding in the Father's love. In the light of His union with the Father, their union with Him will become clear. His life in the Father is the law of their life in Him.

The thought is so high that we can hardly take it in, and is yet so clearly revealed, that we dare not neglect it. Do we not read in John 6 (ver.57), "As I live by the Father, even so he that eateth me, he shall live by me"? And the Savior prays so distinctly (John 17:22), "that they may be one even as we are one: I in them, and Thou in me." The blessed union of Christ with the Father and His life in Him is the only rule of our thoughts and expectations in regard to our living and abiding in Him.

Think first of the origin of that life of Christ in the Father. They were *one*—one in life and one in love. In this His abiding in the Father had its root. Though dwelling here on earth, He knew that He was one with the Father; that the Father's life was in Him, and His love on Him. Without this knowledge, abiding in the Father and His love would have been utterly impossible. And it is thus only that you can abide in Christ and His love. Know that you are one with Him—one in the unity of nature. By His birth He became man, and took your nature that He might be one with you. By your new birth you become one with Him, and are made partaker of His divine nature. The link that binds you to Him is as real and close as bound Him to the Father—the link of a divine life. Your claim on Him is as sure and always availing as was His on the Father. Your union with Him is as close.

And as it is the union of a divine life, it is one of an infinite love. In His life of humiliation on earth He tasted the blessedness and strength of knowing Himself the object of an infinite love, and of dwelling in it all the day; from His own example He invites you to learn that herein lies the secret of rest and joy. You are one with Him: yield yourself now to be loved by Him; let your eyes and heart open to the love that shines and presses in on you on every side. Abide in His love.

Think then too of the mode of that abiding in the Father and His love which is to be the law of your life. "I kept my Father's commandments and abide in His love." His was a life of subjection and dependence and yet most blessed. To our proud self-seeking nature the thought of dependence and subjection suggests the idea of humiliation and servitude; in the life of love which the Son of God lived, and to which He invite us, they are the secret of blessedness. The Son is not afraid of losing aught by giving up all to the Father, for He knows that the Father loves Him, and can have no interest apart from that of the beloved Son. He knows that as complete as is the dependence on His part is the communication on the part of the Father of all He possesses. Hence when He had said, "The Son can do nothing of Himself, except He see the Father do it," He adds at once, "Whatsoever things the Father doeth, them also doeth the Son likewise: for the Father loveth the Son, and showeth Him all things that Himself doeth." The believer who studies this life of Christ as the pattern and the promise of what his may be, learns to understand how the "Without me ye can do nothing," is but the forerunner of "I can do all things through Christ who strengtheneth me." We learn to glory in infirmities, to take pleasure in necessities and distresses for Christ's sake; for "when I am weak, then am I strong." He rises above the ordinary tone in which so many Christians speak of their weakness, while they are content to abide there, because he has learnt from Christ that in the life of divine love the emptying of self and the sacrifice of our will is the surest way to have all we can wish or will. Dependence, subjection, self-sacrifice, are for the Christian as for Christ the blessed path of life. Like as Christ lived through and in the Father, even so the believer lives through and in Christ.

Think of the glory of this life of Christ in the Father's love. Because He gave Himself wholly to the Father's will and glory, the Father crowned Him with glory and honor. He acknowledged Him as His only representative; He made Him partaker of His power and authority; He exalted Him to share His throne as God. And even so will it be with him who abides in Christ's love. If Christ finds us willing to trust ourselves and our interests to His love, if in that trust we give up all care for our own will and honor, if we make it our glory to exercise and confess absolute dependence on Him in all things, if we are content to have no life but in Him, He will do for us what the Father did for Him. He will lay of His glory on us: As the name of our Lord is Jesus is glorified in us, we are glorified in Him (2 Thess.1:12). He acknowledges us as His true and worthy representatives; He entrusts us with His power; He admits us to His counsels, as He allows our intercession to influence His rule of His Church and the world; He makes us the vehicles of His authority and His influence over men. His Spirit knows no other dwelling than such, and seeks no other instruments for His divine work. Blessed life of love for the soul that abides in Christ's love, even as He in the Father's!

Believer! abide in the love of Christ. Take and study His relation to the Father as pledge of what thine own can become. As blessed, as mighty, as glorious as was His life in the Father, can yours be in Him. Let this truth, accepted under the teaching of the Spirit in faith, remove every vestige of fear, as if abiding in Christ were a burden and a work. In the light of His life in the Father, let it henceforth be to you a blessed rest in the union with Him, an overflowing fountain of joy and strength. To abide in His love, His mighty, saving, keeping, satisfying love, even as He abode in the Father's love—surely the very greatness of our calling teaches us that it never can be a work we have to perform; it must be with us as with Him, the result of the spontaneous outflowing of a life from within, and the mighty inworking of the love from above. What we only need is this: to take time and study the divine image of this life of love set before us in Christ. We need to have our souls still unto God, gazing upon that life of Christ in the Father until the light from heaven falls on it, and we hear the living voice of our Beloved whispering gently to us personally the teaching He gave to the disciples. Soul, be still and listen; let every thought be hushed until the word has entered your heart too: "Child! I love thee, even as the Father loved me. Abide in my love, even as I abide in the Father's love. Thy life on earth in me is to be the perfect counterpart of mine in the Father."

And if the thought will sometimes come: Surely this is too high for us; can it be really true? only remember that the greatness of the privilege is justified by the greatness of the object He has in view. Christ was the revelation of the Father on earth. He could not be this if there were not the most perfect unity, the most complete communication of all the Father had to the Son. He could be it because the Father loved Him, and He abode in that love. Believers are the revelation of Christ on earth. They cannot be this unless there be perfect unity, so that the world can know that He loves them and has sent them. But they can be it if Christ loves them with the infinite love that gives itself and all it has, and if they abide in that love.

Lord, show us Thy love. Make us with all the saints to know the love that passeth knowledge. Lord, show us in Thine own blessed life what it is to abide in Thy love. And the sight shall so win us, that it will be impossible for us one single hour to seek any other life than the life of abiding in Thy love.

Obeying His Commandments

"If ye keep my commandments, ye shall abide in my love; even as I kept my Father's commandments, and abide in his love."—JOHN 15:10.

How clearly we are taught here the place which good works are to occupy in the life of the believer! Christ as the beloved Son was in the Father's love. He kept His commandments, and so He abode in the love. So the believer, without works, receives Christ and is in Him; he keeps the commandments, and so abides in the love. When the sinner, in coming to Christ, seeks to prepare himself by works, the voice of the Gospel sounds, "Not of works." When once in Christ, lest the flesh should abuse the word, "Not of works," the Gospel lifts its voice as loud: "Created in Christ Jesus unto good works" (see Eph.2:9,10). To the sinner out of Christ, works may be his greatest hindrance, keeping him from the union with the Savior. To the believer in Christ, works are strength and blessing, for by them faith is made perfect (Jas.2:22), the union with Christ is cemented, and the soul established and more deeply rooted in the love of God. "If a man love me, he will keep my words, and my Father will love him." "If ye keep my commandments, ye shall abide in my love."

The connection between this keeping the commandments and the abiding in Christ's love is easily understood. Our union with Jesus Christ is not a thing of the intellect or sentiment, but a real vital union in heart and life. The holy life of Jesus, with His feelings and. disposition, is breathed into us by the Holy Spirit. The believer's calling is to think and feel and will just what Jesus thought and felt and willed. He desires to be partaker not only of the grace but also of the holiness of His Lord; or rather, he sees that holiness is the chief beauty of grace. To live the life of Christ means to him to be delivered from the life of self; the will of Christ is to him the only path of liberty from the slavery of his own evil self-will.

To the ignorant or slothful believer there is a great difference between the promises and commands of Scripture. The former he counts his comfort and his food; but to him who is really seeking to abide in Christ's love, the commands become no less precious, As much as the promises they are the revelation of the divine love, guides into the deeper experience of the divine life, blessed helpers in the path to a closer union with the Lord. He sees how the harmony of our will with His will is one of the chief elements of our fellowship with Him. The will is the central faculty in the Divine as in the human being. The will of God is the power that rules the whole moral as well as the natural world. How could there be fellowship with Him without delight in His will? It is only as long as salvation is to the sinner nothing but a personal safety, that he can be careless or afraid of the doing of God's will. No sooner is it to him what Scripture and the Holy Spirit reveal it to be—the restoration to communion with God and conformity to Him—than he feels that there is no law more natural or more beautiful than this: Keeping Christ's commandments the way to abide in Christ's love. His inmost soul approves when he hears the beloved Lord make the larger measure of the Spirit, with the manifestation of the Father and the Son in the believer, entirely dependent upon the keeping of His commandments (John 14:15,16,21,23).

There is another thing that opens to him a deeper insight and Secures a still more cordial acceptance of this truth. It is this, that in no other way did Christ Himself abide in the Father's love. In the life which Christ led upon earth, obedience was a solemn reality. The dark and awful power that led man to revolt from his God, came upon Him too, to tempt Him. To Him as man its offers of self-gratification were not matters of indifference; to refuse them, He had to fast and pray. He suffered, being tempted. He spoke very distinctly of not seeking to do His own will, as a surrender He had continually to make. He made the keeping of the Father's commandments the distinct object of His life, and so abode in His love. Does He not tell us, "I do nothing of myself, but as the Father taught me, I speak these things. And He that sent me is with me; He hath not left me alone; for I do always the things that are pleasing to Him." He thus opened to us the only path to the blessedness of a life on earth in the love of heaven; and when, as from our vine, His Spirit flows in the branches, this keeping the commands is one of the surest and highest elements of the life He inspires.

Believer! would you abide in Jesus, be very careful to keep His commandments. Keep them in the love of your heart. Be not content to have them in the Bible for reference, but have them transferred by careful study, by meditation and by prayer, by a loving acceptance, by the Spirit's teaching, to the fleshy tables of the heart. Be not content with the knowledge of some of the commands, those most commonly received among Christians, while others lie unknown and neglected. Surely, with your New Covenant privileges, you would not be behind the Old Testament saints who spoke so fervently: "I esteem all thy precepts concerning all things to be right." Be assured that there is still much of your Lord's will that you do not yet understand. Make Paul's prayer for the Colossians yours for yourself and all believers, "that you might be filled with the knowledge of His will in all wisdom and spiritual understanding"; and that of wrestling Epaphras, "that you may stand perfect and complete in all the will of God." Remember that this is one of the great elements of spiritual growth—a deeper insight into the will of God concerning you. Imagine not that entire consecration is the end—it is only the beginning—of the truly holy life. See how Paul, after having (Rom. 12:1) taught believers to lay themselves upon the altar, whole and holy burnt-offerings to their God, at once proceeds (ver. 2) to tell them what the true—altar-life is: being ever more and more "renewed in their mind to prove what is the good and perfect and acceptable will of God." The progressive renewal of the Holy Spirit leads to growing like-mindedness to Christ; then comes a delicate power of spiritual perception—a holy instinct—by which the soul "quick of understanding (marg. quick of scent) in the fear of the Lord," knows to recognize the meaning and the application of the Lord's commands to daily life in a way that remains hidden to the ordinary Christian. Keep them dwelling richly within you, hide them within your heart, and you shall taste the blessedness of the man whose "delight is in the law of the Lord, and in His law doth he meditate day and night." Love will assimilate into your inmost being the commands as food from heaven. They will no longer come to you as a law standing outside and against you, but as the living power which has transformed your will into perfect harmony with all your Lord requires.

And keep them in the obedience of your life. It has been your solemn vow—has it not?—no longer to tolerate even a single sin: "I have sworn, and I will perform it, that I will keep Thy righteous judgments." Labor earnestly in prayer to stand perfect and complete in all the will of God. Ask earnestly for the discovery of every secret sin—of anything that is not in perfect harmony with the will of God. Walk up to the light you have faithfully and tenderly, yielding yourself in an unreserved surrender to obey all that the Lord has spoken. When Israel took that vow (Exodus 19:8, 24:7), it was only to break it all too soon. The New Covenant gives the grace to make the vow and to keep it too (Jer.31). Be careful of disobedience even in little things. Disobedience dulls the conscience, darkens the soul, deadens our spiritual energies—therefore keep the commandments of Christ with implicit obedience. Be a soldier that asks for nothing but the orders of the commander.

And if even for a moment the commandments appear grievous, just remember whose they are. They are the commandments of Him who loves you. They are all love, they come from His love, they lead to His love. Each new surrender to keep the commandments, each new sacrifice in keeping them, leads to deeper union with the will, the spirit, and the love of the Savior. The double recompense of reward shall be yours—a fuller entrance into the mystery of His love—a fuller conformity to His own blessed life. And you shall learn to prize these words as among your choicest treasures: "If ye keep my commandments, ye shall abide in my love, *even as* I have kept my Father's commandments and abide in His love."

That Your Joy May Be Full

"These things have I spoken unto you, that my joy might abide in you, and that your joy might be full." —JOHN 15:11

Abiding fully in Christ is a life of exquisite and overflowing happiness. As Christ gets more complete possession of the soul, it enters into the joy of its Lord. His own joy, the joy of heaven, becomes its own, and that in full measure, and as an ever-abiding portion. Just as joy on earth is everywhere connected with the vine and its fruit, so joy is an essential characteristic of the life of the believer who fully abides in Christ, the heavenly Vine.

We all know the value of joy. It alone is the proof that what we have really satisfies the heart. As long as duty, or self-interest, or other motives influence me, men cannot know what the object of my pursuit or possession is really worth to me. But when it gives me joy, and they see me delight in it, they know that to me at least it is a treasure. Hence there is nothing so attractive as joy, no preaching so persuasive as the sight of hearts made glad. Just this makes gladness such a mighty element in the Christian character: there is no proof of the reality of God's love and the blessing He bestows, which men so soon feel the force of, as when the joy of God overcomes all the trials of life. And for the Christian's own welfare, joy is no less indispensable: the joy of the Lord is his strength; confidence, and courage, and patience find their inspiration in joy. With a heart full of joy no work can weary, and no burden can depress; God Himself is strength and song.

Let us hear what the Savior says of the joy of abiding in Him. He promises us His own joy: "My joy." As the whole parable refers to the life His disciples should have in Him when ascended to heaven, the joy is that of His resurrection life. This is clear from those other words of His (John 16:22): "I will see you again, and your heart shall rejoice, and your joy shall no man take from you." It was only with the resurrection and its glory that the power of the never-changing life began, and only in it that the never-ceasing joy could have its rise. With it was fulfilled the word: "Therefore thy God hath anointed thee with the oil of gladness above thy fellows." The day of His crowning was the day of the gladness of His heart. That joy of His was the joy of a work fully and for ever completed, the joy of the Father's bosom regained, and the joy of souls redeemed. These are the elements of His joy; of them the abiding in Him makes us partakers. The believer shares so fully His victory and His perfect redemption, that his faith can without ceasing sing the conqueror's song: "Thanks be to God, who always causeth me to triumph." As the fruit of this, there is the joy of the undisturbed dwelling in the light of the Father's love—not a cloud to intervene if the abiding be unbroken. And then, with this joy in the love of the Father, as a love received, the joy of the love of souls, as love going out and rejoicing over the lost. Abiding in Christ, penetrating into the very depths of His life and heart, seeking for the most perfect oneness, these the three streams of His joy flow into our hearts. Whether we look backward and see the work He has done, or upward and see the reward He has in the Father's love that passeth knowledge, or forward in the continual accessions of joy as sinners are brought home, His joy is ours. With our feet on Calvary, our eyes on the Father's countenance, and our hands helping sinners home, we have His joy as our own.

And then He speaks of this joy as abiding—a joy that is never to cease or to be interrupted for a moment: "That my joy might abide in you." "Your joy no man taketh from you." This is what many Christians cannot understand. Their view of the Christian life is that it is a succession of changes, now joy and now sorrow. And they appeal to the experiences of a man like the Apostle Paul, as a proof of how much there may be of weeping, and sorrow, and suffering. They have not noticed how just Paul gives the strongest evidence as to this unceasing joy. He understood the paradox of the Christian life as the combination at one and the same moment of all the bitterness of earth and all the joy of heaven. "As sorrowful, yet always rejoicing": these precious golden words teach us how the joy of Christ can overrule the sorrow of the world, can make us sing while we weep, and can maintain in the heart, even when cast down by disappointment or difficulties, a deep consciousness of a joy that is unspeakable and full of glory. There is but one condition: "I will see you again, and your heart shall rejoice, and your joy shall no man take from you." The presence of Jesus, distinctly manifested, cannot but give joy. Abiding in Him consciously, how can the soul but rejoice and be glad? Even when weeping for the sins and the souls of others, there is the fountain of gladness springing up in the faith of His power and love to save.

And this His own joy abiding with us, He wants to be full. Of the full joy our Savior spoke thrice on the last night. Once here in the parable of the Vine: "These things have I spoken unto you that your joy might be full"; and every deeper insight into the wonderful blessedness of being the branch of such a Vine confirms His Word. Then He connects it (John 16:24) with our prayers being answered: "Ask and ye shall receive, that your joy may be full." To the spiritual mind, answered prayer is not only a means of obtaining certain blessings, but something infinitely higher. It is a token of our fellowship with the Father and the Son in heaven, of their delight in us, and our having been admitted and having had a voice in that wondrous interchange of love in which the Father and the Son hold counsel, and decide the daily guidance of the children on earth. To a soul abiding in Christ, that longs for manifestations of His love, and that understands to take an answer to prayer in its true spiritual value, as a response from the throne to all its utterances of love and trust, the joy which it brings is truly unutterable. The word is found true: "Ask and ye shall receive, and your joy shall be full." And then the Savior says, in His high priestly prayer to the Father (John 17:13), "These things I speak, that they might have my joy fulfilled in themselves." It is the sight of the great High Priest entering the Father's presence for us, ever living to pray and carry on His blessed work in the power of an endless life, that removes every possible cause of fear or doubt, and gives us the assurance and experience of a perfect salvation. Let the believer who seeks, according to the teaching of John 15, to possess the full joy of abiding in Christ, and according to John 16, the full joy of prevailing prayer, press forward to John 17. Let him there listen to those wondrous words of intercession spoken, that his joy might be full. Let him, as he listens to those words, learn the love that even now pleads for him in heaven without ceasing, the glorious objects for which it is pleading, and which through its all-prevailing pleading are hourly being realized, and Christ's joy will be fulfilled in him.

Christ's own joy, abiding joy, fulness of joy—such is the portion of the believer who abides in Christ. Why, O why is it that this joy has so little power to attract? The reason simply is: Men, yea, even God's children, do not believe in it. Instead of the abiding in Christ being looked upon as the happiest life that ever can be led, it is regarded as a life of self-denial and of sadness. They forget that the self-denial and the sadness are owing to the not abiding, and that to those who once yield themselves unreservedly to abide in Christ as a bright and blessed life, their faith comes true—the joy of the Lord is theirs. The difficulties all arise from the want of the full surrender to a full abiding.

Child of God, who seekest to abide in Christ, remember what the Lord says. At the close of the parable of the Vine He adds these precious words:

"These things have I spoken unto you, that my joy might abide in you, and that your joy might be full." Claim the joy as part of the branch life—not the first or chief part, but as the blessed proof of the sufficiency of Christ to satisfy every need of the soul. Be happy. Cultivate gladness. If there are times when it comes of itself, and the heart feels the unutterable joy of the Savior's presence, praise God for it, and seek to maintain it. If at other times feelings are dull, and the experience of the joy not such as you could wish it, still praise God for the life of unutterable blessedness to which you have been redeemed. In this, too, the word holds good: "According to your faith be it unto you." As you claim all the other gifts in Jesus, ever claim this one too—not for your own sake, but for His and the Father's glory. "My joy in you"; "that my joy may abide in you"; "my joy fulfilled in themselves"—these are Jesus' own words. It is impossible to take Him wholly and heartily, and not to get His joy too. Therefore, "Rejoice in the Lord always; and again I say, Rejoice."

And in Love to the Brethren

"This is my commandment, That ye love one another, as I have loved you."—JOHN 15:12.

"Like as the Father loved me, *even* so I have loved you; *like as* I have loved you, *even so* love ye one another." God became man; divine love began to run in the channel of a human heart; it becomes the love of man to man. The love that fills heaven and eternity is ever to be daily seen here in the life of earth and of time.

"This is my commandment," the Savior says, "That ye love one another, as I have loved you." He sometimes spoke of commandments, but the love, which is the fulfilling of the law, is the all-including one, and therefore is called His commandment—the new commandment. It is to be the great evidence of the reality of the New Covenant, of the power of the new life revealed in Jesus Christ. It is to be the one convincing and indisputable token of discipleship: "Hereby shall all men know that ye are my disciples"; "That they may be one in us, that the world may believe"; "That they may be made perfect in one, that the world may know that Thou hast loved them, as Thou hast loved me." To the believer seeking perfect fellowship with Christ, the keeping of this commandment is at once the blessed proof that he is abiding in Him, and the path to a fuller and more perfect union.

Let us try to understand how this is so. We know that God is love, and that Christ came to reveal this, not as a doctrine but as a life. His life, in its wonderful self-abasement and self-sacrifice, was, above everything, the embodiment of divine love, the showing forth to men, in such human manifestations as they could understand, how God loves. In His love to the unworthy and the ungrateful, in His humbling Himself to walk among men as a servant, in His giving Himself up to death, He simply lived and acted out the life of the divine love which was in the heart of God. He lived and died to show us the love of the Father.

And now, just as Christ was to show forth God's love, believers are to show forth to the world the love of Christ. They are to prove to men that Christ loves them, and in loving fills them with a love that is not of earth. They, by living and by loving just as He did, are to be perpetual witnesses to the love that gave itself to die. He loved so that even the Jews cried out, as at Bethany, "Behold how He loved!" Christians are to live so that men are compelled to say, "See how these Christians love one another." In their daily intercourse with each other, Christians are made a spectacle to God, and to angels, and to men; and in the Christlikeness of their love to each other, are to prove what manner of spirit they are of. Amid all diversity of character or of creed, of language or of station, they are to prove that love has made them members of one body, and of each other, and has taught them each to forget and sacrifice self for the sake of the other. Their life of love is the chief evidence of Christianity, the proof to the world that God sent Christ, and that He has shed abroad in them the same love with which He loved Him. Of all the evidences of Christianity, this is the mightiest and most convincing.

This love of Christ's disciples to each other occupies a central position between their love to God and to all men. Of their love to God, whom they cannot see, it is the test. The love to one unseen may so easily be a mere sentiment, or even an imagination; in the intercourse with God's children, love to God is really called into exercise, and shows itself in deeds that the Father accepts as done to Himself. So alone can it be proved to be true. The love to the brethren is the flower and fruit of the root, unseen in the heart, of love to God. And this fruit again becomes the seed of love to all men: intercourse with each other is the school in which believers are trained and strengthened to love their fellow-men, who are yet out of Christ, not simply with the liking that rests on points of agreement, but with the holy love that takes hold of the unworthiest, and bears with the most disagreeable for Jesus' sake. It is love to each other as disciples that is ever put in the foreground as the link between love to God alone and to men in general.

In Christ's intercourse with His disciples this brotherly love finds the law of its conduct. As it studies His forgiveness and forbearance towards His friends, with the seven times seven as its only measure—as it looks to His unwearied patience and His infinite humility—as it sees the meekness and lowliness with which He seeks to win for Himself a place as their servant, wholly devoted to their interests—it accepts with gladness His command, "Ye should do as I have done" (John 13:15). Following His example, each lives not for Himself but for the other. The law of kindness is on the tongue, for love has vowed that never shall one unkind word cross its lips. It refuses not only to speak, but even to hear or to think evil; of the name and character of the fellow-Christian it is more jealous than of its own. My own good name I

may leave to the Father; my brother's my Father has entrusted to me. In
gentleness and loving kindness, in courtesy and generosity, in self-sacrifice
and beneficence, in its life of blessing and of beauty, the divine love, which
has been shed abroad in the believer's heart, shines out as it shone in the life
of Jesus.

Christian! what say you of this your glorious calling to love like Christ?
Does not your heart bound at the thought of the unspeakable privilege of
thus showing forth the likeness of the Eternal Love? Or are you rather ready
to sigh at the thought of the inaccessible height of perfection to which you
are thus called to climb? Brother, sigh not at what is in very deed the highest
token of the Father's love, that He has called us to be like Christ in our love,
just as He was like the Father in His love. Understand that He who gave the
command in such close connection with His teaching about the Vine and the
abiding in Him, gave us in that the assurance that we have only to abide in
Him to be able to love like Him. Accept the command as a new motive to a
more full abiding in Christ. Regard the abiding in Him more than ever as an
abiding in His love; rooted and grounded daily in a love that passeth
knowledge, you receive of its fulness, and learn to love. With Christ abiding
in you, the Holy Spirit sheds abroad the love of God in your heart, and you
love the brethren, the most trying and unlovable, with a love that is not your
own, but the love of Christ in you. And the command about your love to the
brethren is changed from a burden into a joy, if you but keep it linked, as
Jesus linked it, to the command about His love to you: "Abide in my love;
love one another, as I have loved you."

"This is my commandment, That ye love one another, as I have loved
you." Is not this now some of the much fruit that Jesus has promised we shall
bear—in very deed a cluster of the grapes of Eshcol, with which we can prove
to others that the land of promise is indeed a good land? Let us try in all
simplicity and honesty to go out to our home to translate the language of high
faith and heavenly enthusiasm into the plain prose of daily conduct, so that
all men can understand it. Let our temper be under the rule of the love of
Jesus: He can not alone curb it—He can make us gentle and patient. Let the
vow, that not an unkind word about others shall ever be heard from our lips,
be laid trustingly at His feet. Let the gentleness that refuses to take offence,
that is always ready to excuse, to think and hope the best, mark our
intercourse with all. Let the love that seeks not its own, but ever is ready to
wash others' feet, or even to give its life for them, be our aim as we abide in
Jesus. Let our life be one of self-sacrifice, always studying the welfare of
others, finding our highest joy in blessing others. And let us, in studying the

divine art of doing good, yield ourselves as obedient learners to the guidance of the Holy Spirit. By His grace, the most commonplace life can be transfigured with the brightness of a heavenly beauty, as the infinite love of the divine nature shines out through our frail humanity. Fellow-Christian, let us praise God! We are called to love as Jesus loves, as God loves.

"Abide in my love, and love as I have loved." Bless God, it is possible. The new holy nature we have, and which grows ever stronger as it abides in Christ the Vine, can love as He did. Every discovery of the evil of the old nature, every longing desire to obey the command of our Lord, every experience of the power and the blessedness of loving with Jesus' love, will urge us to accept with fresh faith the blessed injunctions: "Abide in me, and I in you"; "Abide in my love."

That You May Not Sin

"In him is no sin. Whosoever abideth in him sinneth not."—1 JOHN 3:5,6.

"Ye know," the apostle had said, "that He was manifested to take away our sin," and had thus indicated salvation from sin as the great object for which the Son was made man. The connection shows clearly that the taking away has reference not only to the atonement and freedom from guilt, but to deliverance from the power of sin, so that the believer no longer does it. It is Christ's personal holiness that constitutes His power to effect this purpose. He admits sinners into life union with Himself; the result is, that their life becomes like His. "In Him is no sin. Whosoever abideth in Him sinneth not." As long as he abides, and as far as he abides, the believer does not sin. Our holiness of life has its roots in the personal holiness of Jesus. "If the root be holy, so also are the branches."

The question at once arises: How is this consistent with what the Bible teaches of the abiding corruption of our human nature, or with what John himself tells of the utter falsehood of our profession, if we say that we have no sin, that we have not sinned? (see I John 1:8,10). It is just this passage which, if we look carefully at it, will teach us to understand our text aright. Note the difference in the two statements (ver. 8), "If we say that we have no sin," and (ver. 10), "If we say that we have not sinned." The two expressions cannot be equivalent; the second would then be an unmeaning repetition of the first. Having sin in verse 8 is not the same as doing sin in verse 10. Having sin is having a sinful nature. The holiest believer must each moment confess that he has sin within him—the flesh, namely, in which dwelleth no good thing. Sinning or doing sin is something very different: it is yielding to indwelling sinful nature, and falling into actual transgression. And so we have two admissions that every true believer must make. The one is that he has still sin within him (ver. 8); the second, that that sin has in former times broken out into sinful actions (ver. 10). No believer can say either, "I have no sin in me," or "I have in time past never sinned." If we say we have no sin at present, or that we have not sinned in the past, we deceive ourselves. But no confession, though we have sin in the present, is demanded that we are doing sin in the present too; the confession of actual sinning refers to the past. It may, as appears from chapter 2:2, be in the present also, but is expected not to be. And so we see how the deepest confession of sin in the past (as Paul's of his having been a persecutor), and the deepest consciousness of having still a vile and corrupt nature in the present, may consist with humble but joyful praise to Him who keeps from stumbling.

But how is it possible that a believer, having sin in him—sin of such intense vitality, and such terrible power as we know the flesh to have—that a believer having sin should yet not be doing sin? The answer is: "In Him is no sin. He that abideth in Him sinneth not." When the abiding in Christ becomes close and unbroken, so that the soul lives from moment to moment in the perfect union with the Lord its keeper, He does, indeed, keep down the power of the old nature, so that it does not regain dominion over the soul. We have seen that there are degrees in the abiding. With most Christians the abiding is so feeble and intermittent, that sin continually obtains the ascendency, and brings the soul into subjection. The divine promise given to faith is: "Sin shall not have dominion over you." But with the promise is the command: "Let not sin reign in your mortal body." The believer who claims the promise in full faith has the power to obey the command, and sin is kept from asserting its supremacy. Ignorance of the promise, or unbelief, or unwatchfulness, opens the door for sin to reign. And so the life of many believers is a course of continual stumbling and sinning. But when the believer seeks full admission into, and a permanent abode in Jesus, the Sinless One, then the life of Christ keeps from actual transgression. "In Him is no sin. He that abideth in Him sinneth not. " Jesus does indeed save him from his sin—not by the removal of his sinful nature, but by keeping him from yielding to it.

I have read of a young lion whom nothing could awe or keep down but the eye of his keeper. With the keeper you could come near him, and he would crouch, his savage nature all unchanged, and thirsting for blood —trembling at the keeper's feet. You might put your foot on his neck, as long as the keeper was with you. To approach him without the keeper would be instant death. And so it is that the believer can have sin and yet not do sin. The evil nature, the flesh, is unchanged in its enmity against God, but the abiding presence of Jesus keeps it down. In faith the believer entrusts himself to the keeping, to the indwelling, of the Son of God; he abides in Him, and counts on Jesus to abide in Him too. The union and fellowship is the secret of a holy life: "In Him is no sin; he that abideth in Him sinneth not."

And now another question will arise: Admitted that the complete abiding in the Sinless One will keep from sinning, is such abiding possible? May we hope to be able so to abide in Christ, say, even for one day, that we may be kept from actual transgressions? The question has only to be fairly stated and considered— it will suggest its own answer. When Christ commanded us to abide in Him, and promised us such rich fruit-bearing to the glory of the Father, and such mighty power in our intercessions, can He have meant anything but the healthy, vigorous, complete union of the branch with the vine? When He promised that as we abide in Him He would abide in us, could He mean anything but that His dwelling in us would be a reality of divine power and love? Is not this way of saving from sin just that which will glorify Him?—keeping us daily humble and helpless in the consciousness of the evil nature, watchful and active in the knowledge of its terrible power, dependent and trustful in the remembrance that only His presence can keep the lion down. O let us believe that when Jesus said, "Abide in me, and I in you," He did indeed mean that, while we were not to be freed from the world and its tribulation, from the sinful nature and its temptations, we were at least to have this blessing fully secured to us—grace to abide wholly, only, even in our Lord. The abiding in Jesus makes it possible to keep from actual sinning; and Jesus Himself makes it possible to abide in Him.

Beloved Christian! I do not wonder if the promise of the text appears almost too high. Do not, I pray, let your attention be diverted by the question as to whether it would be possible to be kept for your whole life, or for so many years, without sinning. Faith has ever only to deal with the present moment. Ask this: Can Jesus at the present moment, as I abide in Him, keep me from those actual transgressions which have been the stain and the weariness of my daily life? You cannot but say: Surely He can. Take Him then at this present moment, and say, "Jesus keeps me now, Jesus saves me now." Yield yourself to Him in the earnest and believing prayer to be kept abiding, by His own abiding in you—and go into the next moment, and the succeeding hours, with this trust continually renewed. As often as the opportunity occurs in the moments between your occupations, renew your faith in an act of devotion: Jesus keeps me now, Jesus saves me now. Let failure and sin, instead of discouraging you, only urge you still more to seek your safety in abiding in the Sinless One. Abiding is a grace in which you can grow wonderfully, if you will but make at once the complete surrender, and then persevere with ever larger expectations. Regard it as His work to keep you abiding in Him, and His work to keep you from sinning. It is indeed your work to abide in Him; but it is that, only because it is His work as Vine to bear and hold the branch. Gaze upon His holy human nature as what He prepared for you to be partaker of with Himself, and you will see that there is something even higher and better than being kept from sin—that is but the restraining from evil: there is the positive and larger blessing of being now a vessel purified and cleansed, of being filled with His fulness, and made the channel of showing forth His power, His blessing, and His glory.

Note

Is daily sinning an inevitable necessity?

"Why is it that, when we possess a Savior whose love and lower are infinite, we are so often filled with fear and despondency? We are wearied and faint in our minds, because we do not look steadfastly unto Jesus, the author and finisher of faith, who is set down at the right hand of God—unto Him whose omnipotence embraces both heaven and earth, who is strong and mighty in His feeble saints.

"While we remember our weakness, we forget His all-sufficient power. While we acknowledge that apart from Christ we can do nothing, we do not rise to the height or depth of Christian humility: I can do all things through Christ which strengtheneth me. While we trust in the power of the death of Jesus to cancel the guilt of sin, we do not exercise a reliant and appropriating faith in the omnipotence of the living Savior to deliver us from the bondage and power of sin in our daily life. We forget that Christ worketh in us mightily, and that, one with Him, we possess strength sufficient to overcome every temptation. We are apt either to forget our nothingness, and imagine that in our daily path we can live without sin, that the duties and trials of our everyday life can be performed and borne in our own strength; or we do not avail ourselves of the omnipotence of Jesus, who is able to subdue all things to Himself, and to keep us from the daily infirmities and falls which we are apt to imagine an inevitable necessity. If we really depended in all things and at all times on Christ, we would in all things and at all times gain the victory through Him whose power is infinite, and who is appointed by the Father to be the Captain of our salvation. Then all our deeds would be wrought, not merely before, but in God. We would then do all things to the glory of the Father, in the all-powerful name of Jesus, who is our sanctification. Remember that unto Him all power is given in heaven and on earth, and live by the constant exercise of faith in His power. Let us most fully believe that we have and are nothing, that with man it is impossible, that in ourselves we have no life which can bring forth fruit; but that Christ is all—that abiding in Him, and His word dwelling in us, we can bring forth fruit to the glory of the Father"—From Christ and the Church. Sermons by Adolph Saphir. The italics are not in the original.

As Your Strength

"All power is given unto me in heaven and in earth."—MATT.28:18. [1]

"Be strong in the lord, and in the power of his might."—EPH.6.10.

"My power is made perfect in weakness."—2 COR.12:9 (R.V.).

There is no truth more generally admitted among earnest Christians than that of their utter weakness. There is no truth more generally misunderstood and abused. Here, as elsewhere, God's thoughts are heaven-high above man's thoughts.

The Christian often tries to forget his weakness: God wants us to remember it, to feel it deeply. The Christian wants to conquer his weakness and to be freed from it: God wants us to rest and even rejoice in it. The Christian mourns over his weakness: Christ teaches His servant to say, "I take pleasure in infirmities; most gladly will I glory in my infirmities." The Christian thinks his weakness his greatest hindrance in the life and service of God: God tells us that it is the secret of strength and success. It is our weakness, heartily accepted and continually realized, that gives us our claim and access to the strength of Him who has said, "My strength is made perfect in weakness."

When our Lord was about to take His seat upon the throne, one of His last words was: "All power is given unto me in heaven and on earth." Just as His taking His place at the right hand of the power of God was something new and true—a real advance in the history of the God-man—so was this clothing with all power. Omnipotence was now entrusted to the man Christ Jesus, that from henceforth through the channels of human nature it might put forth its mighty energies. Hence He connected with this revelation of what He was to receive, the promise of the share that His disciples would have in it: When I am ascended, ye shall receive power from on high (Luke 24:49; Acts 1:8). It is in the power of the omnipotent Savior that the believer must find his strength for life and for work.

It was thus with the disciples. During ten days they worshiped and waited at the footstool of His throne. They gave expression to their faith in Him as their Savior, to their adoration of Him as their Lord, to their love to Him as their Friend, to their devotion and readiness to work for Him as their Master. Jesus Christ was the one object of thought, of love, of delight. In such worship of faith and devotion their souls grew up into intensest communion with Him upon the throne, and when they were prepared, the baptism of power came. It was power within and power around.

The power came to qualify for the work to which they had yielded themselves—of testifying by life and word to their unseen Lord. With some the chief testimony was to be that of a holy life, revealing the heaven and the Christ from whom it came. The power came to set up the Kingdom within them, to give them the victory over sin and self, to fit them by living experience to testify to the power of Jesus on the throne, to make men live in the world as saints. Others were to give themselves up entirely to the speaking in the name of Jesus. But all needed and all received the gift of power, to prove that now Jesus had received the Kingdom of the Father, all power in heaven and earth was indeed given to Him, and by Him imparted to His people just as they needed it, whether for a holy life or effective service. They received the gift of power, to prove to the world that the Kingdom of God, to which they professed to belong, was not in word but in power. By having power within, they had power without and around. The power of God was felt even by those who would not yield themselves to it (Acts 2.43; 4:13; 5:13).

And what Jesus was to these first disciples, He is to us too. Our whole life and calling as disciples find their origin and their guarantee in the words: "All power is given to me in heaven and on earth." What He does in and through us, He does with almighty power. What He claims or demands, He works Himself by that same power. All He gives, He gives with power. Every blessing He bestows, every promise He fulfils, every grace He works—all, all is to be with power. Everything that comes from this Jesus on the throne of power is to bear the stamp of power. The weakest believer may be confident that in asking to be kept from sin, to grow in holiness, to bring forth much fruit, be may count upon these his petitions being fulfilled with divine power. The power is in Jesus; Jesus is ours with all His fulness; it is in us His members that the power is to work and be made manifest.

And if we want to know how the power is bestowed, the answer is simple: Christ gives His power in us by giving His life in us. He does not, as so many believers imagine, take the feeble life He finds in them, and impart a little strength to aid them in their feeble efforts. No; it is in giving His own life in us that He gives us His power. The Holy Spirit came down to the disciples direct from the heart of their exalted Lord, bringing down into them the glorious life of heaven into which He had entered. And so His people are still taught to be strong in the Lord and in the power of His might. When He strengthens them, it is not by taking away the sense of feebleness, and giving in its place the feeling of strength. By no means. But in a very wonderful way leaving and even increasing the sense of utter impotence, He gives them along with it the consciousness of strength in Him. "We have this treasure in earthen vessels, that the excellency of the power may be of God and not of us." The feebleness and the strength are side by side; as the one grows, the other too, until they understand the saying, "When I am weak, then am I strong; I glory in my infirmities, that the power of Christ may rest on me."

The believing disciple learns to look upon Christ on the throne, Christ the Omnipotent, as his life. He studies that life in its infinite perfection and purity, in its strength and glory; it is the eternal life dwelling in a glorified man. And when he thinks of his own inner life, and longs for holiness, to live well pleasing unto God, or for power to do the Father's work, he looks up, and, rejoicing that Christ is his life, he confidently reckons that that life will work mightily in him all he needs. In things little and things great, in the being kept from sin from moment to moment for which he has learned to look, or in the struggle with some special difficulty or temptation, the power of Christ is the measure of his expectation. He lives a most joyous and blessed life, not because he is no longer feeble, but because, being utterly helpless, he consents and expects to have the mighty Savior work in him.

The lessons these thoughts teach us for practical life are simple, but very precious. The first is, that all our strength is in Christ, laid up and waiting for use. It is there as an almighty life, which is in Him for us, ready to flow in according to the measure in which it finds the channels open. But whether its flow is strong or feeble, whatever our experience of it be, there it is in Christ: All power in heaven and earth. Let us take time to study this. Let us get our minds filled with the thought: That Jesus might be to us a perfect Savior, the Father gave Him all power. That is the qualification that fits Him for our needs: All the power of heaven over all the powers of earth, over every power of earth in our heart and life too.

The second lesson is: This power flows into us as we abide in close union with Him. When the union is feeble, little valued or cultivated, the inflow of strength will be feeble. When the union with Christ is rejoiced in as our highest good, and everything sacrificed for the sake of maintaining it, the power will work: "His strength will be made perfect in our weakness." Our one care must therefore be to abide in Christ as our strength. Our one duty is to be strong in the Lord, and in the power of His might. Let our faith cultivate large and clear apprehensions of the exceeding greatness of God's power in them that believe, even that power of the risen and exalted Christ by which He triumphed over every enemy (Eph. 1: 19-21). Let our faith consent to God's wonderful and most blessed arrangement: nothing but feebleness in us as our own, all the power in Christ, and yet within our reach as surely as if it were in us. Let our faith daily go out of self and its life into the life of Christ, placing our whole being at His disposal for Him to work in us. Let our faith, above all, confidently rejoice in the assurance that He will in very deed, with His almighty power, perfect His work in us. As we thus abide in Christ, the Holy Spirit, the Spirit of His power, will work mightily in us, and we too shall sing, "*Jehovah* is my strength and song: *in Jehovah* I have righteousness and strength." "I can do all things through Christ, which strengtheneth me."

[1] The word power in this verse is properly authority (R.V.), but the two ideas are so closely linked, and the authority as a living divine reality is so inseparable from the power, that I have felt at liberty to retain the word power.

And Not in Self

"In me, that is, in my flesh, dwelleth no good thing." —Rom. 7:18.

To have life in Himself is the prerogative of God alone, and of the Son, to whom the Father hath also given it. To seek life, not in itself, but in God, is the highest honor of the creature. To live in and to himself is the folly and guilt of sinful man; to live to God in Christ, the blessedness of the believer. To deny, to hate, to forsake, to lose his own life, such is the secret of the life of faith. "I live, yet NOT I, but Christ liveth in me"; "*not* I, but the grace of God which is with me": this is the testimony of each one who has found out what it is to give up his own life, and to receive instead the blessed life of Christ within us. There is no path to true life, to abiding in Christ, than that which our Lord went before us—through death.

At the first commencement of the Christian life, but few see this. In the joy of pardon, they feel constrained to live for Christ, and trust with the help of God to be enabled to do so. They are as yet ignorant of the terrible enmity of the flesh against God, and its absolute refusal in the believer to be subject to the law of God. They know not yet that nothing but death, the absolute surrender to death of all that is of nature, will suffice, if the life of God is to be manifested in them with power. But bitter experience of failure soon teaches them the insufficiency of what they have yet known of Christ's power to save, and deep heart-longings are awakened to know Him better. He lovingly points them to His cross. He tells them that as there, in the faith of His death as their substitute, they found their title to life, so there they shall enter into its fuller experience too. He asks them if they are indeed willing to drink of the cup of which He drank—to be crucified and to die with Him. He teaches them that in Him they are indeed already crucified and dead—all unknowing, at conversion they became partakers of His death. But what they need now is to give a full and intelligent consent to what they received ere they understood it, by an act of their own choice to will to die with Christ.

This demand of Christ's is one of unspeakable solemnity. Many a believer shrinks back from it. He can hardly understand it. He has become so accustomed to a low life of continual stumbling, that he hardly desires, and still less expects, deliverance. Holiness, perfect conformity to Jesus, unbroken fellowship with His love, can scarcely be counted distinct articles of his creed. Where there is not intense longing to be kept to the utmost from sinning, and to be brought into the closest possible union with the Savior, the thought of being crucified with Him can find no entrance. The only impression it makes is that of suffering and shame: such a one is content that Jesus bore the cross, and so won for him the crown he hopes to wear. How different the light in which the believer who is really seeking to abide fully in Christ looks upon it. Bitter experience has taught him how, both in the matter of entire surrender and simple trust, his greatest enemy in the abiding life, is *self*. Now it refuses to give up its will; then again, by its working, it hinders God's work. Unless this life of self, with its willing and working, be displaced by the life of Christ, with His willing and working, to abide in Him will be impossible. And then comes the solemn question from Him who died on the cross: "Are you ready to give up self to the death?" You yourself, the living person born of God, are already in me dead to sin and alive to God; but are you ready now, in the power of this death, to mortify your members, to give up self entirely to its death of the cross, to be kept there until it be wholly destroyed? The question is a heart-searching one. Am I prepared to say that the old self shall no longer have a word to say; that it shall not be allowed to have a single thought, however natural—not a single feeling, however gratifying—not a single wish or work, however right?

Is this in very deed what He requires? Is not our nature God's handiwork, and may not our natural powers be sanctified to His service? They may and must indeed. But perhaps you have not yet seen how the only way they can be sanctified is that they be taken from under the power of self, and brought under the power of the life of Christ. Think not that this is a work that you can do, because you earnestly desire it, and are indeed one of His redeemed ones. No, there is no way to the altar of consecration but through death. As you yielded yourself a sacrifice on God's altar as one alive from the dead (Rom.6:13, 7:1), so each power of your nature—each talent, gift, possession, that is really to be holiness to the Lord—must be separated from the power of sin and self, and laid on the altar to be consumed by the fire that is ever burning there. It is in the mortifying, the slaying of self, that the wonderful powers with which God has fitted you to serve Him, can be set free for a complete surrender to God, and offered to Him to be accepted, and sanctified, and used. And though, as long as you are in the flesh, there is no thought of being able to say that self is dead, yet when the life of Christ is allowed to take full possession, self can be so kept in its crucifixion place, and under its sentence of death, that it shall have ho dominion over you, not for a single moment. Jesus Christ becomes your second self.

Believer! would you truly and fully abide in Christ, prepare yourself to part for ever from self, and not to allow it, even for a single moment, to have aught to say in your inner life. If you are willing to come entirely away out of self, and to allow Jesus Christ to become your life within you, inspiring all your thinking, feeling, acting, in things temporal and spiritual, He is ready to undertake the charge. In the fullest and widest sense the word life ever can have, He will be your life, extending His interest and influence to each one, even the minutest, of the thousand things that make up your daily life. To do this He asks but one thing: Come away out of self and its life, abide in Christ and the Christ life, and Christ will be your life. The power of His holy presence will cast out the old life.

To this end give up self at once and for ever. If you have never yet dared to do it, for fear you might fail of your engagement, do it now, in view of the promise Christ gives you that His life will take the place of the old life. Try and realize that though self is not dead, you are indeed dead to self. Self is still strong and living, but it has no power over you. You, your renewed nature—you, your new self, begotten again in Jesus Christ from the dead—are indeed dead to sin and alive to God. Your death in Christ has freed you completely from the control of self: it has no power over you, except as you, in ignorance, or unwatchfulness, or unbelief, consent to yield to its usurped authority. Come and accept by faith simply and heartily the glorious position you have in Christ. As one who, in Christ, has a life dead to self, as one who is freed from the dominion of self, and has received His divine life to take the place of self, to be the animating and inspiring principle of your life, venture boldly to plant the foot upon the neck of this enemy of yours and your Lord's. Be of good courage, only believe; fear not to take the irrevocable step, and to say that you have once for all given up self to the death for which it has been crucified in Christ (Rom.6:6). And trust Jesus the Crucified One to hold self to the cross, and to fill its place in you with His own blessed resurrection life.

In this faith, abide in Christ! Cling to Him; rest on Him; hope on Him. Daily renew your consecration; daily accept afresh your position as ransomed from your tyrant, and now in turn made a conqueror. Daily look with holy fear on the enemy, self, struggling to get free from the cross, seeking to allure you into giving it some little liberty, or else ready to deceive you by its profession of willingness now to do service to Christ. Remember, self seeking to serve God is more dangerous than self refusing obedience. Look upon it with holy fear, and hide yourself in Christ: in Him alone is your safety. Abide thus in Him; He has promised to abide in you. He will teach you to be humble and watchful. He will teach you to be happy and trustful. Bring every interest of your life, every power of your nature, all the unceasing flow of thought, and will, and feeling, that makes up life, and trust Him to take the place that self once filled so easily and so naturally. Jesus Christ will indeed take possession of you and dwell in you; and in the restfulness and peace and grace of the new life you shall have unceasing joy at the wondrous exchange that has been made—the coming out of self to abide in Christ alone.

Note

In his work on Sanctification, Marshall, in the twelfth chapter, on "Holiness through faith alone," puts with great force the danger in which the Christian is of seeking sanctification in the power of the flesh, with the help of Christ, instead of looking for it to Christ alone, and receiving it from Him by faith. He reminds us how there are two natures in the believer, and so two ways of seeking holiness, according as we allow the principles of the one or other nature to guide us. The one is the carnal way, in which we put forth our utmost efforts and resolutions, trusting Christ to help us in doing so. The other the spiritual way, in which, as those who have died, and can do nothing, our one care is to receive Christ day by day, and at every step to let Him live and work in us.

"Despair of purging the flesh or natural man of its sinful lusts and inclinations, and of practicing holiness by your willing and resolving to do the best that lieth in your own power, and trusting on the grace of God and Christ to help you in such resolutions and endeavors. Rather resolve to trust on Christ to work in you to will and to do by His own power according to His own good pleasure. They that are convinced of their own sin and misery do commonly first think to tame the flesh, and to subdue and root out its lusts, and to make their corrupt nature to be better-natured and inclined to holiness by their struggling and wrestling with it; and if they can but bring their hearts to a full purpose and resolution to do the best that lieth in them, they hope that by such a resolution they shall be able to achieve great enterprises in the conquests of their lusts and performance of the most difficult duties. It is the great work of some zealous divines in their preachiness and writings to stir up people to this resolution, wherein they place the chaffiest turning point from sin to godliness. And they think that this is not contrary to the life of faith, because they trust in the grace of God through Christ to help them in all such resolutions and endeavors. Thus they endeavour to reform their old state, and to be made perfect in the flesh, instead of putting it off and walking according to the new state in Christ. They trust on low carnal things for holiness, and upon the acts of their own will, their purposes, resolutions, and endeavors, instead of Christ; and they trust to Christ to help them in this carnal way; whereas true faith would teach them that they are nothing, and that they do but labor in vain."

As the Surety of the Covenant

"Jesus was made a surety of a better testament."—Heb 7:22

Of the old Covenant, Scripture speaks as not being faultless, and God complains that Israel had not continued in it; and so He regarded them not (Heb.8:7-9). It had not secured its apparent object, in uniting Israel and God: Israel had forsaken Him, and He had not regarded Israel. Therefore God promises to make a New Covenant, free from the faults of the first, and effectual to realize its purpose. If it were to accomplish its end, it would need to secure God's faithfulness to His people, and His people's faithfulness to God. And the terms of the New Covenant expressly declare that these two objects shall be attained. "I will put my laws into their mind": thus God proposes to secure their unchanging faithfulness to Him. "Their sins I will remember no more" (see Heb.8:10-12): thus He assures His unchanging faithfulness to them. A pardoning God and an obedient people: these are the two parties who are to meet and to be eternally united in the New Covenant.

The most beautiful provision of this New Covenant is that of the surety in whom its fulfilment on both parts is guaranteed. Jesus was made the surety of the better covenant. To man He became surety that God would faithfully fulfil His part, so that man could confidently depend upon God to pardon, and accept, and never more forsake. And to God He likewise became surety that man would faithfully fulfil his part, so that God could bestow on him the blessing of the covenant. And the way in which He fulfils His suretyship is this: As one with God, and having the fulness of God dwelling in His human nature, He is personally security to men that God will do what He has engaged. All that God has is secured to us in Him as man. And then, as one with us, and having taken us up as members into His own body, He is security to God that His interests shall be cared for. All that man must be and do is secured in Him. It is the glory of the New Covenant that it has in the Person of the God-man its living surety, its everlasting security. And it can easily be understood how, in proportion as we abide in Him as the surety of the covenant, its objects and its blessings will be realized in us.

We shall understand this best if we consider it in the light of one of the promises of the New Covenant. Take that in Jer.32:40 : "I will make an everlasting covenant with them, that I will not turn away from them, to do them good; but I will put my fear in their hearts, that they shall not depart from me."

With what wonderful condescension the infinite God here bows Himself to our weakness! He is the Faithful and Unchanging One, whose word is truth; and yet more abundantly to show to the heirs of the promise the immutability of His counsel, He binds Himself in the covenant that He will never change: "I will make an everlasting covenant, that I will not turn away from them." Blessed the man who has thoroughly appropriated this, and finds his rest in the everlasting covenant of the Faithful One!

But in a covenant there are two parties. And what if man becomes unfaithful and breaks the covenant? Provision must be made, if the covenant is to be well ordered in all things and sure, that this cannot be, and that man too remain faithful. Man never can undertake to give such an assurance. And see, here God comes to provide for this too. He not only undertakes in the covenant that He will never turn from His people, but also to put His fear in their heart, that they do not depart from Him. In addition to His own obligations as one of the covenanting parties, He undertakes for the other party too: "I *will cause* you to walk in my statutes, and ye shall keep my judgments and do them" (Ezek.36:27). Blessed the man who understands this half of the covenant too! He sees that his security is not in the covenant which he makes with His God, and which he would but continually break again. He finds that a covenant has been made, in which God stands good, not only for Himself, but for man too. He grasps the blessed truth that his part in the covenant is to accept what God has promised to do, and to expect the sure fulfilment of the divine engagement to secure the faithfulness of His people to their God: "I will put my fear in their hearts, that they shall not depart from me."

It is just here that the blessed work comes in of the surety of the covenant, appointed of the Father to see to its maintenance and perfect fulfilment. To Him the Father hath said, "I have given thee for a covenant of the people." And the Holy Spirit testifies, "All the promises of God IN Him are yea, and in Him are Amen, to the glory of God by us." The believer who abides in Him hath a divine assurance for the fulfilment of every promise the covenant ever gave.

Christ was made surety of a better testament. It is as our Melchisedec that Christ is surety (see Heb.7). Aaron and his sons passed away; of Christ it is witnessed that He liveth. He is priest in the power of an endless life. Because He continueth ever, He hath an unchangeable priesthood. And because He ever liveth to make intercession, He can save to the uttermost, He can save completely. It is because Christ is the Ever-living One that His suretyship of the covenant is so effectual. He liveth ever to make intercession, and can therefore save completely. Every moment there rise up from His holy presence to the Father, the unceasing pleadings which secure to His people the powers and the blessings of the heavenly life. And every moment there go out from Him downward to His people, the mighty influences of His unceasing intercession, conveying to them uninterruptedly the power of the heavenly life. As surety with us for the Father's favor, He never ceases to pray and present us before Him; as surety with the Father for us, He never ceases to work, and reveal the Father within us.

The mystery of the Melchisedec priesthood, which the Hebrews were not able to receive (Heb.5:10-14), is the mystery of the resurrection life. It is in this that the glory of Christ as surety of the covenant consists: He ever liveth. He performs His work in heaven in the power of a divine, an omnipotent life. He ever liveth to pray; not a moment that as surety His prayers do not rise Godward to secure the Father's fulfilment to us of the covenant. He performs His work on earth in the power of that same life; not a moment that His answered prayers—the powers of the heavenly world—do not flow downward to secure for His Father our fulfilment of the covenant. In the eternal life there are no breaks—never a moment's interruption; each moment has the power of eternity in it. He ever, every moment, liveth to pray. He ever, every moment, liveth to bless. He can save to the uttermost, completely and perfectly, because He ever liveth to pray.

Believer! come and see here how the possibility of abiding in Jesus every moment is secured by the very nature of this ever-living priesthood of your surety. Moment by moment, as His intercession rises up, its efficacy descends. And because Jesus stands good for the fulfilment of the covenant—"I will put my fear in their heart, and they shall not depart from me"—He cannot afford to leave you one single moment to yourself. He dare not do so, or He fails of His undertaking. Your unbelief may fail of realizing the blessing; He cannot be unfaithful. If you will but consider Him, and the power of that endless life after which He was made and is a High Priest, your faith will rise to believe that an endless, ever-continuing, unchangeable life of abiding in Jesus, is nothing less than what is waiting you.

It is as we see what Jesus is, and is to us, that the abiding in Him will become the natural and spontaneous result of our knowledge of Him. If His life unceasingly, moment by moment, rises to the Father for us, and descends to us from the Father, then to abide moment by moment is easy and simple. Each moment of conscious intercourse with Him we simply say, "Jesus, surety, keeper, ever-living Savior, in whose life I dwell, I abide in Thee." Each moment of need, or darkness, or fear, we still say, "O thou great High Priest, in the power of an endless, unchangeable life, I abide in Thee." And for the moments when direct and distinct communion with Him must give place to needful occupations, we can trust His suretyship, His unceasing priesthood, in its divine efficacy, and the power with which He saves to the uttermost, still to keep us abiding in Him.

The Glorified One

"Your life is hid with Christ in God. When Christ, who is our life, shall appear, then shall ye also appear with him in glory."—COL.3:3-4

He that abides in Christ the Crucified One, learns to know what it is to be crucified with Him, and in Him to be indeed dead unto sin. He that abides in Christ the Risen and Glorified One, becomes in the same way partaker of His resurrection life, and of the glory with which He has now been crowned in heaven. Unspeakable are the blessings which flow to the soul from the union with Jesus in His glorified life.

This life is a life of perfect victory and rest. Before His death, the Son of God had to suffer and to struggle, could be tempted and troubled by sin and its assaults: as the Risen One, He has triumphed over sin; and, as the Glorified One, His humanity has entered into participation of the glory of Deity. The believer who abides in Him as such, is led to see how the power of sin and the flesh are indeed destroyed: the consciousness of complete and everlasting deliverance becomes increasingly clear, and the blessed rest and peace, the fruit of such a conviction that victory and deliverance are an accomplished fact, take possession of the life. Abiding in Jesus, in whom he has been raised and set in the heavenly places, he receives of that glorious life streaming from the Head through every member of the body.

This life is a life in the full fellowship of the Father's love and holiness. Jesus often gave prominence to this thought with His disciples. His death was a going to the Father. He prayed: "Glorify me, O Father, with Thyself, with the glory which I had with Thee." As the believer, abiding in Christ the Glorified One, seeks to realize and experience what His union with Jesus on the throne implies, he apprehends how the unclouded light of the Father's presence is His highest glory and blessedness, and in Him the believer's portion too. He learns the sacred art of always, in fellowship with His exalted Head, dwelling in the secret of the Father's presence. Further, when Jesus was on earth, temptation could still reach Him: in glory, everything is holy, and in perfect harmony with the will of God. And so the believer who abides in

Him experiences that in this high fellowship his spirit is sanctified into growing harmony with the Father's will. The heavenly life of Jesus is the power that casts out sin.

This life is a life of loving beneficence and activity. Seated on His throne, He dispenses His gifts, bestows His Spirit, and never ceases in love to watch and to work for those who are His. The believer cannot abide in Jesus the Glorified One, without feeling himself stirred and strengthened to work: the Spirit and the love of Jesus breathe the will and the power to be a blessing to others. Jesus went to heaven with the very object of obtaining power there to bless abundantly. He does this as the heavenly Vine only through the medium of His people as His branches. Whoever, therefore, abides in Him, the Glorified One, bears much fruit, for he receives of the Spirit and the power of the eternal life of his exalted Lord, and becomes the channel through which the fulness of Jesus, who hath been exalted to be a Prince and a Savior, flows out to bless those around him.

There is one more thought in regard to this life of the Glorified One, and ours in Him. It is a life of wondrous expectation and hope. It is so with Christ. He sits at the right hand of God, expecting till all His enemies be made His footstool, looking forward to the time when He shall receive His full reward, when His glory shall be made manifest, and His beloved people be ever with Him in that glory. The hope of Christ is the hope of His redeemed: "I will come again and take you to myself, that where I am there ye may be also." This promise is as precious to Christ as it ever can be to us. The joy of meeting is surely no less for the coming bridegroom than for the waiting bride. The life of Christ in glory is one of longing expectation: the full glory only comes when His beloved are with Him.

The believer who abides closely in Christ will share with Him in this spirit of expectation. Not so much for the increase of personal happiness, but from the spirit of enthusiastic allegiance to his King, he longs to see Him come in His glory, reigning over every enemy, the fill revelation of God's everlasting love. "Till He come," is the watchword of every true-hearted believer. "Christ shall appear, and we shall appear with Him in glory."

There may be very serious differences in the exposition of the promises of His coming. To one it is plain as day that He is coming very speedily in person to reign on earth, and that speedy coming is his hope and his stay. To another, loving his Bible and his Savior not less, the coming can mean nothing but the judgment day—the solemn transition from time to eternity, the close of history on earth, the beginning of heaven; and the thought of that manifestation of his Savior's glory is no less his joy and his strength. It is

Jesus, Jesus coming again, Jesus taking us to Himself, Jesus adored as Lord of all, that is to the whole Church the sum and the center of its hope.

It is by abiding in Christ the Glorified One that the believer will be quickened to that truly spiritual looking for His coming, which alone brings true blessing to the soul. There is an interest in the study of the things which are to be, in which the discipleship of a school is often more marked than the discipleship of Christ the meek; in which contendings for opinions and condemnation of brethren are more striking than any signs of the coming glory. It is only the humility that is willing to learn from those who may have other gifts and deeper revelations of the truth than we, and the love that always speaks gently and tenderly of those who see not as we do, and the heavenliness that shows that the Coming One is indeed already our life, that will persuade either the Church or the world that this our faith is not in the wisdom of men, but in the power of God. To testify of the Savior as the Coming One, we must be abiding in and bearing the image of Him as the Glorified One. Not the correctness of the views we hold, nor the earnestness with which we advocate them, will prepare us for meeting Him, but only the abiding in Him. Then only can our being manifested in glory with Him be what it is meant to be—a transfiguration, a breaking out and shining forth of the indwelling glory that had been waiting for the day of revelation.

Blessed life! "the life hid with Christ in God," "set in the heavenlies in Christ," abiding in Christ the glorified! Once again the question comes: Can a feeble child of dust really dwell in fellowship with the King of glory? And again the blessed answer has to be given: To maintain that union is the very work for which Christ has all power in heaven and earth at His disposal. The blessing will be given to him who will trust his Lord for it, who in faith and confident expectation ceases not to yield himself to be wholly one with Him. It was an act of wondrous though simple faith, in which the soul yielded itself at first to the Savior. That faith grows up to clearer insight and faster hold of God's truth that we are one with Him in His glory. In that same wondrous faith, wondrously simple, but wondrously mighty, the soul learns to abandon itself entirely to the keeping of Christ's almighty power, and the actings of His eternal life. Because it knows that it has the Spirit of God dwelling within to communicate all that Christ is, it no longer looks upon it as a burden or a work, but allows the divine life to have its way, to do its work; its faith is the increasing abandonment of self, the expectation and acceptance of all that the love and the power of the Glorified One can perform. In that faith unbroken fellowship is maintained, and growing conformity realized. As with

Moses, the fellowship makes partakers of the glory, and the life begins to shine with a brightness not of this world.

Blessed life! it is ours, for Jesus is ours. Blessed life! we have the possession within us in its hidden power, and we have the prospect before us in its fullest glory. May our daily lives be the bright and blessed proof that the hidden power dwells within, preparing us for the glory to be revealed. May our abiding in Christ the Glorified One be our power to live to the glory of the Father, our fitness to share to the glory of the Son.

And Now,
Little Children,
Abide in Him,
That, When He Shall Appear, We May Have
Confidence, and Not Be Ashamed
Before Him at His Coming.

www.ingramcontent.com/pod-product-compliance
Lightning Source LLC
Chambersburg PA
CBHW030911090426
42737CB00007B/159